The

# WISDOM

of

# YOUR DREAMS

# The
# WISDOM
## of
# YOUR DREAMS

*Using Dreams to Tap into Your Unconscious*
*and Transform Your Life*

⚮

# JEREMY TAYLOR

JEREMY P. TARCHER/PENGUIN
*a member of Penguin Group (USA) Inc.*
*New York*

JEREMY P. TARCHER/PENGUIN
Published by the Penguin Group
Penguin Group (USA) Inc., 375 Hudson Street, New York, New York 10014,
USA • Penguin Group (Canada), 90 Eglinton Avenue East, Suite 700, Toronto,
Ontario M4P 2Y3, Canada (a division of Pearson Penguin Canada Inc.) • Penguin Books Ltd,
80 Strand, London WC2R 0RL, England • Penguin Ireland, 25 St Stephen's Green,
Dublin 2, Ireland (a division of Penguin Books Ltd) • Penguin Group (Australia),
250 Camberwell Road, Camberwell, Victoria 3124, Australia (a division of Pearson
Australia Group Pty Ltd) • Penguin Books India Pvt Ltd, 11 Community Centre,
Panchsheel Park, New Delhi–110 017, India • Penguin Group (NZ),
67 Apollo Drive, Rosedale, North Shore 0632, New Zealand (a division of
Pearson New Zealand Ltd) • Penguin Books (South Africa) (Pty) Ltd,
24 Sturdee Avenue, Rosebank, Johannesburg 2196, South Africa

Penguin Books Ltd, Registered Offices: 80 Strand, London WC2R 0RL, England

Previously published as *Where People Fly and Water Runs Uphill*, 1992, Warner Books
Copyright © 1992, 2009 by Jeremy Taylor

Most Tarcher/Penguin books are available at special quantity discounts for bulk
purchase for sales promotions, premiums, fund-raising, and educational needs.
Special books or book excerpts also can be created to fit specific needs.
For details, write Penguin Group (USA) Inc. Special Markets,
375 Hudson Street, New York, NY 10014.

Library of Congress Cataloging-in-Publication Data

Taylor, Jeremy, date.
The wisdom of your dreams : using dreams to tap into your unconscious
and transform your life / Jeremy Taylor.
p.      cm.
Rev. ed. of: Where people fly and water runs uphill. New York, NY: Warner Books, c1992.
Includes index.
ISBN 978-1-58542-754-3
1. Dreams.   I. Taylor, Jeremy, date. Where people fly and water runs uphill.   II. Title.
BF1078.T36      2009                    2009024320
154.6'3—dc22

Printed in the United States of America
1   3   5   7   9   10   8   6   4   2

BOOK DESIGN BY AMANDA DEWEY

*To*
*My wife, Kathryn,*
*My daughter, Trismegista,*
*and*
*Joan and Myrin Borysenko*
*with*
*gratitude for their*
*support and enthusiasm*

# CONTENTS

# BRIEF INTRODUCTION AND ACKNOWLEDGMENTS

Curiosity has ruled my life since childhood—curiosity about life, about love, about the great possibilities and frustrating limits of creative expression. I have always wondered about the obvious and not-so-obvious connections that weave individual psychology, family, society, and history together into a single complex phenomenon. Just what *are* these subtle, shaping psychospiritual energies and patterns, mostly hidden, but revealing themselves often enough to demonstrate that they really *are* there, just below and beyond the surface of obvious waking appearance? What are these archetypes that influence and arrange the events in the material world, just as they also organize and form the deepest foundations of my own character and personality? All these intriguing, lifelong questions have found a unifying focus in my endless curiosity and ever-increasing excitement about the deeper meanings and implications of dreams.

Careful and sustained exploration of the multiple layers of deeper meaning that inhere in every dream remembered from sleep (and in every spontaneous upwelling of interior life in waking life as well) has occupied my passionately focused professional and personal attention for more than forty years. (In 2008, I turned sixty-five. I began my sustained inquiry into dreams and dreaming in my early twenties; so the math is inescapable.)

I continue to be buoyed up and renewed by all I have learned and continue to learn from this inquiry into the nature and the multiple meanings and implications of dreams, and the way they simultaneously reflect and influence my own actions as well as the actions and behaviors of others, and events in the wider world. This investigation has taught me some very important things, particularly about the possibilities and limits of human freedom.

We human beings, regardless of gender, language, age, ethnic heritage, intelligence, physical capabilities, beliefs, and so on, *are only as free as we are conscious and self-aware.* Our actions are "predetermined," "automatic," and "unfree" to the precise extent that we remain unconscious and unaware of our deeper interior drives and dramas. It is a continuum: as we become more conscious, self-aware, and aware of our multilayered relationships with others, and with the depths of our own unconscious psyches, we are also provided with the expanding opportunity to become more free, creative, compassionate, and expressive in the outer world.

No matter where we may fall on this continuum of evolving consciousness, we are *always free* to either follow or ignore the subtle and startling suggestions that our dreams make about how we might become more healthy and whole, while at the same time we are *never free* to avoid the consequences, both calculated and unintended, of these choices.

As I contemplate the release of this new book, I am filled with great excitement and enthusiasm. It is a significant undertaking, a major updating of my earlier work, *Where People Fly and Water Runs Uphill: Using Dreams to Tap the Wisdom of the Unconscious,* woven together with a significant amount of new material in the main body of the text. It includes a correction (it was, of course, Annie Besant who hailed the young Krishna Murti as the "avatar of the age," not her distinguished predecessor, Madame Blavatsky), along with a new chapter addressing the connections between developing individual consciousness and self-awareness, and the development of human consciousness as a whole. There is also an updated reference and bibliographic guide.

This new work includes an extended discussion of some aspects of my work exploring dreaming and working with dreams that have developed and become "more speech-ripe" in the years since the original publication of *Where People Fly* in 1992.

I am particularly grateful to Susan Rosen, the founder and director of Miriam's Well, the wonderfully welcoming, multifaceted spiritual retreat and action-oriented conference center in Saugerties, New York, where I have been privileged to work for many years, and also to her husband, Richard. Susan and Richard and the staff and participants in the Miriam's Well programs have been unfailingly supportive of my work. Susan has been especially helpful in advocating the publication of this book. Thank you, Susan.

I also want to thank all my friends and dream work colleagues who responded so generously to my request that they tell me what books and other resources they have come to rely on and make most use of over the years in their explorations of dreams. I am also grateful to my editor at Tarcher/Penguin, Joel Fotinos, whose deft support and sensitive guidance have improved this book beyond my expectations.

My greatest gratitude is to Kath, my wife, life partner, and cosmic cocreator. Thank you, my love, for *everything* that you have done, that you do, and that you are and are becoming as we continue to grow together (all puns intended).

I must also express my profound debt and gratitude once again to all the dreamers over the decades who have trusted me, and the consciously projective way of work I teach and practice, enough to have opened your hearts, minds, and lives to me, to one another, and (anonymously) to you, the reader. Thank you all—you know who you are. Without you, without your trust, generosity, and exemplary courage, none of this exciting, life- and world-shaping work would have been possible.

# AN INITIAL WORD
# ABOUT ANONYMITY AND
# CONFIDENTIALITY

In order to work successfully with dreams, either one to one or in a group setting, it is absolutely necessary that the people sharing their dreams feel safe. The simplest way to promote this sense of individual and collective safety is for all dream work to be strictly confidential—in other words, for it to be understood and agreed at the outset that there will be *no discussion* of the dreams, or the work with the dreams, outside regular group meetings.

Over the years, however, I have become convinced that although strict confidentiality does promote this necessary sense of safety, it also tends to violate an equally important need: the freedom to be open, spontaneous, and intimate in all communication with friends and loved ones. To be healthy and whole, we must be free to discuss and explore candidly the details of our inner and outer experience with the people we care most about, whether those people were initially present for all those experiences or not.

To balance these two equally important needs, I always encourage the individuals and groups with whom I do dream work to agree to *anonymity* in all conversations about dream work outside the group. Under such an agreement, the people involved in group dream work are free to discuss and write about their insights and experiences, provided no individual dreamer is identifiable, and with the clear understanding that it only takes one request for confidentiality for everyone involved to shift into that more restricted mode. Such agreements encourage free and open communication. The freedom to speak openly and anonymously about the details of working with dreams also tends to spread information and enthusiasm about the exciting possibilities of working with dreams in groups.

Over the several decades I have been working with dreams, many people have agreed to anonymity in their work with me. I am most grateful to all of you. Without your confidence and generosity of spirit, it would be impossible for me to talk or write about dreams and dreaming in anything but the most abstract and lifeless way. Some of you will find accounts of your dreams in the pages that follow, always with sufficient details withheld or altered to ensure your continued anonymity.

I would like to offer all of you whose dreams I have quoted a word of caution in reading and discussing this book: please read the *whole text* before you break the anonymity that has been preserved here. At some later point in the book there may be comments and suggestions relating to your dreams and the work with your dreams with which you may not wish to be identified.

The

# WISDOM

of

# YOUR DREAMS

*Chapter One*

# WHAT YOU SHOULD
# KNOW ABOUT DREAMS:
# TEN BASIC ASSUMPTIONS

*Dreams are impartial products of the unconscious psyche, outside the control of the will. They are pure nature; they show us the unvarnished, natural truth, and are therefore fitted, as nothing else is, to give us back an attitude that accords with our basic human nature when our consciousness has strayed too far from its foundations and run into an impasse.*

—C. G. JUNG

There are already many books available about dreams and dreaming. They vary widely in quality and sophistication and present many different ideas about the ways in which dreams convey meaning. Some even question whether dreams have any meaning at all. The available literature ranges from "dictionaries" where mechanical, stereotyped interpretations are offered for common dream images, to abstract theoretical treatises about neurobiology and the nature of metaphor and symbol. A few books offer rudimentary ideas about how to begin to explore the dream world for yourself, and even fewer attempt to bring some of these many approaches and perspectives together into a coherent presentation. In Appendix I, I offer my assessments of the most interesting and informative books and periodicals devoted to dream work currently available in English.

So why another dream book? For several reasons. I have been working with dreams for more than forty years and I have explored more than one hundred fifty thousand dreams. From this experience, I have developed ideas, insights, and techniques which are not discussed in other books. I have also developed unique examples of dream work, along with unique ways of thinking about and explaining the multiple meanings of dreams.

I believe that people in Western society do not sufficiently value their dreams. Our dreams are more important, more useful and interesting than we generally acknowledge. In this book, I attempt to show you why you should pay more attention to your nightly dream adventures. Despite all the other dream books, we still undervalue our dreams, and this book is an effort to change that.

The ideas in this book are primarily focused on exploring dreams with other people. *Sharing dreams and searching cooperatively for their meanings regularly creates deeper intimacy and understanding between and among people participating in the process.* Dreams reveal the projections and self-deceptions that so often interfere with honest, intimate, successful relating between and among parents, children, lovers, friends, coworkers, authorities, and casual acquaintances.

The ideas presented in this book are distilled from my extensive experience as a dream worker and teacher of dream work. I have done this work mostly in private groups and classes, but also in more traditional one-to-one counseling and group work in institutional and clinical settings. As an ordained Unitarian Universalist minister I have taught dream work to seminary students, ministers, social workers, and therapists at the Starr King School for the Ministry, and at other affiliated schools of the Graduate Theological Union at the University of California at Berkeley, and at the Institute in Culture and Creation Spirituality and its successor, Wisdom University, in Oakland. I regularly conduct dream-work groups in churches, schools, overseas study tours, day and residential treatment and care programs, hospitals, and community service organizations. I have also led dream groups in prisons, including San Quentin, the California Medical Facility at Vacaville, and the Federal Correctional Facility at Pleasanton. (For an in-depth discussion of a dream group meeting in San Quentin, see Chapter 6.) In all of these diverse settings, the work with dreams has proven to be of immense and ongoing use and value to a wide variety of people.

The ideas touched on briefly in this introductory chapter are discussed in much greater detail with multiple, concrete examples in the chapters that follow.

My experience has led me to ten basic, important assumptions about dreams.

The single most important conclusion I have come to in my work is that all dreams come in the service of health and wholeness. In other words, there really is no such thing as a "bad dream." On the face of it, of course, the dreams we call nightmares do not seem to have anything even remotely to do with our health and wholeness. However, my experience convinces me beyond doubt that the primary reason for the existence of nightmares is that the information they contain is of particular importance and value to you. A dream assumes the form of a "nightmare" to ensure that the content of the dream will not be forgotten.

One of the things that separates "nightmares" from "ordinary dreams" is that when you wake from a nightmare, it is "in your face." You can't forget it even if you wanted to, in marked contrast to most of the rest of your dreams, which have a distressing tendency to disappear from consciousness, even when you are making a concerted effort to remember them. This, I believe, is a large part of the point. It is as though every nightmare says to the dreamer upon awakening: "Pay attention! This is worth remembering, whether you happen to think so at this moment or not!" In those rare instances where the dreamer awakens from a "nightmare" with no concrete images, only the overwhelming sense of having had a nasty dream, the dream is still saying urgently: "Pay attention to your feelings! They matter! They are important, even if you don't like them, or what provokes them!"

What is true of nightmares is true of all dreams: what is remembered ✳ is worth remembering because it always contains valuable information. All dreams bring us creative energies and insights into the meaning of confusing emotions. The ideas and techniques in this book for exploring the meanings in dreams all derive from this basic understanding of the universal inherently positive quality of all dreams and dreaming experience, despite any surface appearances to the contrary. The generic message of every remembered dream is wake up; pay attention; there is a potentially creative, positive, useful, effective, elegant, (the list of positive adjectives is quite long) role for the dreamer's waking mind to play in the further unfolding of ALL the issues that are given symbolic shape in this dream (whether or not the dreamer was consciously aware of them at the time). At this level, the generic message of every remembered dream is: Pay attention! There is an important, transformative, effective role for your waking mind in the further unfolding of whatever is being given symbolic shape in this dream.

In the same way that all dreams come in the service of health and wholeness, it is also true that *no dream ever comes just to tell you what you already know.* All dreams carry new information and energy in their metaphors and symbols. All remembered dreams will make some reference to what you already consciously know and understand about your life, but always in the context of moving you further along in your growth and development.

The only apparent exception to this truth comes in those instances where you already "know" something intellectually about the deeper truth of your life, but for some reason you have failed to *act* on that knowledge. In such circumstances, your dreams are likely to reemphasize what you already know, often picturing the situation in a seemingly "exaggerated" form, to help you move beyond mere intellectual understanding into the realm of creative response and appropriate action.

For example, a woman in an ongoing dream group knew intellectually that it really was inappropriate for her to continue to provide total financial support for her unemployed college-graduate son, but she simply could not bring herself to "cut him off" when he had not yet "found himself." This woman shared a disturbing dream in which she sees her son drowning in a swimming pool filled with soup she knew she had cooked, while she watches impassively from a lawn chair without making any effort to help him. Upon awakening, she was shocked at the vision of herself as "uncaring," merely watching calmly as her son drowned. This "exaggerated" picture of her life was clearly designed to move her beyond a merely intellectual grasp of the "inappropriateness" of her seemingly generous and loving action, into a fuller awareness of the actual damage she was doing to her son, in order to move her to change her *behavior.*

In this instance, it is easy to see that the only thing that *matters* is whether or not the dreamer grasps the import of the dream. It would have been an exercise in futility to argue with this woman that her dream was calling for her to cut back on her "generous" support of her son if she could not see this implication herself when it was suggested to her. It is an absolute waste of time and energy to argue with anyone about the meanings you see in his or her dreams.

As a practical matter, *only you the dreamer can say with any certainty what meanings your dreams may hold*. Other people's suggestions are likely to be interesting and useful, but in the final analysis, only you can say what your dreams mean.

This does not mean that there are not excellent theories about the unconscious in general and dreams in particular that will yield interesting and important insights most of the time, or that there are not dream workers, counselors, and therapists who are particularly skilled, well trained, intuitive, articulate, and caring people who will have interesting and important things to say most of the time. What it does mean is that the only person who is right about the meanings of a dream all the time is you, the person who had the dream to begin with.

*This certainty about the meaning(s) in a dream usually comes as a wordless "aha" of recognition.* When you discover some part of the truth that your dream is trying to convey, there is almost always a confirming "pop" or "tingle" or "felt shift" of recognition. *I believe that this "aha" is a function of memory*.

The metaphoric meanings of a dream are there from the very beginning. They are not manufactured after the fact by the effort to understand. When someone suggests an accurate interpretation of a dream, or when you discover for yourself some true thing about a dream, you are likely to experience the aha of recognition because, in that moment, you *remember*, consciously for the first time, what you *already knew unconsciously* the dream meant at the time it first occurred.

This previously existent, unconscious knowledge about the significance of a dream is the only reliable source of insight into the many levels of meaning and significance that reside in all dreams. In other words, only you the dreamer can remember with certainty what you already know. The aha of recognition of the dreamer himself or herself is the only reliable touchstone of dream work.

The crucial confirmation of the dreamer's own aha is particularly important to bear in mind because *all dreams have multiple meanings and layers of significance*. There is no such thing as a dream with only one meaning. All dreams (and indeed, all dream images) have multiple meanings that are simultaneously "true." Dreams are like puns and always suggest multiple truths about your life.

In the case of the woman who dreamed about her adult son drowning in the swimming pool full of soup, she also recognized that the figure of "her son" represented a picture of her own creative, masculine side, which she was allowing to "remain submerged" as she focused on nurturing other people.

The technical name for this quality of simultaneous, multiple meanings is "overdetermined." Because all dreams and dream images are overdetermined, it is impossible to say when, or even if, you have "unpacked" a dream fully and touched on all its levels of meaning. For this reason, all ways of concluding the exploration of a dream are arbitrary, and all interpretations of a dream must be considered incomplete, no matter how satisfying and internally consistent and "complete" they may seem.

Sometimes, these multiple levels of truth, and the ahas that reveal and confirm them, may appear to be in conflict, or even mutually exclusive. This is because the very nature of unfinished, still-evolving, and developing human consciousness and self-awareness is ambiguous, multivalent, and often confusingly self-contradictory. The true and full nature of our individually and collectively developing human consciousness, hovering as it always does between the already known and the not yet imagined, cannot be adequately represented or symbolized in any other fashion. The discovery of seemingly contradictory insights into the meanings of a dream is always an indication that your life is moving into a radically new phase, where previously unquestioned assumptions and values are being reshaped by your unanticipated experience.

Even though all dreams have multiple meanings, and always reflect our unique personalities and life circumstances, it is also true that we all share a deep common humanity with many fundamental similarities and feelings. The process of exploring dreams in cooperation with others is made possible by the fact that at this deep, shared, "archetypal" level, *all dreams speak a universal language of metaphor and symbol.*

This universal language of dreams unites us all, even across those barriers of age, gender, race, sexual orientation, conviction, and social/cultural background that we habitually use to separate ourselves from meaningful contact with each other. In fact, the dream unites us even across the boundaries of profound mental and emotional illness and distress. Dreams address all people in essentially the same way, regardless of the things that make us appear radically different from each other.

This universal quality of the images and energies in all dreams means that work unpacking the multiple layers of possible meaning in a dream is of great benefit to *all* the people involved, and not just the original dreamer. In fact, it is often easier to do your own work on your own personal issues in projected form while exploring someone else's dream.

This "universal language" of symbol and metaphor has been charted and described in a rudimentary fashion by many different explorers. I believe that the Swiss psychiatrist and historian of culture Carl G. Jung has left us more accurate and reliable maps, and sketches of maps, than any other explorer, but the only way to verify any explorer's reports is to travel the territory and see for ourselves.

Leading group expeditions and solitary scouting trips into the terra incognita of the dream world over the past forty years has led me to conclude that *all dreams reflect the dreamer's inborn creativity and ability to solve life's problems*. Over and over again, creative energies and ideas emerge from even the most unexpected and obscure corners of the dream experience. There is even substantial reason to suppose that dreams themselves may be "the workshop of evolution" and that new forms of individual and collective life may emerge first as images and experiences in dreams.

One of the most immediately compelling metaphors of the dreaming process comes from folklore: a dream is "the magic mirror that never lies." This ability of the dream to reflect the deepest truths of our lives, despite any denials and conscious self-deceptions we may be trapped in, is both the dream's greatest gift and its greatest challenge.

It is particularly challenging because the picture the dream reflects of your life is as much *collective* as it is personal. The dream always reflects the realities of our social and cultural circumstances with the same clarity and metaphoric candor with which it depicts our individual psychological and emotional responses. *All dreams reflect society as a whole, as well as the individual dreamer's relationship to it*. Some of the most potentially productive, yet generally neglected, aspects of dream work lie in this area of symbolic reflection of the deep social, cultural, and archetypal patterns below the surface appearances of our shared, collective view of reality.

In the course of exploring dreams for some of their many meanings, thousands of people have discovered that *working with dreams in voluntary groups builds community, intimacy, support, and understanding.* The dream not only embodies creative energies and possibilities for individual dreamers but cooperating in the exploration of dreams also provides a unique opportunity for those gifts of dream energy and insight to take form and practical shape in community. Dream groups offer a safe space for exploring even the most difficult and emotionally charged issues in an individual dreamer's life. They also provide nurture and support for creative expression and shared growth that lead inevitably to changes of behavior in family, school, workplace, church, and the larger society. Eventually, these changes in attitude and behavior and increased recognition of common humanity begin to echo far beyond the individual's separate life. Working with dreams in groups helps us overcome the sense of isolation that we all feel from time to time, bringing us into more meaningful contact with one another. This renewal of community has an effect on the shape of society as a whole.

Appendix III at the end of this book offers an account of a "typical" ongoing dream group meeting from beginning to end, so that the reader may get a sense of the communication and interactions that usually accompany group work with dreams. This account will be more meaningful if it is read after the rest of the book, but you may want to turn to it directly to get a sense of how group exploration of dreams works in practice.

In summary, the ten basic assumptions are:

1. All dreams come in the service of health and wholeness.
2. No dream comes just to tell the dreamer what he or she already knows.
3. Only the dreamer can say with any certainty what meanings his or her dream may hold.
4. The dreamer's aha of recognition is a function of previously unconscious memory and is the only reliable touchstone of dream work.
5. There is no such thing as a dream with only one meaning.
6. All dreams speak a universal language of metaphor and symbol.

7. All dreams reflect inborn creativity and ability to face and solve life's problems.
8. All dreams reflect society as a whole, as well as the dreamer's relationship to ːt.
9. Working with dreams regularly improves relationships with friends, lovers, partners, parents, children, and others.
10. Working with dreams in groups builds community, intimacy, and support and begins to impact on society as a whole.

*Chapter Two*

# EXPLORING THE MANY LAYERS OF DREAMS—THE BASIC ASSUMPTIONS IN ACTION

*This is the reason why I take carefully into account the symbols produced by the unconscious mind. They are the only things able to convince the critical mind of modern people. They are convincing for very old-fashioned reasons. They are overwhelming, which is an English rendering of the Latin word* convincere. *The thing that cures a neurosis must be as convincing as the neurosis; and since the latter is only too real, the helpful [dream] experience must be of equal reality.*

—C. G. JUNG

As I stated in Chapter 1, the single most important thing to understand about dreaming is that *all dreams come in the service of health and wholeness.* Every dream is a completely natural and spontaneous instinctive expression, welling up from your unconscious depths, directed toward bringing conscious awareness to neglected or repressed aspects of your experience. The greater awareness of these inadequately appreciated elements of your life that comes from paying more attention to your dreams always turns out to foster psychological and emotional growth and increasing maturity, creative expression, and developing awareness of your life's fullest potentials. There is also always an aspect of every dream that provides an exquisitely accurate "readout" of your physical health and the condition of your body at the moment of the dream.

In fact, even the nasty dreams we call nightmares take the emotionally dramatic form they do to ensure that the content of the dream will be *remembered*, at least for a little while after the dreamer awakens. They do this because the content of the dream is of *particular* potential value and importance.

Let me offer a dramatic and concrete example to illustrate the point. A woman—to preserve her anonymity I will call her Barbara—dreamed:

> I am alone in my kitchen. I hear the sounds of a party going on down in my basement. I think to myself, "There haven't been any impromptu parties in my basement since my kids lived at home. What's going on down there!" I go down the cellar stairs to see what's happening. I get down into the basement and see all these strange people standing around talking and drinking, but now I can't hear anything—it's as though I have gone deaf! I move around and it is as though I have turned into a ghost—no one seems to be able to see or hear me. I realize that I am carrying my handbag now. I didn't have it with me before, but now I have it, and I know that there is a piece of rotting meat inside the bag, and I'm afraid to open it up for fear the smell will offend everyone, so I wander around in the basement feeling more and more anxious and frustrated and hopeless until I finally wake up in a sweat.

This dream was particularly upsetting to Barbara, and when she shared it at the ongoing dream group at her church, there was a collective response of concern among the members, because they held a generally shared projection that the dream might have to do with Barbara's physical health. The group's projections centered on the possibility of cancer (a thought evoked by the "rotting meat" and the menacing, somber quality of "turning into a ghost at the suddenly silent party"), possibly in the lower abdomen (suggested by "the basement"), perhaps localized in the uterus (one of the stronger implications of the image of the handbag).

In waking life, Barbara felt fine, both physically and mentally. In fact, she was taking great pleasure in preparing for a much anticipated trip to Europe. Initially she dismissed the group's reflections on her dream, but in fact she experienced a subtle aha of recognition when they raised the question of her physical health in association with the dream, a tingle of confirmation she ignored and suppressed at the time.

However, when she returned home, she found she could not forget the dream or dismiss from her mind the group's suggestions about the possibility that it had to do with her physical health. Before her trip she made sure to get a checkup, "just to reassure herself."

Her Pap test turned out negative. However, to her surprise and annoyance, her anxiety was not relieved. The lingering, nagging aha about the somber meaning of her dream remained with her as strong as ever and caused her to insist on a further evaluation.

At this point, she was faced with one of the generic problems that often confront people who begin to take their dreams seriously while continuing to live in a society that generally disparages them and dismisses them as "meaningless." She decided to press for further tests but to keep silent about the fact that her insistence was based on an intuition born in a dream, lest she be dismissed as a hysterical hypochondriac.

In the face of her firm, continued insistence, her doctors resorted to a sonogram. This test detected a curious overall thickening of the lining of her uterus, a condition clearly calling for a biopsy. The biopsy detected a malignant and quickly metastasizing cancer. She had immediate surgery, which apparently caught the cancer in the nick of time. As of this writing, she has been in full remission for more than fifteen years.

In her own view, this "nasty" nightmare and her subsequent work with it, supported by her ongoing dream group, saved her life. When she later asked the doctors what would have happened if she had postponed a checkup until after her European trip, the doctors cautiously said that a month or so later would probably have been "too late."

In my experience, there is tremendous benefit to working on dreams regularly in an ongoing group. Group dream work leads to an intensity and intimacy among the participants that provides creative inspiration and deep emotional support for everyone, particularly when they are going through difficult life transitions (as was Barbara, on a number of levels, at the time when she had and shared her dream). *Working with dreams in voluntary groups builds community, deep supportive intimacy, and provides a place where creative responses to life's challenges can be brought to consciousness.*

The depth of intimacy, quality of candid communication, and strength of the emotional support coming to Barbara from the other members of her group as she worked on her dream (to say nothing of afterward, when she went through the traumatic diagnosis and subsequent surgery)

were important in bringing about a positive outcome. The deep connection she experienced with the other members of her dream group, and
their intimate connections with her, were instrumental in helping her
find the courage and emotional strength to bring her understanding of
the dream to fuller consciousness, go through the ordeal of her cancer,
and to come out on the other side more centered in her awareness of the
complex truths of her life.

The story of the work with Barbara's dream also illustrates the third
assumption to bear in mind when remembering and working with
these nocturnal adventures: *only the dreamer can say with any certainty what
meanings his/her dreams may have*. This certainty usually comes to the
dreamer, as it did for Barbara, in the form of an aha experience of insight
and recognition—a wordless "felt shift"—when something true and
on-the-case is suggested about the possible meaning(s) of one's dream.
This aha is the only consistently reliable touchstone in determining the
multiple meanings of a dream.

The many layers of meaning in any dream are already there, woven
into the fabric of the dream experience at the time it occurs. The meanings
are not manufactured after the fact by the effort to remember and understand. The aha reaction can be understood as a function of *memory*. You
experience an aha of recognition when an accurate and evocative comment is offered on a dream because you *remember* (for the first time consciously) what you already knew *unconsciously* the dream meant when you
first dreamed it. Barbara recognized the truth in the comments of her group
because in her heart, she *already knew,* unconsciously, that her dream was
telling her that there was "nasty, rotting meat" (cancer) in her "handbag"
(uterus). The only person who can remember with any clarity or certainty
what his/her dream means is the person who originally experienced it.

The primacy of the aha, your preconscious memory of what your
dream means, is particularly important to bear in mind when you are
working with dreams with the guidance and support of an analyst, therapist, pastoral counselor, spiritual director, psychic consultant, or the like.
Unless it is clearly understood by everyone involved that the aha born
of your preconscious understanding of your dream is the only reliable
touchstone in this work, there is an ironic and distressing tendency for
dream work to become an instrument of tyranny in the dreamer's life.
This tendency is ironic because it is in direct proportion to the quality of

the work with the dreams—the better the work, the more tyrannical it tends to become.

This is because if the dreamer (or the dream worker) thinks that he or she is getting these deeply meaningful and potentially life-shaping insights *from someone else,* then the better the insights, the more dependent the dreamer is likely to become on the relationship with that "guru." In this situation, the cumulative result of months and years of excellent, insightful dream work is often to postpone indefinitely the dreamer's arrival at the center of his or her own life, with his or her emotional and imaginative powers intact, ready to live creatively, expressively, fully, and freely. For this reason, I cannot stress strongly enough that the only one who *knows* what your dreams mean is you. An aha will tip you off that you are "remembering" what you always knew, because you cre-ated your dream in the first place. Others can help you find this inborn, unconscious knowledge, but only the dreamer can be the final judge.

The deep unconscious wisdom that is the source of all meaningful insights into the multiple meanings of dreams is available to all people. *Dream work is not an activity just for an elite, educated few.*

Much of this universally available unconscious wisdom is located in the body. Each cell in the body has a life of its own and contributes its unconscious "readout" to the total experience of the dream each night. In my experience, every dream has many layers of meaning, and there is always a level of every dream that "reports" on the physical condition of the dreamer's body at the moment of the dream. In the vast majority of instances, this level of the dream is virtually invisible. It fades harmoni-ously into the background of the dream, like the old town crier's call "Four A.M. and all's well." Having heard it all their lives, the townspeople don't even wake when they hear it each night as they sleep.

However, when something is physically wrong, the dream places the level of "health readout" in the foreground, tinged with unusual urgency. This often causes the dreamer to awaken with a start, just as our forebears responded to the town crier's urgent call "Four A.M.! Batten your shut-ters and get your livestock to shelter! There's a great storm on the hori-zon!" In this sense, Barbara's dream cried, "Four A.M. and there's a silent, menacing gathering in the basement and a piece of rotting meat in your purse!" and she awoke with a start, already unconsciously aware of the urgency and meaning of this seemingly cryptic message.

The healing and helpful work done by the members of the ongoing dream group with Barbara's dream was made possible by the fact that the symbolic language of dreams really is universal. As Barbara told her dream, the group members imagined their own versions of it and experienced their own ahas of insight born of what that dream would have meant to them if each of them had dreamed it. The comments they offered turned out to be accurate and awakened an answering aha in Barbara because of the deep layers of universal, shared symbolic significance of the images themselves, both in Barbara's dream and in everyone else's imagined versions.

In fact, it is quite likely that many of you reading this book had a similar "tingle" of intuitive/imaginative response to the "feel" and symbolic resonance of the images in Barbara's dream, even before going on to read any of this discussion. Such aha reactions are a result of encountering the universal symbolic quality of the images themselves; such insights are available to us through our shared human sense of the subtle, archetypal, metaphoric language that dreams embody. Dreams speak alike to us all.

The language of the dream is our original native tongue, a common language shared by all human beings. There is every reason to suppose that we have been dreaming in essentially the same fashion for millions of years. (Richard Leakey places *Homo habilis,* the earliest tool-using human ancestors yet discovered, in what is now Olduvai Gorge, at somewhere around two million years B.C.) We all share a deep, unconscious, intuitive understanding of this common language that we can access with a minimum of effort, particularly if this effort is undertaken in the company of others seeking the same kind of self-knowledge.

This universal, cross-cultural, common language of the dream is also shared by the world's mythology and religious texts and rituals. The sacred narratives of world myth and religion are filled with simultaneous levels of symbolic meaning and implication in exactly the same way that dreams are. *Myths and dreams speak the same language of symbol and metaphor and have multiple meanings and multiple layers of significance.* There is no such thing as a dream or a myth with only one meaning. All the images and elements in dreams and myths are "overdetermined," that is, they have multiple reasons for assuming the specific forms they do in any particular instance. As Joseph Campbell says, "A myth is a public dream; a dream is a private myth."

Once again, Barbara's dream may serve as a case in point. The day the group worked with the dream, our first set of projections about the possible meaning of her dream focused on the physical level, and these suggestions were dismissed by Barbara as irrelevant. The group then went on to explore other layers of possible meaning, and several of these other suggestions were confirmed by Barbara with immediate and strong ahas.

Barbara had a strong conscious aha when one person in the group suggested that if it were her dream, it would be important that it start with her being "alone in the kitchen." This person suggested that hearing the sounds of a party in her own house to which she had not been invited, accompanied by the thought that such a thing hadn't happened "since my kids lived at home," might be a picture of the "empty-nest syndrome." For her, she said, her children's growing up and leaving home means the end of her safe, clear role as mother, and her feelings of worth are undermined. The fact that even when Barbara arrived at the party, she was ignored and treated as though she were invisible, led the woman to suggest that if it were her dream, she would think that she had not yet found a new focus for her considerable creative energies, which for more than thirty good years she had devoted to active, daily parenting.

Barbara confirmed that being "alone in the kitchen" was indeed a picture of the "empty nest" when the last teenage child left home. She felt "the sounds of the party in the basement" represented an intuitive call to explore "downward" into the less-lived-in depths of her personal/psychological/spiritual/creative identity.

Barbara's "descent into the basement" strongly suggests the universal archetypal mythological theme of the "descent into the underworld." The hero/heroine of myth often has to descend into the depths (of the unconscious) to find the "treasure" (wisdom, courage, strength, and creativity) that is needed to revitalize the "upper world" (of waking life). Barbara's dream is an excellent example of how this kind of mythological motif will appear "in modern dress" in the dreams of contemporary people, still carrying the same deep and essential symbolic meaning that it has always carried in even the most ancient stories. This collective, archetypal level of meaning is always present to some degree in every dream.

Barbara confirmed that for her the "failure to hear and be heard" once she arrived in the lower level was a symbol of the fear that she had no real worth or importance, either to herself or to others, beyond the now outdated role of active daily mothering. At this level of symbolic meaning, the "rotting meat in the handbag" was a blunt metaphor of the exclusive identification with the role of mother/nurturer, carried in the purse, the place where most women carry their "official identity papers." The "meat," whose only real use would be as nourishment, was "rotting" because it was not being used for the one thing it was good for. Its "nourishment" was no longer needed. Barbara added that for her the question of self-worth and identity through "productive" activity was a particularly pressing emotional issue at the time of the dream. She had recently been forced to quit the part-time job she had taken on a few years earlier when her older children first left home.

All suggestions regarding the meaning of a dream may be simultaneously "correct" and have relevance to one layer of significance in the dream or another. Only the aha of the dreamer can confirm the truth or relevance of an interpretation. In the instance of Barbara's "silent party" dream, she verified *both* the psychological and somatic layers of interpretation.

It seems to me that the continuing academic controversy over the meanings of dreams (or indeed, whether dreams have any inherent meanings at all) must be seen against the backdrop of this ambiguous, overdetermined, multilayered quality of dreams and dream images. My experience convinces me that *all* the major schools of thought regarding the meaning of dreams are essentially correct. All the schools bring massive and persuasive evidence to bear to prove the validity of their points of view. The problem arises when the dream theoreticians suggest, "Having demonstrated beyond reasonable doubt that all dreams mean thus and so, we have somehow magically proven that all other ideas about the meanings in dreams must be false." Good science, like good art, doesn't try to close down the universe of discourse or exclude new possibilities, but rather tries to discover and interpret previously unappreciated patterns and connections.

Freud is right—all dreams *do* have an element of sexual energy and "libidinal" desire woven into their imagery and emotional impact; Adler is also on-the-case—all dreams do have an element depicting the dreamer's "will to power and competence" and his/her relative success or failure in achieving that goal in the multiple arenas of waking life. In addition, Jung is also right—all dreams do include a reflection of the dreamer's psychospiritual development toward "individuation" and his/her search for deeper communion with the archetypal energies of the "collective unconscious" (regardless of the dreamer's conscious attitudes and opinions about "religion"). The contemporary laboratory researchers Winson, Hobson, McCarley, et al., are also on the right track when they say that every dream is the result of the transfer of "random" short-term memory traces into the categories of long-term memory. All these theories are quite useful, and none need be excluded from our investigations. Do we throw away an orange because it isn't an apple or a peach? They are all tasty and nourishing, and they all enhance our appreciation of the category "fruit."

The fact that all dreams exhibit multiple, interdependent meanings raises an interesting further possibility regarding the cancer "diagnosed" in Barbara's dream and its relationship to the other layers of meaning in her dream and her waking life. In physical fact, cancer is a "growth disorder." Cells grow wildly, without regard for the development of the organism as a whole. From a symbolic point of view (treated as a myth/dream image) cancer is a metaphoric expression of life energies finding inappropriate, self-destructive expression in "uncontrolled, unbalanced, and unintegrated growth." In this sense, it may be useful to think of cancer as "the revenge of suppressed, unlived life." Natural energies of growth and creative development manifest themselves in dangerous and disproportionate ways, in part at least because they have not been able to find expression in healthy, balanced, and integrated ways.

In many instances in my experience, cancer appears to play this kind of metaphoric, "compensatory" role in the lives of people in whom more healthy and appropriate channels of growth and expression are blocked. Most often, these blockages take the form of an injured self-image that is too restricted, limited, and small: "I couldn't do something like that. . . . I'm too old to start anything new. . . . Oh, I'm not an artist."

My experience with dreams over the last thirty-five-plus years has led me to conclude that the *symbolic* qualities of physical disease and disorder are a significant factor in their genesis, and thus potentially in their healing and resolution as well. I have seen increased conscious awareness of these symbolic elements (often as a result of working with dreams) serve as an apparently major factor in the resolution of many physical health problems. (For an example of a dream leading to overcoming an addiction to smoking, see Chapter 8.) Repeated experiences of this kind convince me that interior explorations that lead to increased self-awareness and self-understanding, and to more accepting, forgiving, and consciously creative self-concepts, can and regularly do have a profound and positive effect on physical health and healing.

In the case of Barbara's dream, it is a useful thought that a fundamental link may exist between the psychology of the "empty nest," and a swiftly growing uterine cancer that "solves" the problem by mimicking pregnancy. However, this idea can be used as an oppressive "New Age tyranny." The victim of accident, illness, and disease is made "to blame" for his or her distress, with the assertion that "they made their own reality," and attributing it to some sort of unconscious but ultimately avoidable psychospiritual "failure of nerve." Even when there is an element of truth to it, this attitude lacks what the injured person most needs: compassion. In searching for the symbolic energies involved in illness, injury, and healing, it is vital always to focus attention on the possibility of healing and reconciliation, rather than on blame.

Many people shy away from consciously examining these "subtle" symbolic and metaphoric aspects of physical illness and injury, because it is intellectually suspect on the one hand, and because it is potentially distressing and emotionally disrespectful to the person struggling to heal him/herself on the other. In my experience, however, the rewards of including attention to psychospiritual healing, particularly the transformation of injured and limited self-image, far outweigh the potential dangers. An aha regarding the deeper symbolic significance of a disease or injury is often accompanied by noticeable and immediate increased physical healing, to say nothing of the positive consequences in other areas of the person's life.

At this juncture, the question of the multiple layers of meaning in every dream may also be extended to include the impact that larger social and cultural patterns have on the health and psychospiritual wholeness of individual dreamers, and the ways in which dreams regularly reflect and reveal these larger collective forces.

Our dreams always include layers of "collective" significance, which is to say dreams not only provide an accurate picture of the individual dreamer's personal circumstances, but also portray the culture and society in which the dreamer resides. This reflection of society as a whole in dreams is rendered with the same precision and "objectivity" with which the dreams reflect individual situations and emotions.

The "empty-nest syndrome" revealed in Barbara's dream touches on this societal level of meaning. The images of her dream clearly reflect cultural forces, most particularly oppression by the collective structures of sexism and sex-role stereotyping. Despite the advances made by the women's movement in recent years, our masculinist society still conspires to persuade women that their worth as people resides wholly in restricted gender-defined roles as sex partners, family nurturers, and mothers. There is compelling reason to suppose that a large part of the sinister quality of the "silent party in the basement" (in addition to representing Barbara's initial "deafness" to the subtle messages of her body with regard to the cancer) may also represent her primarily unconscious but deeply felt experience of her culture as a whole; in the midst of seemingly normal and polite socializing, society as a whole conspires to "ignore" her true personhood as an older woman, just as it tends to ignore the true personhood of all women as a class.

The emotions of intense "hopelessness" and "frustration" that Barbara experienced at the end of her dream are particularly poignant in this regard. At one level, these feelings reflect an intuitive knowledge that her physical health was in deep jeopardy. Here we can see another example of the dream employing what appears to be "exaggeration for effect" in order to move her from passive consideration to action. Her extreme emotions of hopelessness reflect feelings most usually evoked when human beings "look death in the face." We all know our own physical deaths are inevitable; however, any experience that focuses our attention on that knowledge almost always brings forth such emotions.

At another level, Barbara's deep feelings of hopelessness and frustration reflect what a woman may experience when she begins to explore the question of just how much of her authentic life has gone ignored and unlived because she has chosen socially acceptable, middle-class accommodations to the oppressions of sexism. When a woman asks herself "Has my chosen lifestyle limited my imagination and my perception of possibilities to the ones on the 'approved list' provided by my parents, school, church, and the larger society?" the authentic answer, particularly when this question is asked later in life, often leads to a profound sense of frustration, anger, and hopelessness.

Understood at this level, Barbara's dream stands together with thousands of dreams I have heard from women over the years that embody in their metaphors vivid pictures of the woman's experience of sexist oppression, regardless of their intellectual convictions on the subject in their waking lives. Barbara had always deeply enjoyed her life as a "typical" wife and mother, resented the implication of certain feminists that it was a trivial occupation or a waste of her creative energies, and for this reason had never had much sympathy for the so-called women's movement. Yet it is interesting to note that her initial thought in the dream is that the sounds of the "party" remind her of the impromptu gatherings of adolescents that took place when her children lived at home, but when she gets down into the basement, it is composed entirely of adults. Barbara was willing to consider that this might reflect the fact that sexism is an "adult" phenomenon, a way in which adults ignore each other's authentic humanity and train children to do likewise.

It is interesting to speculate that at this level, the "deafness" that she experiences in the dream, in addition to being a picture of her experience as an older woman in a patriarchal society, may also be a metaphor of her internalized oppression and her reluctance in waking life to consider the ways in which she has been injured by sexism. Prior to the dream and her bout with cancer, Barbara always preferred to think that because of her relatively privileged class status, and the happiness of her marriage, that she had pretty much escaped the oppressions that other women experienced. With the dramatic changes in her life reflected by the dream and her cancer, based on her ahas in the dream work, Barbara has been increasingly willing to reconsider many of these opinions, and to seek more dramatic and expressive outlets for her considerable creative energies.

It is important to note that the dreams of men are regularly and equally eloquent about the collective experience of sexism, and the oppressive consequences of gender-role inequality as viewed from a masculine perspective. Let me offer a brief example.

A man in his late thirties reported the following dream:

I am a warrior, riding on a big black horse. I have just fought in a terrible, fierce battle, and I have many deep, bloody wounds. I am riding back to my home village. I come over a hill and see that the village is a smoking ruin—all my struggles to protect my home community have been for nothing.

I ride slowly down toward the ruins. The few people who have survived see me coming, but they do not recognize me. They flee in terror. One man is too old and crippled to flee. As I ride toward him, he cringes in terror, but as I get closer, he suddenly recognizes me. He straightens up and asks, "Where are the others?" I look at him, but I can not bring myself to speak. He understands my silence—I am the only one of the group of men who left the village to go off and fight who has survived and returned home. He looks up at me in shocked horror as I ride slowly past him.

Ahead of me now is a woman carrying a small boy and holding a roasting spit that she is wielding as a spear. She is protecting the boy. She holds up her "spear" in a menacing, defensive gesture as I approach, but then she recognizes me as I draw closer, and she drops her spear and comes toward me. She tells me to dismount so that she can help me and bind up my wounds, but I know that if I dismount, I will never be able to mount again. I just keep riding slowly forward.

Now the old man calls out to the fleeing villagers, "Follow him! He will show us the way!" The people, including the woman and the boy, all start to fall in and walk behind me as I continue to ride slowly forward. I struggle and manage to lift my head and look toward the far horizon. Mountains rise in the distance. Perhaps we will be able to find some safety in the mountains, if we can get there.

Like all dreams, this one has many layers of meaning, ranging from the personal to the collective. It was dreamed by "Peter," a man recovering from a protracted, debilitating physical and emotional illness. These illnesses appeared to have been caused in large measure by his being permanently laid off from his "rust belt" industrial employment. There is substantial reason to suppose that Peter was experiencing a masculine equivalent of Barbara's "empty nest" as his fundamental sense of value and worth as a man was jeopardized by the loss of his job when his company closed its plant.

At one level, the wounds he carries in his dream are unique and personal, but at another level, as with Barbara's dream, the metaphoric shape of his dream reveals collective wounds received from the internalization of sexist values prevalent in the culture, most particularly the traditional male sex role.

Virtually all men in contemporary, patriarchal society bear their own versions of Peter's "warrior wounds" and the accompanying emotions: an increasing sense of hopelessness and numbness, a nagging awareness that their immense and debilitating efforts are resulting in an increasingly sterile and futile outcome, an inability to "speak" or give spontaneous expression to feeling and emotion, a paralyzing inability to seek and accept human support and contact, particularly at moments of greatest stress and pain, a separation from the nurturing and healing feminine within and without, etc. All of this leads to a tragically limited "heroic" self-image as a "victorious" but badly crippled warrior with *no real choices or options*—even in victory—only the prospect of continuing on in silence with the one difficult, painful course leading deeper into hopeless (but "honorable") misery.

Although this dream deserves more detailed attention, I offer it here primarily as a clear example of a dream that, in addition to the other layers of significance it conveys, dramatically reveals the distressingly common, collective shape of some of the most debilitating psychospiritual consequences of sexism for men as a group.

I regularly see similar reflections of the unacknowledged collective oppressions of society in the dreams of children, ethnic minorities, poor people, and institutionalized populations in hospitals and prisons, among others.

Like the layer of dreaming that always reflects the state of the dreamer's physical health, this level of meaning picturing society as a whole is present in every dream. Most often, it tends to blend into the background of the dream, much as our waking awareness of society tends to form the unconscious "background" of our decisions and actions, emerging into the foreground only when something is noticeably "amiss" in our relationship to our larger society and culture. There is compelling reason to suppose this was the case for both Barbara and Peter at the times when they had their respective dreams.

Another related archetypal aspect of dreams and dreaming holds great promise for the future of humankind: *dreams are reflections of our inborn creativity*. Creativity is our universal human birthright. All creativity has its source deep in the unconscious. Dreams have always been one

of the major vehicles for the appearance of the creative impulse in waking
imagination and awareness. This creativity is easily seen in the incredibly
clever, dramatic, symbolic "reframing" of our waking lives and activities
that our dreams always provide us. It also appears in the form of "creative
inspiration" for specific projects and acts of self-expression.

Most people think of the creative inspiration of dreams solely in terms
of traditional artistic productions. Dreams do in fact regularly serve as a
source of "artistic" inspiration, but all too often this popular understanding has obscured the larger truth that dreams have tremendous value as
creative inspirations in *all* aspects of life. The archetypal creative impulse
given shape in our dreams provides creative energy and innovation, not
just in the arts, but in all areas of human endeavor, specifically including
the inventions and discoveries of "hard" science and technology.

For example, most people are aware that Robert Louis Stevenson
composed many of his novels and stories, and particularly the "psychological masterpiece" *Dr. Jekyll and Mr. Hyde,* by transcribing and rework-
ing events that took place in his dreams. People are also generally aware
that many composers, including Mozart and Beethoven, made extensive
use of the music they first heard in their dreams. Some will recall that the
composer Tartini received the inspiration for his famous "Devil's Trill"
by dreaming that he was engaged in a musical competition with "Old
Nick," watching and listening to him improvise on the violin.

Students of Romantic literature will remember that Samuel Taylor
Coleridge composed the poem "Kubla Khan" by directly transcribing
his dream inspiration and that this composition remains unfinished today
because the dream recording was interrupted by the infamous "person
from Porlock." Like so many of our own dream memories, Coleridge's
dream inspiration had disappeared from his memory by the time he got
rid of his unwanted visitor and returned to his poetic dream record.

For the most part, these stories of "artistic" dream inspirations are
much better known than the equally dramatic and historically attested to
stories of scientific and technical inspiration from dreams. However, the
truth of the matter is that dreams have been and continue to be a source
of genuinely innovative thinking, invention, and discovery in fields
ranging from philosophy to physics, from architecture and agriculture to
electronics and zoology.

In the nineteenth century, the aristocratic Russian academician

Dimitri Mendeleyev was investigating the nature of the fundamental building blocks of the physical world, the basic "elements" that combine in various forms to make up all physical matter. Mendeleyev sought in vain for some overall organizing principle to explain and predict their complex and seemingly random properties and appearances.

It was the habit of the Mendeleyevs (as it is among the upper classes in Russia even today) to spend their summers in the countryside at their dacha outside Odessa on the Black Sea. It was also the regular practice of Mendeleyev's extended family to pass the hottest part of the afternoon playing chamber music together.

One day, Mendeleyev excused himself from the family musicale and retired to an adjoining room where he lay down on a divan to take a nap. From the adjoining room, he could still hear the strains of their music as he slept. In Mendeleyev's now-famous dream, he suddenly "saw" that the basic elements of the physical universe disposed themselves in relation to one another in an orderly and beautiful pattern, like repeating phrases of music. He awakened from his dream in a state of great excitement and sketched the first model of the periodic table, that staple of all introductory chemistry texts.

Half a century later, a Dane, Niels Bohr, was examining essentially the same question as Mendeleyev. Building on Mendeleyev's earlier insight, Bohr formulated the question for himself in a slightly different fashion. He asked himself, Why are there such things as "basic elements" in the first place? What is the physical principle that allows for the existence of discrete elements at all? Why, for example, is there hydrogen over here on Mendeleyev's periodic table, and then an empty space, and then helium? Why isn't there something in between the two that constitutes a transitional state between them?

Having exhausted all the ideas that were currently available without coming up with any satisfactory hypothesis, Bohr had a dream.

He dreamed that he was at the races. (In some versions of the story, he is reported to have been dreaming he was eating ice cream—a homely touch that I find most appealing.) As he was thus occupied in his dream, he heard an announcement over the public address system that a race he was particularly interested in was about to start. (I have always assumed that it was a race he had bet money on.) On hearing the announcement, he climbed into the wooden grandstand to view the race, and while he was standing there, he noticed that the lanes in which the horses were to run were heavily marked out with white calcium dust.

Looking at these exaggerated lane markers, he "remembered" in the dream that it was the rule at this particular track that the horses had to run within the marked lanes. Horses could change lanes, provided they were sufficiently separated not to bump, but any horse that was observed to be running outside a marked lane, kicking up the white powder as it ran, was immediately disqualified.

At this point in his dream, Bohr reports that he was filled with tremendous excitement. He suddenly understood that embedded in this curious "rule of the track" was a symbolic solution to his question about the basic "rules" of physics that determined the discrete nature of the elements. Bohr suddenly grasped that the orbits of the electrons around the nucleus of an atom are as rigidly and arbitrarily "marked" as the lanes on the track. Like the horses, the electrons are not "free" to rotate in any orbit, but only in the predetermined orbits defined by the discrete and specific amounts, or "quanta," of energy necessary to move them from one specific orbit to another. These unvarying and discrete "quanta" of energy define the particular paths of the orbiting electrons, which in turn determine the discrete and unvarying qualities of the basic elements themselves. He awoke from this dream and hastily sketched the first formulation of "quantum theory" (for which he later won the Nobel Prize in physics) on the back of an envelope.

Albert Einstein was asked by the journalist Edwin Newman when he had the first inkling of the idea for his theory of relativity. Einstein replied that the basis of the idea had first come to him years ago, when he was an adolescent back in Germany, flunking math, and being counseled by his family to take up a career as a plumber so that he wouldn't be a financial burden on them. During this difficult period of his life, Einstein reported he had a particularly riveting and memorable dream:

In his dream, he was sledding with his friends at night. They would climb the hill, whisk down the snowy slope, then climb to the top again to repeat the pleasurable slide. At one point, Einstein climbed the hill and started to slide down once again, only this time he became aware that his sled was traveling faster and faster. (Those familiar with

Einstein's life and work will recognize the basic shape of, and presumably the earliest inspiration for, his famous "thought experiment," demonstrating the fundamental principle of "relativity" in the particular metaphor of this dream.)

In his dream, as he sped down the hill faster and faster, he realized that he and his sled were approaching the speed of light. He looked up at that point and saw the stars—they were being refracted into a spectra of colors that Einstein had never seen before. He felt filled with a sense of awe and numinosity. He understood that in some way he was looking at the most important meaning in his life.

"I knew that I had to understand that dream, and," he concluded to Edwin Newman, "you could say, and I would say, that my entire scientific career has been a meditation on that dream!"

My favorite example of scientific discovery through dreams involves Elias Howe's invention of that staple of modern life, the sewing machine. When James Hargreaves and Edmund Cartwright invented the spinning jenny and the power-driven loom in the mid-1700s, the industrial revolution was off and running. However, the absence of the third necessary invention—a machine that could sew with the same increased efficiency that the other two machines could spin and weave—meant that the industrial revolution was stymied; in order to actually produce finished goods that could be sold, all the mountains of machine-made cloth still had to pass through the skilled hands of the medieval Guild of Tailors. The economic and social bottleneck was immense.

The economic pressure to invent a machine that could sew with the same mechanical speed and quality control with which the other machines could produce cloth focused a tremendous amount of creative energy on the problem all around the world, but for more than half a century, the problem went unsolved.

Here in the United States, Howe began to work on the problem, lured by the immense amount of money being offered as a reward by the cloth barons for a solution to their long-standing problem. Having exhausted all the conventional ideas about building a machine that could sew, none of which could be made to work, he continued to struggle with the problem, still without results. Then, some seventy-five years after the invention of the first spinning and weaving machines, Howe had a dream.

As he recounted it, his memory of the dream picked up in the middle of the action (as so many dream memories do).

Howe finds himself in Africa, fleeing from cannibals. They pursue him through the jungle. He flees in desperation, but the natives capture him, tie him up hand and foot, and carry him back to their village slung from a pole. There they dump him into a huge iron pot full of water. They light a fire under the pot and start to boil him alive.

In his dream, as the water starts to bubble and boil around him, he discovers that the ropes have loosened enough for him to work his hands free. He tries repeatedly to take hold of the edge of the pot and haul himself out of the hot water, but every time he manages to heave himself up over the edge of the pot, the natives reach across over the flames and forcibly poke him back down into the pot again with their sharp spears.

When Howe awoke from this "nightmare," part of his mind noted with some distance and objectivity, "That's odd—those spears all have holes in the points." As he came more fully awake, he realized, "Holes in the points . . . holes in the points! That's it! That's the answer!"

Howe realized as he awoke from his dream that he and all his rivals had been blinded by the conventional idea of the sewing needle. As a hand tool, the thread transport hole must be back at the blunt end, where it is most convenient for the human hand, but all that was required to make a machine that would sew was to move the thread transport hole up to the point of the needle, where it would be most convenient for a machine. Then it was a relatively simple matter to design a system of gears that would cause the needle to poke the thread down through the layers of cloth, wrap it around a second thread, and then pull it up again, all very neatly and efficiently.

Unfortunately, we do not know enough about Howe's personal life and emotional history to make anything more than vaguely educated guesses about the layers of meaning and significance in this historic dream that refer to his personal psychology. However, for us, the primary significance of the dream is its collective impact. This dream released the pent-up energies of the industrial revolution. With the invention of the sewing machine, the last bottleneck in the first fully industrial process was broken open.

A friend of mine has pointed out that at this collective level of meaning, the "hot water" the "cannibals" were "cooking" him in might ironically be a metaphor for the "sweat" and misery of the "sweatshops" that were the social consequence of his invention. The "hot water" was also likely a metaphor for the "sweat" of Howe's intense mental efforts.

At the level of Freudian sexual imagery, the sewing machine itself is a prime example of the "sublimation" of "primitive" libidinal energy into creative expression and cultural artifacts, and the specific imagery of the dream evokes that layer of possible meaning strongly.

Even more important, the dream offers an extraordinary example of the Jungian archetype of the "Shadow" and its creative and gift-giving aspect. It is far from accidental that the creative solution to the technical problem is literally in the hands of the darkest, most repugnant, and scary figures in the dream—the "cannibals." In Howe's dream, the cannibalistic natives manifest one of the deepest truths about the archetypal energy of the Shadow: that from the point of view of conventional waking consciousness, everything that is unconscious and not yet clearly manifested and understood in the world of the ego appears nasty, ugly, frightening, "dark," and dangerous. However, since the deep unconscious contains all that waking consciousness desires and longs for the most—the energies of love, creativity, and felt communion with the Divine, to name only the most salient and obvious—then the dark and frightening mask of the Shadow always hides the thing devoutly wished and sought.

In this case, the "cannibals" are the ones who carry the technical solution to the industrial design problem, but it requires psychological clarity of heroic proportions to see past the upsetting emotions of the "nightmare" (which, once again, mark the dream as being of particular interest and value) in order to see the gift that is literally being thrust in the dreamer's face. How many of us have had equally gripping "nightmares" but failed to see the healing and creative possibilities that the dream was thrusting at us?

I find these four anecdotes particularly interesting and compelling because they demonstrate how the creative impulse is given shape in dreams. There are literally hundreds of similar stories of dream-inspired innovation in science and technology that could be used equally well as examples of the archetypal creative impulse that is always woven into the total fabric of our dreams. Of course, each of these four dreams has many threads of meaning in addition to the element of creative inspiration, as all dreams do, but these four examples do show how the creative impulse is "delivered" to consciousness in essentially the same symbolic/metaphoric form that the dreams employ with the other layers of meaning they embody.

The dream experiences of Howe, Mendeleyev, Bohr, and to a lesser extent, Einstein, also demonstrate another important principle of dream inspiration. Each one spent immense effort and time examining the basic problem from all the angles suggested by conventional wisdom before their creative-breakthrough dreams occurred. In many other stories of scientific and technological dream inspiration (from Otto Loewi's dream inspiration for the experiment that demonstrated the chemical activity associated with the functioning of the nerves, to Friedrich Kekule's discovery that the molecular structure of benzine is ring shaped, prompted by a dream image of a snake biting its own tail), the creative breakthrough stimulated by the imagery of the dream appears in recognizable form only after all the possibilities of conventional thought and analysis have been carefully reexamined and exhausted.

Priming the pump works. It isn't just artists and scientists who are rewarded with creative "breakthroughs" as a result of paying attention to their dreams. All of us prime the dream pump each time we ask ourselves honest questions about our most important life issues. Being ready and open to the dream's healing and creative messages allows all of us to touch the archetypal creative impulse that is woven into our dreams every night.

Dreams exhibit a wisdom, good humor, cleverness, and creativity that is truly astonishing when viewed in the light of waking consciousness. The benefits of paying more regular attention to our dreams will be great, both at the level of the personal details of our lives, and the larger, collective level of our shared reality and interdependent existence. To quote the old Universalist maxim, the dream comes in the service of health and wholeness to promote "the reconciliation of each with all."

*Chapter Three*

# DREAMS AND THE EVOLUTION
# OF CONSCIOUSNESS

*Only the [one] who can consciously consent to the power of the inner voice
becomes a personality.*

—C. G. JUNG

The scientific evidence is in: *all* human beings dream, whether they tend to recall their regular nightly adventures or not. The discovery in the sleep laboratory of the University of Chicago by Eugene Aserinsky and Nathaniel Kleitman in 1958 that their young experimental subjects regularly exhibited "rapid eye movement" (REM) in sleep when they were dreaming, and not during other periods of the sleep cycle, made it possible for other researchers around the world to verify through direct observation in the controlled environment of the laboratory the ancient wisdom that "all people dream."

The discovery of REM sleep (also called paradoxical sleep in the literature) and its fundamental association with dreaming ushered in a new era of laboratory research focused on dreaming. Prior to the REM discoveries, academic dream research had been limited to examination of people's subjective dream reports—highly unreliable and unverifiable data from an experimental scientific point of view, since they can't be measured or duplicated. This fundamental lack of a means of collecting reliable, objective data about dreams and dreaming meant that interest in the scientific community in dream studies was

understandably low and that money to support such research was not
readily forthcoming.

After the publication of Aserinsky's and Kleitman's discoveries, however, it became possible for scientific researchers to study the physiologi-
cal phenomenon of dreaming in the laboratory on a regular basis, without
recourse to the subjective and highly suspect reports of dreamers themselves. On the one hand, this breakthrough has focused a great deal of
creative attention and financial support on the physiology and biochem-
istry of dreaming, for the first time making dream studies a legitimate
and respected field of scientific/academic inquiry; but on the other hand,
it has also tended to divert attention away from the all-important questions of the symbolic content and meaning of dreams and the dreaming
process, in favor of an almost exclusive focus on the physical aspects of
dreaming.

By its very nature, laboratory research is limited to an exclusive
concern with measurable and quantifiable physical data. This inherent
restriction has even led some laboratory researchers into the odd assertion that the process of dreaming is "meaningless" in itself. Many laboratory investigators (such as Crick, Mitcheson, Hobson, McCarley, and
the rest) view the phenomenon of the dream as the product of random
neurological activity, or at best, as "noise" associated with the transfer of
short-term memory traces into the categories of long-term memory. As
I have already stated, my own work leads me to conclude that dreams are
in fact laden with multiple meanings and layers of significance. Certainly,
the evidence is clear that *one* of these layers of significance observable in
all dreams is that short-term memory traces are being integrated into the
long-term memory, but this in no way contradicts the overwhelming
evidence that *other* meaningful mental and emotional energies are being
given shape in the experience of dreaming *at the same time*.

Extensive research into the functioning of waking consciousness
strongly suggests that the practical limit of short-term human memory
is about an hour and a half. Studies repeatedly show that no matter how
well motivated and dedicated a person may be, no one can maintain sustained attention on any given activity for more than about ninety minutes. Every hour and a half or so, awake or asleep, the brain has to go
"off-line" and "reprocess" the experience of the immediate past into
the categories and structures of long-term memory. The approximately

ninety-minute regularity of the REM sleep/dreaming cycle appears to be determined in large measure by the limitations of "space" on the "blackboard" of short-term memory.

It seems to me that the strong evidence that dreams are associated with the restructuring of short-term memory into long-term memory, far from indicating that dreams are meaningless, is one of the strongest indications that the dreaming process is central to the creation of meaning in human consciousness. How do human beings perceive meaning? We use the categories of long-term memory: sequential ordering, cross-referencing through intellectual comparison for difference and similarity, establishing linked associations through perception of underlying structural homology, symbolic/emotional "charge" and cathexis, etc. These categories themselves *are* the basic structures of human perception of meaning. The categories of long-term memory comprise the basic definition of meaning. The regular, rhythmic reflection of these fundamental categories in the seemingly bizarre imagery and experience of the dream is in itself proof positive of the inherently meaningful nature of dreams and dreaming.

The experience of dreaming is not "rational," but this does not mean that it is not meaningful. Quite the contrary; the seemingly irrational imagery and emotion and thought in the dream experience reflect, and are primary manifestations of, the processes of association from which all possibilities of meaningful self-awareness arise in the first place.

As a result of Aserinsky's and Kleitman's discovery of the REM sleep cycle and its positive correlation with dreaming, a number of other important discoveries about the nature of the dreaming process have been made. For instance, ethologists (animal-behavior specialists) have observed animals' behavior during their sleeping cycles more closely and discovered that REM is a regular part of the sleep cycle in virtually all animals with eyelids that close in sleep. This discovery suggests not only that all human beings dream but that *all* complex, warm-blooded, viviparous mammalian species regularly exhibit periods of REM in sleep and may therefore be assumed to dream regularly as well.

There are reports that the echidna, the warm-blooded "spiny anteater" of Australia that reproduces by laying eggs like a bird, may not exhibit rapid eye movement in sleep and therefore may not dream. However, all other mammalian and marsupial species have been observed to exhibit rapid eye motion in sleep and are therefore assumed to dream. Continued research in cross-species communication, such as Francine Patterson's work with Koko the Gorilla and Washoe the Chimpanzee's computer-assisted interactions with the ethologists at the Yerkes Primate Center, have reportedly yielded dream reports from other animals. Researchers working with Koko the Gorilla have reported that Koko once awoke from sleep in apparent distress, and that when asked in sign, "What's the matter?" she is reported to have signed back, "Dark, bad, dirty, awful." When the gorilla watchers asked for further elaborations, Koko reportedly signed, "I don't want to talk about it . . ." It seems to me that to deny that this is an authentic interspecies dream report—more specifically, an interspecies report of an emotionally distressing nightmare—is to deny everything we know about dreams and dreaming. Reports such as this ask us to acknowledge the deep psychological and emotional kinship we humans have with all living things, and most particularly with our closest primate relatives.

Laboratory research and field observation also show that during the REM cycle, the metabolic activity of the dreaming organism regularly increases to levels approaching those of waking life. These anomalous "spindles" of metabolic activity are part of the reason why the REM dreaming cycle is also sometimes referred to as paradoxical sleep. If one looks exclusively at these fluctuations in metabolism and electrochemical activity during dormancy periods, then the evidence is quite dramatic that *all living things dream*—even those organisms that do not have eyelids, or even eyes, to exhibit REM. Once again, modern science appears to be confirming the ancient folk wisdom: not only do all people dream, but dreaming is an experience shared by all living organisms.

The analysis of electroencephalographic evidence (the readout of so-called brain waves during REM sleep in both human and animal subjects) has also clearly shown that the responses of the brain to the illusory experience of the dream are the *same* as the responses of the brain to waking events. In other words, if you are dreaming that you are running in the Boston Marathon, your whole metabolism stimulated, and your brain is urgently pumping out exactly the same instructions to your major muscles to run as it would if you were *actually running* in the race. The only thing that prevents the dreamer of such a dream from jumping out of bed and hitting the floor to run is the presence of neural inhibitors in the bloodstream during REM periods.

These inhibitors isolate the voluntary nervous system and prevent the impulses that come from the cerebral cortex in response to the experience of the dream from activating the muscles. The inhibitors are highly unstable and break down within microseconds, leaving no discernible trace. Produced continuously, they are immediately replaced all during the experience of the dream, while REM sleep occurs. As soon as the dream and the REM sleep cycle end, the production of neural inhibitors ceases. The last molecules break down and disappear immediately, the period of temporary paralysis comes to an end, and once again voluntary control of the major muscles is restored to the impulses generated in the cerebral cortex. This is one of the reasons why a sleeper will lie quite still while he or she is dreaming, then tend to stir around as soon as the dream is over.

Once these neural inhibitors were discovered, a number of nasty experiments were undertaken with cats and other research subjects where the production and release of these neural inhibitors was prevented, and sure enough, when the subjects entered the dream state, they began to act out their dreams physically with great energy and intensity. These experiments demonstrated positively what the electroencephalographic evidence had so strongly suggested: the neuromotor response of the sleeping brain to the experience of the dream is fundamentally the same as that of the fully alert brain to the experiences of waking life.

Sometimes, however, the endocrine system malfunctions and continues to produce neural inhibitors even after the dream ends and the brain has returned to a state of full alertness. When this happens, the awakened sleeper experiences total paralysis—one literally "cannot move a muscle." Usually when people experience this distressing sleep disorder, they struggle to move and become more and more agitated with repeated failure, until at the height of their distress, they somehow succeed in overcoming the paralytic effect and finally regain conscious, voluntary control of their bodies.

The typical frantic struggles to overcome the continuing dream paralysis are ironically counterproductive, because it is precisely those urgent cerebral commands to the large muscles to move that are most effectively blocked by the inhibitors. Oddly enough, experience shows

that the most effective way to "break the spell" of dream paralysis is to
make a face, because it is the small muscles of the face and neck that are
least affected by the paralysis, and moving them voluntarily appears to be
the easiest and most effective way to send the missed "signal" to the endocrine system that the dream is over and it is time to restore command of
the voluntary muscles to the cerebral cortex. It may even be the case that
it is the unintentional facial expressions of distress and frustration that
accompany the unsuccessful efforts to move that actually accomplish the
release from the "spell" of continuing paralysis in these circumstances.

Such malfunctions of the dream paralysis system, although they are
often quite distressing when they occur, shrink to relative insignificance
in comparison with another more sinister implication of this phenomenon: sudden infant death syndrome (SIDS). Although, for obvious reasons, a full-blown SIDS attack has never been observed in a controlled
clinical setting, some clinicians are suggesting that what happens in SIDS
is that the infant, often born prematurely, goes to sleep, enters the dream
state, and the dream neural inhibitors enter the bloodstream in inappropriate amounts, or inappropriate concentrations. When this happens, not
only are the voluntary nervous impulses associated with the dreaming
experience blocked, but the *in*voluntary nervous impulses, which are
normally unaffected by the inhibitors are blocked as well, and the child
smothers to death because the heart stops pumping, the diaphragm stops
contracting, and the child stops breathing.

The fact that premature infants are particularly at risk for SIDS also
strongly suggests the dream paralysis system is the locus of the problem: it
seems highly likely that the basic distinction between voluntary and involuntary nervous impulses, upon which the proper functioning of the dream
paralysis system depends, has not had sufficient time to develop in some
premature infants. In these cases, even an otherwise appropriate amount or
intensity of inhibitors has a lethal effect because the neurological structure of
the premature infant is not sufficiently differentiated to respond properly.

In any case, these facts and inferences about the dream paralysis system and its absolute link with dreaming present a curious anomaly: here
is a perfectly normal and natural bodily system that, even when it is functioning at peak efficiency, renders the organism totally paralyzed, helpless, vulnerable, and at risk several times a night. Furthermore, when
this system malfunctions, it significantly extends those periods of risk

and vulnerability and (in the distressingly common occurrence of SIDS) can even *kill* you. Yet there is not one complex, evolved, warm-blooded, viviparous species that has evolved to abandon this seemingly anomalous and dangerous behavior in favor of the increased chances of survival that one might well imagine would come from the reduction or elimination of these regular periods of physical risk and danger that accompany the process of dreaming.

This odd state of affairs points to an interesting conclusion: if you take the idea of the evolution of the species at all seriously—if you think there is anything at all to the idea that species alter both behavior and physical structure to enhance their ability to survive in particular ecological/environmental circumstances—then there must also be something about dreaming itself that is of primary and fundamental importance from a collective evolutionary survival point of view, because in spite of these multiple, serious, and dangerous drawbacks associated with dreaming, there is not a single relatively evolved species that has found it of increased survival value to abandon this seemingly anomalous and dangerous behavior.

Sandor Ferenczi, the Hungarian colleague of Freud and Jung, looked at the evidence related to dreams and evolution and concluded that not only is dreaming significant from an evolutionary point of view, "dreaming itself is the workshop of evolution." Ferenczi suggests that the human species may have evolved into the condition we recognize as human today because our prehuman, hominid ancestors *dreamed* about articulate speech, making the first neurological/synaptic connections and first laying down the neural pathways necessary for speech in the dream state.

This is, admittedly, a difficult proposition to demonstrate at the level of species evolution. However, it is not at all difficult to demonstrate at the level of the evolution and development of individual consciousness and self-awareness. Regardless of the other issues our dreams may constellate, they are *always* centered on revealing the character of the person the dreamer is developing and growing into. No matter what else the dream may do, it always asks and symbolically answers the same question: "Who am I, now, in this moment, how did I get to be this way, and who am I becoming as I grow and mature?"

The fact that this is universally the case at the level of individual consciousness, together with the overwhelming inferential evidence that there is something of equal significance about dreaming at a collective level, suggests that Ferenczi and the others are correct, that the "dream is the workshop of evolution" and that dreaming itself provides the venue where the evolutionary developments and survival strategies of entire species are first formed and manifested.

The implication is inescapable: in addition to the personal/psychological and social/cultural layers of significance that regularly manifest in dreams, there is also a layer concerned with the evolution and development of the species as a whole. This also points to one important answer to the question of why dreams regularly appear so "obscure" and "meaningless" when we first recall them. Our dreams appear "confused" and "pointless," in part at least, because they regularly address possibilities of evolutionary growth and development that we are not yet sufficiently conscious of and sophisticated enough to recognize and appreciate.

This is clearly the case at the level of individual growth and development. We regularly recognize in retrospect that our dreams were speaking about developments in our personal lives that we were not yet consciously aware of at the time, and there is significant reason to suppose that this may be so at a collective level as well.

In this connection, I often imagine our hominid ancestors of more than 4 million years ago waking up from their dreams to the first rays of dawn over the rolling savannah and stretching and scratching and blinking and wondering, "What was *that* all about! What were all those strange noises in my dreams? They weren't insect noises or bird noises or the sounds the wind and water make, although they sound a little like all of those—no, they were definitely animal noises, but not like any animal sounds I've ever heard before. . . . What were they?"

I imagine hominids having these dreams full of strange sounds and idly pondering the question of their meaning at moments of sufficient comfort and leisure from time to time throughout their lives. Perhaps this process of dreaming and pondering continued for generations, perhaps even millennia, until at last some supergenius of the hominid pack had the astonishing original thought: "Oh! I get it! Those sounds *mean* something! They are the *names* of things! They're *words!*" It seems to me that this marvelous creature—was it a woman?—has claim to the title of First Human, Original Ancestor of the Race *Homo Sapiens*, Adam and/or Eve, as the case may be.

Clearly, we are still dreaming. Evolution is not done with us. We are not finished or completed, either as individuals or as a species. To put it into theological terms, the Book of Revelations is not yet closed; the Divine (or the still-unconscious and as-yet-unmanifested potentialities of full humanity, if you prefer) is not yet as consciously developed and self-aware within us as it longs to be. One of the more dramatic proofs of this ongoing evolutionary process is the continuing archetypal drama of our dream lives.

As discussed in Chapter 2, our dreams regularly bring us gifts of creative inspiration and energy, greater understanding of confusing emotions, insight into the more problematic areas of both our personal and our shared, collective lives, and more conscious awareness and appreciation of our deeper, authentic unconscious nature. Our dreams also regularly provide a glimpse of the hidden roots of our self-awareness that touch what Paul Tillich has called "the basic ground of our being," that-which-is-beyond-naming, _____ the fundamental "Within," without which it would be impossible to draw the next breath or have the next thought, even though we seldom consciously recognize or feel this aspect of our psyches when we are awake.

Indeed, one of the better ways of defining "spiritual development" is by relating it to this divine evolutionary energy we sometimes feel in our lives. Dreams regularly bring us the next step closer to such a conscious felt-sense. However, they perform this function with a kind of playful ruthlessness that often produces shocking results (as the "drowning in the swimming pool of soup" dream discussed in Chapter 1, Barbara's dream of "the silent party in the basement," and Peter's dream of the "wounded warrior," discussed in Chapter 2, begin to demonstrate).

The "shocking" impression that so many of our most important dreams leave with us is one of the reasons why dreaming itself is the source of so many of humankind's deepest religious and spiritual beliefs and intuitions. Because we regularly *dream* that we meet the spirits of the recently dead, and dream of ghosts, demons, angels, and divine guides and protectors, these "archetypal ideas" appear in the beliefs of people around the world.

One of the best metaphors of the dreaming process itself is the fairy-tale image of "the magic mirror that never lies" that appears in the tale *Snow White* and other folktales. Dream images that reflect the complexities of the self may be ambiguous, seemingly trivial and banal, or even disturbing and distressing on first encounter, but at some deep level or another, like the magic mirror, they always speak *truth*. This image of the magic mirror that never lies suggests both the reliable truth that dreams always reflect and the shocking way that truth often strikes us.

As you may recall, in *Snow White*, the Wicked Queen looks into the magic mirror that never lies every morning and always asks the same question: "Mirror, mirror, on the wall, who's the fairest of them all?" The mirror tells the Wicked Queen that she is the fairest until Snow White grows to puberty, at which time it informs her that the title now belongs to Snow White. The Wicked Queen is enraged and spends the rest of the story attempting to murder Snow White, first by sending a series of assassins and then by trying to kill Snow White herself. She fails, primarily because Snow White is aided by all of Nature, from the dwarfs to the birds and forest animals.

It is far from accidental that the Wicked Queen in Snow White looks into the magic mirror that never lies *every morning* or that she responds to what she sees with such misguided ferocity. She responds as we all do from time to time when confronted with uncomfortable, "shocking," and unpleasant truths springing from our unconscious depths. She refuses to see the truth reflected as referring to her and instead *projects* the unconscious energy outward onto other people. The reflection in the magic mirror is always true and accurate, but she/we do not wish to acknowledge its relevance to our own interior lives.

Most often, we are not the "fairest in the land" (of our own selves). This is not a comparative judgment, but rather a reference to the possibilities that lie undeveloped within us. All too often, like the Wicked Queen, we prefer to see only that aspect of the complex truth the dream presents that relates to other people. However, because the reflection *is* true at all its levels of reference, it can be seen as coming in the service of individual and collective evolving health and wholeness, no matter how negative and unprepossessing it may seem at first glance.

Some years ago I was invited to lead a series of Lenten retreat days at a Jesuit retreat center in the San Francisco Bay area. I began the first day with a pep talk about the value of becoming more aware of the depths of our unconscious interior lives through paying closer attention to dreams. We discussed the theory, along with practical suggestions for improving dream recall (see Chapter 4), and the retreat participants went off at the end of the first day primed to remember and write down accounts of their dreams.

The next day, when they returned, a collective wail of protest arose from the group as soon as we reconvened. In essence, they said, we are pious folk; we are coming here over the Lenten period to try to enhance our felt sense of the presence of the Divine in our lives, and now you've asked us to pay more attention to our dreams, and yet when we do, they are so "yucky" and nasty and noxious that they are having precisely the opposite effect from what we wanted and hoped, and from what you had suggested would happen.

The response that occurred to me at the time, and that seems even more true in retrospect, is that dreams always come to bring us to a deeper experience of the Divine and that they always start wherever the sense of transcendent presence is injured or broken. If, for example, I am separated from my deepest self because of unresolved resentments toward my family, then I will have to experience those feelings fully and transform my understanding of those childhood events before I can hope to have a greater awareness of the deeper archetypal divine energies hidden below the obvious surface events of my current life. Therefore, in the name of health and wholeness, my dreams will respond to my desire to become more conscious of the divine energies at work and play in my life by taking me directly to my unresolved emotional dramas that stand between me and that larger, deeper sense of archetypal self and cosmos.

There is a potentially unbroken continuity of experience stretching from the ordinary, limited awareness of "me" (my seemingly small and separate waking "self"), all the way to a transcendent awareness of completeness and oneness and self-identification with the ALL—the Divine. In my experience, all dreams are ultimately aimed at this transcendent, direct, conscious, creative participation in the collective, archetypal, divine energies that are given shape in the cosmic dance of all life. At the very least, this is a way of conceptualizing the scope of the complete, transpersonal "health and wholeness" toward which our dreams are always striving.

Viewed in this light, it is possible to see that the inherent multilayered quality of the "hidden" meanings in dreams are all related to one another, and to the transpersonal, archetypal energies of the collective unconscious. Any dream, and any work done with any dream that results in anything less than this sort of total awareness of the divinity in the self, and in all things, is incomplete, because in the final analysis, this is the order of health and *wholeness* that all dreams strive for, whether they achieve this aim in full view of waking consciousness or not. To reach this level of healthy, whole experience and understanding, every step of the way must be traversed. No steps can be left out—anything less would be only theory and would not be authentic and complete.

Thus, our dreams are always going back and forth along the road, so to speak, between our limited, "blind" sense of egocentric, anguished, existentially separate self that tends to characterize our waking experience, and this transcendent, deeply unconscious experience of direct, meaningful participation in the larger life of ALL. Wherever a "roadblock" exists along this path, wherever a bridge is washed out or a rock slide has covered the roadway, it is there that the dreams set up their tents and begin to put on their little "morality plays" in an effort to motivate the dreamer to freely choose to do the work to clear the way and move closer to that transcendent/creative realization experience. Whenever we succeed in removing a roadblock, the dreams skip on ahead to the next place that needs "repair work" and set up their traveling tent show again.

One of the strongest indications that this is so is that as an individual begins to undertake this work of psychospiritual development, the experience of the remembered dream life tends to get more and more "mythic," and to echo more and more not only with the dreamer's personal life and dilemmas, but with the life and collective dilemmas of the species as a whole.

In this context, it is also important to remember that the magic mirror does not lie in its positive reflections either. When the dream suggests that I *am* the fairest in the land, I can believe it. It is important to understand that the "land" referred to is the land of the deep, authentic self. Being the fairest in the land is *not a comparative* judgment; it means that I am living in deep and creative rapport and harmony with the truest parts of *myself*, regardless of what others may think, or what I may think of them. Ironically, these positive reflections offered by the dreams are often the more difficult to embrace and integrate. Owning to and giving creative expression to our strengths and superior abilities is usually far more problematic than admitting to our failures and foibles, troublesome though that may be.

The single most common "blockage" in this continuum of potential self-awareness stretching from individual/personal/"separate" experience to the consciously felt-sense of the presence of the Divine, simultaneously within and without, is *self-deception*. As it occurred to me to say to the Lenten seekers years ago, it seems grotesque to imagine that anyone can make up and act out of a false identity, then have any legitimate expectation that the "fake person" will be able to have any sort of an authentic, transcendent experience of deep meaning in his/her life.

It is only the *real me*, the authentic and consciously developed person that I am capable of being, who has any chance of seeing into the depths of my experience and consciously sensing the energy and presence of the Divine in my life. Inauthentic, faked behavior, including fake piety (a piety based on the imitation of external forms, rather than on the spontaneous response to the felt-presence of the Divine—a response that, in my experience, must be discovered and rediscovered anew in each new encounter), will militate against the very result it is trying to achieve.

In this all-important sense, all dreams, particularly the dreams of sincere seekers of spiritual experience, will guide them directly to the "roadblocks"—to their histories of childhood injury, their current self-deceptions, and their repressed "secret" desires and opinions—in short, to all the things that "block the way" and separate them from the felt-sense of transcendent meaning in their lives. This dreaming experience of looking into the "magic mirror that never lies" may feel "yucky" on first encounter, but it exists precisely to bring conscious, moral, creative, purposeful self-awareness to the "problems" that block psychological awareness and emotional growth and cloud spiritual vision. The dreams do this not to make psychospiritual growth more difficult, but rather to resolve the "blockages" one by one, "in order," so to speak, to ensure that none is overlooked. Each time a "personal" or "merely psychological" issue is resolved, it brings the dreamer that much closer to genuine spiritual/"religious" experience, whose hallmark is full aliveness and transcendent conscious awareness of and participation in a universe of all-encompassing meaning and significance. This kind of spiritual experience is essentially the same for all people who experience it, whether they define themselves as "religious" or not.

The fact that all dreams regularly carry this wide range of meanings, from the intensely personal to the transcendently collective, should be enough to warrant much deeper and closer attention to our dream lives than we usually tend to bring to them. When you add to this the fact that sharing our dreams with other people tends to bring us closer to each other and to build reliable and lasting communities of support and mutual aid, the prospect of experimenting with dream recall and dream sharing becomes more and more attractive and potentially worthwhile.

Let me offer the following story as a case in point.

Years ago, when I had been teaching my course, The Meanings in Dreams and Dreaming, for about five years, a young man came to me at the Starr King School for the Ministry in Berkeley and asked if there was any point in his taking my class if he never had any dreams to share.

"You don't have to give your speech about how 'everybody dreams.' I've read the literature," he said, "and I know that I actually do dream every night and just don't ever remember it. From what I've read, I have the idea that my dreams might be very interesting and useful to me, if I could only remember them. My question to you is, is there any point in my taking your class if I never have any dreams to share?"

I blithely answered that he should go ahead and sign up for the class because simply having a place where he was regularly expected to have a dream to share would increase his recall. I said this to him because my experience up to that point had convinced me that the main reason why most adults do not recall their dreams with any frequency, even though they are dreaming regularly (the laboratory researchers tell us we all regularly dream five or six or even more times every night), is that they have no socially and emotionally supportive contexts in their lives in which to share and think about their dreams. As soon as such a context is created—for example, by signing up for a class where remembering and sharing a dream once a week with other class members is part of the "homework"—it almost invariably has the effect of increasing even the most stubbornly dim recall of dreams.

However, I turned out to be wrong. The young man—I will call him Mike—did take the class. His attendance was exemplary. He was there every week, bright-eyed and interested, and quite articulate about his ideas regarding the possible meanings in other people's dreams, but he never had a dream of his own to share.

Eventually, I began to have some qualms about his participation in and experience of the class. Though his suggestions often provoked substantial ahas of insight for other dreamers, he was still relatively aloof from the process in important emotional ways. By never allowing himself to be at the emotional center of everyone else's caring attention by working on a dream of his own, he was missing out on an important social and emotional dimension of the work.

The point of the formal, academic classes in dream work that I teach at various institutions of higher learning in the San Francisco Bay area and elsewhere is not simply to develop an intellectual facility at the analysis of symbolic forms and structures. That kind of skill is important, but is far from the main point of the work. Equally if not even more important is the experience of authentic emotional contact and the building of reliable communities of creative intimacy and psychospiritual support. The fundamental element in the building of this kind of authentic community is the willingness to be emotionally vulnerable—to experience the risk and acceptance that goes with sharing one's own dreams.

For this reason, I almost always share and work with my own dreams in those groups that I facilitate. In my view, Mike was missing this basic aspect of the work because of his inability to remember and share his dreams. So, I started to hassle Mike about his lack of dream recall much more aggressively than I ordinarily do. I started to question him closely at the beginning of every class about his lack of recall: What had the awakening been like? Had any fleeting impressions of the mental activity just prior to waking up been left at all? Finally, when the answers to these questions turned up no new information, I suggested to him that he simply *make up* a dream: "What would your dream have been like this morning if you had been able to remember it?"

I went on to point out that this was not as bizarre a suggestion as it might at first appear. All forms of interior imagery and experience come from essentially the same unconscious place that the dreams come from, and for this reason, they inevitably carry essentially the same freight of symbolic meaning and import as the "real" dreams remembered from sleep. Had Mike been willing and relaxed enough to take me up on my playful but serious suggestion, it is quite likely he would have produced a conscious fantasy narrative that would have lent itself quite well to the same group process of exploration that we were using with the regular nighttime dreams shared by the other members of the class. This, however, was not to be.

Mike sidestepped the suggestion by saying that, yes, he understood the theory, and that it was probably even correct, but that he didn't want to do it "because it felt too much like cheating."

As I was sitting there, wondering what to do next, Mike suddenly said that it was odd, but while we were talking, he had a curious thought:

"Maybe there were some pastel colors in my dreams last night."

I thought to myself, "maybe pastel colors"! I've heard some *skinny* dream fragments in my time, but this one is definitely the skinniest! We probably won't get anywhere trying to work on something this insubstantial, but it is the *only* opening he has offered all semester to be the center of everyone's attention, so on grounds of group process alone, I'm going to go for it.

At that time in my life, I was under the mistaken impression that there were two kinds of dreams—the kind that appeared to have a beginning, a middle, and an end, which were worth working with, and the kind that were only "random" fragments, which were not worth working with. I fully expected the work with Mike's dream to stir genuine emotions in Mike and the rest of us, but I anticipated that it would not be particularly productive from the point of view of actually "unpacking" any substantial meanings from the tiny fragment that he offered.

When we started to work on the fragment, I tried hard to think of questions to ask and things to suggest, and so did everyone else in the class, all to little avail. Finally one of the class members spoke up and asked, "Is there any association in your mind between the word *pastel* and the word *pastoral?*" (The technical name for such a not-quite-rhyming word similarity is a *klang association*, and dreams make use of klang associations all the time.)

Mike made a funny face—the sort of face that I have come to recognize over the years as an expression of an aha—and said, "Well, yes. Now that you mention it, there is."

Everyone wanted to know what the association was, but Mike said it was "embarrassing" and that he wasn't sure he wanted to share it.

At that point, without any prompting from me, the class began to push him good-humoredly, assuring him it couldn't be any worse than any of the other things that had come up in the group.

Mike laughed and said, "Okay! Okay! I'll tell you! When you asked me that question, I had this aha that everybody's been talking about all semester, and my aha is that my commitment to the 'pastoral life' is distinctly 'pastel'. . . . I'm here in theological school not because I really want to be a Unitarian Universalist minister, the way I always thought I wanted to, but because I am fulfilling the expectations of my parents!"

I was stunned by the depth, strength, and significance of this revelation, coming as it did out of a tiny little dream "fragment"—a fragment that I had been just as willing as everyone else to disparage and toss aside as "meaningless"—but now that we had spent the time and energy to work with it a little, it had yielded this amazingly elegant and succinct metaphor of what I perceived to be his greatest problem at that moment. In fact, I was not really surprised by the content of the revelation. I had already concluded on the basis of our several interactions that it was likely that Mike didn't really have his heart in being a minister the way he seemed to think he did. What surprised me was the way in which this seemingly innocuous little dream fragment brought him to understand consciously that this was the case.

From that point on, I became very interested in working with such seemingly meaningless dream fragments. I told my classes that I didn't want to hear any more of their "epics" for a while—I just wanted to hear and work with their fragments—because I wanted to see if the experience with Mike's dream was an anomaly, or whether all dream fragments had this amazingly concise quality of "Zen telegraphy."

The people in my classes were obliging. We quickly discovered that the experience we had with Mike's dream fragment was not an anomaly; most fragments had the same condensed quality, as if they had been edited down into the same sort of charged and dramatically revealing metaphors that Mike's "fugitive pastel colors" had turned out to be.

The work with Mike's dream fragment also reveals one of the short-term "problems" when working with dreams. Having admitted to himself, wide awake, in front of attentive witnesses, what he truly felt in his heart about not wanting to go on with his ministerial training, he found it impossible to go back to the old denial system that had provided structure and meaning to his life for so long. His behavior, and even his appearance and personality, suddenly deteriorated. He was no longer "Mr. Nice Guy." He ceased arriving on time for classes and appointments.

He stopped turning in his written assignments and even stopped being particularly civil when spoken to in the hall or on the street.

He struggled more and more with the conflicted feelings that the work with the tiny dream fragment had revealed and released, until finally at the end of the semester, he couldn't stand it any longer. He called his parents and told them that despite their lifelong shared enthusiasm about his becoming a minister, he now realized that he didn't like it and was not going to carry it through.

Having broken the news to them, he left school and moved across the bay to San Francisco and got a job in a bank. Subsequent reports of his life suggest that he is much happier and more productive in the world of banking and finance than it appears he would ever have been in the ministry.

To this point, the story is all verified by Mike's own ahas of insight and can thus be presented as a "true story" about the meaning of his dream. From here, the story becomes an exercise in theory. Dreams come with multiple levels of meaning and subtlety to expand and develop our individual and collective consciousness and serve our evolving health and wholeness. Knowing this, I found myself thinking that there was more to Mike's dream than just the struggle with being a minister.

That night, when we first unpacked the "pastel colors" at the level relating to Mike's vocational "call," a thought ran through my mind. If it were my dream, one of the "pastel colors" I wouldn't be remembering might be lavender, and another of the things I might be doing, just to satisfy my parents' lifelong expectations and not because my heart was really in it, would be being straight. If this were my dream, it might also be about being gay.

However, that evening, it seemed to me to be too much to push the work with the fragment any further, so I kept my fleeting thought to myself, and subsequently there was never any easy opportunity to share it with Mike. In retrospect, it seems to me that the issue could probably have been raised in a gentle, supportive, and productive way, but at the time, I was still so stunned at the result of the work with the fugitive fragment that I didn't gather my wits to do so.

However, a few years after Mike left school and moved away, word came back that he had "come out of the closet" and become a fairly well-known political figure in the gay community. So, it seems to me that my original thought may have had some validity, though, of course, the only way to be certain would be to have Mike's own aha of verification.

In any case, even if this is not an accurate speculation about Mike's dream, it is a clear example of the larger truth that *all* dreams and dream fragments can support projections of multiple meanings. It is not a question of their size or apparent complexity; the "overdetermined" quality of the dream is inherent in the structure and nature of the dreaming experience itself, no matter how small or "fragmentary" the memory of that experience may appear.

Let me expand the point even further. We know from Mike's own aha that the tiny dream dealt with a fairly profound self-deception about his desire to become a minister. There is also strong inferential reason to believe that it carried a level of meaning about his sexual orientation. By inference, I believe that at least two more distinct layers of significance were woven into this tiny dream fragment as well.

Whenever anyone erects a "fake identity" in the world and begins to believe and behave as though it is his/her "true self," this self-deception (like all sustained efforts of thought and feeling, be they conscious or unconscious) requires increasing amounts of psychological and emotional *energy* to maintain. The greater the disparity between the false idea we are harboring and putting forth about ourselves, and the true nature of our circumstances and interior life, the greater the energy required to maintain the denial. This energy drain must be unconscious, or at least preconscious to a great extent, because to admit this energy drain consciously would result in a conscious recognition of the falsehood, thus defeating its original "purpose." Maintaining a system of denial *always* drains more energy from consciousness than is appreciated.

For this reason, one of the most ubiquitous "symptoms" of denial and self-deception is an all-pervasive feeling of "tiredness," a feeling of always being just on the brink of some physical illness, and a sense of depression and irritation that despite all efforts to streamline things and make them more efficient, there are simply not enough hours in the day to get even the most necessary and pressing things accomplished, let alone to have any time for leisure and spontaneity.

Because this is always the case, Mike's self-deception about the validity of his vocational choice (let alone his denial of his authentic sexual/relational orientation) would inevitably make him feel "tired" all the

time. Therefore, there is also substantial theoretical reason to suppose that
the pallid, forgotten "pastel colors" of his dream also make direct metaphorical reference to his physical health, as well as to his vocation and his
sexual orientation. At this level, the dream reveals a "washed-out," "pastel" picture of his general lack of physical vitality, caused by the continuous drain of his preconscious denial and self-deception.

By the same token, I believe the dream gives us a poignant picture of
Mike's spiritual life as well. The original family drama that cast Mike in
the role of "the spiritual one" and the "would-be minister" was shaped
not only by his father's and mother's projections of their own unlived
creative potentials onto their "hero son," but also by Mike's own genuine
sensitivity and attraction to spiritual life and experience. However, when
he actually arrived at seminary, he discovered to his dismay that being
a seminary student tended to alienate him from the very spiritual life
that had attracted him there in the first place. The somewhat repressed,
fragile, competitive, and hypocritical lifestyle of many of his brother and
sister seminary students, combined with the intense but bloodlessly theoretical and abstract academic studies—experiences that he had imagined
would bring him closer to satisfying the spiritual longings of his childhood
and young adulthood—tended to alienate him from any felt-sense of the
presence of the Divine, rather than to support and enhance it.

In this sense, I believe the "pastel colors" represented Mike's increasingly pallid sense of spiritual connection and religious commitment in
response to the disappointing realities of seminary life. I believe that
Mike's departure from seminary and his subsequent coming out of the
closet as a gay man made it possible for him to fulfill his call to ministry
in a much more authentic and powerful way than would have been possible had he stepped into any "off the rack" ministry fresh out of seminary. Although it may have appeared initially to some people that the
revelations of his tiny dream and his work with it in the dreams class
"destroyed" his shining plan to become a minister, later developments
prove that his call was clarified and deepened in his subsequent work as a
community religious leader.

Mike's work with his fragment points out clearly once again that the
magic mirror does not lie. Even the tiniest splinters of the shattered mirror reflect deeply true images. The dreams do not support the fantasies
and self-deceptions of the ego, even when that ego is shaped by massive

energies of denial and repression. The dream does not come to flatter and support the dreamer's conscious worldview or self-image (unless, of course, that is what is required to truly serve the dreamer's evolving health and wholeness).

The dreams unfailingly reflect the dreamer's authentic self and true circumstances, even if while performing that service, the comfortable short-term security of the dreamer's life is sometimes disrupted and shattered. Years down the road, dreamers who have had this kind of disorienting experience usually look back with a certain rueful humor at the short-run results of getting involved in dream work, but so it is with everyone in the uncomfortable but necessary process of "shedding the skin" of the old personality and becoming more conscious of the new.

Consciousness itself evolves in this fashion. In all the individual instances of evolving self-awareness, the collective archetypes of the deep unconscious progressively find more conscious and creative expression in our choices, actions, and increasing appreciation of paradox. To the extent that partially evolved consciousness itself rejects paradox, puts up barriers to further development, and prematurely closes the universe of discourse, the dreams will come to break down those barriers to further poignant perceptions of ambiguity. Where consciousness is partial and still evolving, irony and paradoxical ambiguity are inevitable, and since this is always the case to some major extent, we might as well cultivate a taste for them.

The structure and content of any person's conscious worldview (the pattern of his/her rational thoughts, and the shape of the emotions and feelings that he or she habitually allows into waking self-awareness) will inevitably reveal the pattern of whatever self-deceptions, denials, and premature limitations have been placed in the way of the further development of consciousness. For this reason, the rationally held worldview, and the styles of thought and feeling that are woven into it, are always threatened by the new parts of the whole complex truth that have been systematically edited out. Often, this new information comes flowing into one's awareness through the medium of dreams.

This often distressing encounter with previously suppressed and tabooed ideas and feelings is always experienced at a personal level, but it has collective aspects as well. The startlingly frequent occurrence of the image of "telepathy" in dreams of people who don't believe in the possibility of "thought transference" may serve as an illustration of this level of collective metaphor.

Most people do not believe in telepathy, but at the same time, most people also have the experience of communicating "telepathically" with other figures in their dreams almost every night. In dreams, more often than not, the characters with whom we communicate seem to be "talking," but we seldom see their lips move. Occasionally, the dream experience will even be one of gazing at their faces and "listening" to them, and specifically noticing that their lips are *not* moving. Often, particularly if one shares one's dreams with others on a regular basis, the dream will turn out to have "spooky," seemingly "telepathic" resonances with the previously unknown thoughts and dreams of others.

This waking experience of "spookiness" is a further extension of the meaning of the dream. It is itself a legitimate "dream metaphor," even though the experience of "verifying" the seeming telepathy takes place in waking life. Experiences of this kind fall clearly under the rubric of what Carl Jung called "sychronicity"—seeming coincidences in waking life that awaken a strong sense that they are meaningful, even though there is no discernible chain of cause and effect leading up to them.

Setting aside for a moment the question of whether or not telepathy is a real phenomenon, what I wish to emphasize here is the *symbolic* import of the seeming "telepathy" in dreams and subsequent waking connections with dreams. The idea that thoughts and other states of mind and being can be communicated across physical distances without obvious physical means has fascinated human beings throughout history. However, in recent times, this notion has been relegated to the rubbish heap of "occultism" and "hysterical self-deception" by the failure of contemporary laboratory research to devise strategies for isolating, measuring, and replicating the experience.

In this way, the *idea* and *image* of telepathy itself becomes an extraordinarily apt metaphor for *all* the emotional, psychological, and spiritual experiences and ideas currently outside the mainstream of the rationalist/scientific worldview. The startlingly common occurrence of the image of telepathy in the dreams of large numbers of people serves as a constant subtle challenge to the unconscious dominance of the limited exclusively rationalistic worldview. The *metaphor* of telepathy in dreams is a symbolic emotional reminder that the book of scientific revelation is not closed either, despite its "fundamentalist" position in the contemporary Western industrial world. In this way, the startlingly common dream experience of telepathic communication keeps opening the door to the idea that "there are more things between heaven and earth than are dreamed of in your philosophy, Horatio."

Whether or not human beings (and other species) actually have any evolving telepathic propensities, the incidence of the *image* of telepathy is an example of the dreams coming to modern, sophisticated people in the service of our individual and collective health and wholeness. Any premature closure of thought, feeling, and experience in the name of "security" or "conventional wisdom" stands in opposition to the possibilities of as-yet-unevolved consciousness, and as such it will be challenged and called into question by the experience of the dream. Just as Mike had to face the fact that his lifelong fantasy of being a minister was based on prematurely closed assumptions about himself and the professional ministry, so humankind as a whole is regularly forced to relinquish cherished traditional ideas about what is right, proper, and possible, as the developing energies of our deep, authentic human nature continue to manifest themselves in new and challenging ways. Our dreams are one of the primary servants of this individual/collective evolutionary process.

An important political connection can also be drawn here. One of the primary "justifications" of the ongoing imperialism and colonialism of the Western industrial nations is the idea that the exploited and oppressed peoples are "primitive" and require the "helping hand" of "higher civilization" to "bring them into the modern world." The assertion that the oppressed peoples are "primitive" is almost always bolstered by reference to their "superstitious beliefs," particularly their beliefs about the "spirits" that supposedly inhabit inanimate objects, and the beliefs of such peoples regarding their dream experiences—particularly that they involve "telepathy" and communication with the spirits of the natural world and of the dead. However, when sophisticated Westerners begin to pay the same kind of careful attention to their own dreams that "primitives" in virtually all traditional nonindustrial societies do, Westerners discover they have much in common.

The reduction of "primitive people" to less than fully human status is based to a great degree on our acts of psychological self-deception. The primary mechanism of this self-deception is known as "repression and projection." The "primitive" part of our psyche that is primarily involved in the experience of the dream is denied and repressed in an act of self-hatred. However, the act of self-deceptive repression in no way alters the actual state of affairs. The rejected energy within is still present and active and in turn *projects* itself outward, particularly onto those people we can most easily label as "unlike us."

The despised and rejected "primitive" part of *ourselves* is thus seen in the "natives," and the oppressions visited on them are symbolic representations of our own *self-hatred*. In rejecting and denying our own basic humanity, it becomes a psychological necessity to deny the common humanity we share with others. Hitler hated Jews, whom he suspected of wanting to take over and rule the world; early American settlers hated the Indians, whom they believed were untrustworthy and greedy; adults view children as property; men and women mistrust each other because of their differing emotional responses; human beings generally tend to view other species as expendable, etc. Each of these is an example of projected self-hatred, despising the parts of ourselves we can see most easily projected onto others.

In this endlessly repeating drama of repression and projection, we can see the roots of all varieties of human oppression, including classism, racism, ageism, sexism, imperialism, and fascism. Through repression and projection our metaphoric self-hatred is expressed and acted out in the world.

The idea that thoughts and feelings can be communicated among human beings without any physical connection stands high on the list of "ridiculous notions" rejected by the exclusively rationalistic worldview. It appears with such surprising frequency in the dreams of people who subscribe more or less consciously to that worldview in large measure because it is a symbol of all the levels of reality that are tabooed and ignored in that global stance.

However, at the level of unconscious struggles for collective survival and species evolution, the analogy between the possibility that dream telepathy may be entering the dreams of contemporary humans and the idea that our hominid ancestors may have dreamed about articulate speech at a similar nexus of evolutionary development is quite striking. If human beings were to develop a capacity for more conscious "remote sensing" (to use the military term for this whole area of possibility), then the course of future events would certainly be radically altered from its present apparent course. To say the least, the bottom would certainly fall out of the used-car market, and since the "used-car market" is a fairly apt metaphor for so much of our global military/industrial economic and political life, one can imagine the ways in which the fundamental nature of human social interactions would be changed. As a strategy for collective evolutionary survival, it seems to have quite a bit to recommend it.

Now, for people such as myself who have actually had the experience of seemingly "telepathic" connections in their dreams (connections later confirmed in waking experience), this idea does not seem bizarre. Those who have had the experience repeatedly know that something, which one might as well call "telepathy," is very real. As Carl Jung once said in a moment of unusual passion and candor that strained his Germanic English (to John Freeman of the BBC in the midst of a filmed interview), "Only ignorants deny these things!"

Let me offer just one brief example from the literally hundreds of experiences of this sort I have shared with my wife over the almost thirty years we have lived together. On one occasion, my wife and I both dreamed on the same night of full-size elephants with proportionally huge human hands at the ends of their forelegs. Neither of us had been reading about elephants with human hands, nor had we seen any reference to this image on TV, nor had we talked about anything remotely resembling this image before going to sleep. In Kath's dream, the beast looked like a woolly mammoth, and in my dream it was an Indian elephant, which sat back on its haunches and waved at me with its huge hands.

With regard to the meanings and significance of these shared dreams (which seem to merge and become a single dream experience after the fact), all I can say is that over the years I have come to suspect that, in general, such experiences emphasize and confirm the depth of shared emotion and evolving symbolic drama that link the dreamers. Specifically, the image of the "elephant(s) with human hands" led me to the archetypal figure of Ganesha in Hindu mythology. Subsequent to this dream, I began to research the mythology of Ganesha, the Indian elephant-headed god, the Master of Overcoming Obstacles, Patron of Commerce and successful enterprise. Prior to the dream and its spooky corollary in my wife's dreams, Ganesha had been only another curious image among many in the confusing pantheon of shape-changing Hindu deities.

For my wife, the woolly mammoth was primarily an image of plenty and freedom from want and anxiety derived from the Ice Age hunter/gatherer societies, the source of food, clothing, tools, and ritual communion. For me, Ganesha emerged as an image of the archetypal masculine in *harmony* with the feminine, rather than at war with it, as so many other archetypal masculine figures appear to be.

Rudolf Steiner has suggested that animal/human hybrid figures (such as the animal-headed human gods of ancient Egypt, and the human-headed animal gods of Sumer and Mesopotamia) represent the evolution of unconscious instinctive energies into increasingly "human" and self-aware forms. Carl Jung has made a similar suggestion with regard to all the hybrid figures in myth and dream (such as the chimera and the manticore). In the case of the shared image of the "elephant with human hands" in Kath's and my dreams, at one level it was a clear image of our shared development of "masculine" energies in our life together—energies associated with "providing" and "sacrificing" in order to meet the needs of family and community on a reliable basis. The cross-dream(s) suggested an emphasis on "the hands," and by implication, the creative and economic "work of the hands," our ability to "manipulate" our lives toward secure and successful outcomes. We both felt that the dream(s) affirmed our mutual efforts to support one another in this regard.

Our regular, seemingly telepathic cross-dreaming of curious and compelling images of this kind is, I believe, a kind of "barometric reading" of the intensity of our evolving relationship. The stories that other people tell me about their seemingly telepathic experiences lead me to the same conclusion: this kind of thing happens regularly and appears to be associated with the intensity of emotional relationship and shared response to similar symbolic material.

However, as William Dement, the famous contemporary dream researcher, has been heard to complain on many occasions in connection with similar assertions about the reality of telepathy in dreams, "I ask for *proof* and all I get is *anecdotes!*" From the limited perspective of laboratory research, it is a legitimate complaint, but it fails to appreciate the wholeness, and the developing quality, of the human psyche. I suspect that Dr. Dement would not raise the same objection with regard to "proofs" for such concepts and experiences as "creativity" or "love." These crucially important human activities exist only in particular cases and thus can appear only as "anecdotes."

There has been at least one pioneering attempt to demonstrate the telepathic phenomenon in the dream state through a laboratory experiment. Stanley Krippner, Montague Ullman, and Alan Vaughan collaborated in a series of experiments at Maimonides Medical Center in Brooklyn, recounted in their fascinating book, *Dream Telepathy* (New York: Macmillan, 1973). They devised a series of elaborate protocols whereby subjects were recruited to sleep and dream in the laboratory and "receive" images that were "sent" to them by other people who had no waking relationship with the sleepers. (The accepted shorthand term for this lack of conscious relationship is "blind.") The images to be "sent" were selected at random from groups of pictures previously assembled by other "blind" participants in the study. The dreams of the subjects were recorded, and the dream reports were then sent off to a third set of "blind" evaluators, together with the whole set of pictures from which the "target" image had been selected. These outside evaluators were then asked to judge which of the pictures might have been the "target," based on the dream reports of the laboratory dreamers. For example, on one of the most "successful" nights, the randomly selected target image was a print of George Bellows's murky, violent, prizefight painting *Both Members of This Club*. That night the dreamer reported several dreams that the independent "blind" judges all thought were fundamentally related to the stimulus image.

This study yielded statistically significant results, strongly suggesting that the number of times that the "triple-blind" evaluators selected the picture that had in fact been used as the "target image" was well beyond what could reasonably be attributed to chance. The idea is, of course, that having carefully ruled out all other possible causes except chance and telepathy, if chance can legitimately be ruled out by application of rigorous statistical standards, then telepathy is the only possible explanation left.

It is not surprising that the study produced statistically significant evidence for the existence of telepathic phenomena, or that having accomplished this extraordinary feat, the work has been substantially ignored in the scientific research community (with the possible exception of the mostly secret military research, if the media stories are to be believed). What does surprise me is that the study was as successful as it was in demonstrating the telepathic phenomenon, given what seem to me to be the significantly flawed assumptions upon which it was based.

The researchers, by their own admission, developed their experiments based on the theory that telepathy is a kind of "transmission," using the analogy of radio waves. They sought out experimental subjects with inherent "talent" for telepathic communication, drawing analogies to people born with unusual musical or mathematical talent. My own experience is quite the contrary. "Transmission" and "talent" have virtually nothing to do with it. Everyone is born with an undeveloped potential for intuitive expression. My experience is that telepathic connections are born of deep feeling and emotion. The strength of emotional association determines who will have telepathic communion with another person. Parents and children separated by war and natural disaster, lovers and mortal enemies, people who share the same deeply felt phobias and passions—in my experience it is these people who most often report the dreams in which telepathy appears to play a major role, and it is always in association with the "anecdotal" material related to their most personal deep feelings and emotions.

For this reason, it seems to me that the heroic efforts made in this study to remove any relational or emotional connection between the "receivers" and the "senders," in the name of scientific objectivity and reliability, was in itself most likely to produce negative results. All my own experience with the phenomenon of telepathy, particularly the incidence of telepathy in dreams, is that it is precisely over these bridges of deep emotional connection and relationship that the researchers were trying to "control" that the "telepathy" appears to "travel." From that perspective, the success of the Maimonides experiments is an even more impressive demonstration of the reality and *commonness* of the phenomenon. It is so common that even when the most important emotional factors that promote it are specifically weeded out, it still happens often enough to meet statistical standards for validation.

My experience persuades me that the Maimonides experiments succeeded as dramatically as they did because from time to time, the images that were randomly selected from the previously assembled sets of potential target images were symbolically charged and associated with unresolved psychospiritual issues in the personal development of both the "senders" and the "receivers" who were "on duty" that night. Once again, it is the *anecdotes* in the book about the nights when the experiments proved to be particularly successful that convince me of this. It appears that the experiments succeeded on these occasions because the elaborate efforts to weed out all the emotional/relational factors *failed*, and on those particular evenings, the randomly selected image turned out to be one that evoked emotionally charged symbolic material in the psyches of *both* the participants. For example, on the night when the bloody prizefight painting was the target image, I strongly suspect that both the men directly involved in the experiment had unresolved *personal* issues connected with controlling and expressing violent and competitive feelings. Almost all men struggle with this archetypal issue to some extent, so even though the "sender" and the "receiver" did not know each other, they still "communicated telepathically" over the shared bridge of the strong symbolic image of the prizefight.

Supported by laboratory and other evidence of this sort, we can speculate that one of the more radical evolutionary strategies currently being "experimented" with in our collective dream lives is the ability to be more consciously telepathic. The "rational" ridicule that this idea often elicits reminds me of the ridicule and hostility that Ignaz Semmelweis, the nineteenth-century Hungarian medical reformer, encountered when he proposed the germ theory of disease transmission. His assertion that there were tiny invisible organisms that carried illness, and that the solution to the problem was "obsessive washing," caused his contemporaries to dismiss him as a lunatic. Invisible organisms that couldn't be seen or measured sounded like "spooks." Semmelweis's insistence on washing between every examination and surgery on the basis of an unproven idea looked too much like the perseverating behavior of a lunatic for most of his contemporaries even to experiment with the behavior and look at the results. Poor Semmelweis was eventually driven to suicide to prove his point. He purposely cut himself with a septic scalpel and publicly predicted his own eventual death from septicemia.

The people who reject such speculative notions "on principle" are invariably the same people who do not pay attention to their dreams, thus being systematically removed from the very experiences that form the basis of the evidence.

As yet, we have discovered no corollary to the "rapid eye motion" associated with dreaming that corresponds to the telepathic experience.

Many people assume that this apparent failure to isolate and measure tele-pathic communication means that the experience does not exist. How-ever, it is worth remembering that in some scientific circles (prior to the publication and verification of Aserinsky's and Kleitman's research on REM), it was believed by many that there really was no such thing as dreaming either, because there had been no way to isolate and measure it. At that time, it was generally believed that what people experienced as a "dream" was actually only a momentary spurt of cerebral activity upon awakening, a sort of "starter-motor noise" associated with awakening, which did not take place in sleep at all.

Subsequent discoveries proved this "rational" and "hardheaded" view to be incorrect. To believe that current science has all the correct assumptions is a species of inflation (the ancient Greeks called it hubris), and it always turns out to be in error.

The repetitive story of old, prematurely closed ideas giving way before the superior claims of newer, more integrated ideas, which in turn tend to become the "received conventional wisdom," against which the next generation of innovation must struggle, is in itself an archetypal, mythic drama. It takes place in the evolution of individual character and personality, and simultaneously plays itself out in the dramas of history and cultural development. Dreams play a central role in this evolution of consciousness, and we can play an increasingly active, creative, and conscious part in the process if we begin to pay more attention to the experience of the dream.

*Chapter Four*

# TECHNIQUES FOR IMPROVING
# DREAM RECALL

*But regardless of one's philosophical orientation, there is one aspect of dream study upon which scientists, spiritualists, psychologists, and dream therapists agree, and it is the value and importance in keeping a dream journal. The significance of the dream inspires it, its fragile nature demands it, and one can only learn to read what has been written.*
—BARBARA ANDREWS AND MARY MICHAEL

The single most important step in encouraging and enhancing dream recall is deciding cleanly and wholeheartedly that you really *are* interested and really *do* want to remember your dreams. You need to decide clearly that you really want to know more about your unconscious depths and creative energies, even if that means facing potentially disturbing and disruptive information that the dreams may bring into conscious awareness. As I hope I have begun to demonstrate by the accounts of dream work already presented, dreams always come in the service of health and wholeness, and they will always move toward integrating and transforming your denials and self-deceptions, no matter how cherished and well defended they may be.

Like the dream itself the decision to remember dreams is an act of creative imagination. Occasionally, this decision is born of nightmare desperation, but more often than not, it is inspired by a growing sense of curiosity, creative possibility, and excitement.

The simplest and most effective technique for encouraging dream recall is to *imagine* yourself remembering and writing down your dreams, and experiencing the satisfying ahas of insight. The more vividly this is imagined, the more likely it is to take place upon awakening. The best time to imagine is just before drifting off to sleep, but the more often you imagine, the more likely it is to produce the desired effect. Reading books about dreams and dreaming often helps too.

Deciding to share and explore one's dreams with other people on a regular basis, and/or entering into therapy or analysis with a professional who is interested in dreams, will often release previously ignored and forgotten dream memories. I find that any exploration of dreams undertaken with others tends to stimulate recall.

A primary reason why most adults in industrial societies do not remember their dreams is that they have no socially and emotionally supportive contexts in which to do so. My experience of more than twenty years is that as soon as such a context is created (say, for example, by their taking a class in dream psychology, or joining an ongoing dream group), then even the most stubborn failure to recall dreams is usually overcome.

It is important to remember that the people with whom you undertake exploration of the dream world do not have to be trained professionals. Exciting, emotionally profound, insight-producing results may be expected from sharing and talking about dreams regularly with friends. Even if you start out sharing dreams with relative strangers, the members of the newly formed dream group will tend to become intimates and friends very quickly.

In addition to simply inviting your friends to share and explore dreams, you might draw a dream group together by publishing an announcement in a church newsletter or posting one on a dormitory bulletin board. How the group is drawn together is relatively unimportant. What matters most is the willingness of all participants to share dreams openly, to show basic respect for one another, and to keep in mind the "if it were my dream" format in the discussions and projections that follow. However, whether you belong to a dream group or not, focusing conscious attention on the desire and decision to recall dreams, particularly as you are falling asleep, will almost always increase the number and quality of dream memories upon awakening, which you will want to record immediately.

Your tools for recording initial dream memories should be placed right at hand, so that you don't have to get out of bed or even move around much. These tools can be as simple as a pencil stub and the back of an old envelope or as complex as a voice-activated tape recorder.

Tape-recording dream narratives has some drawbacks and some special benefits. Sound-activated tape recorders have come down in price and are more readily available than ever before. They are exceptionally easy to use, even in the middle of the night, since you don't have to turn on a light or even fumble with a switch in the dark. Such a machine will also catch and record *sleep talking* without the dreamer's even waking up. Sleep talking tends to be garbled, but sometimes the words, or even the tone of voice, will stimulate dream recall. Without the help of such a machine, sleep talking is invariably forgotten, unless it is overheard and remembered by someone else. Of course, an ordinary manually operated tape recorder can also be a valuable tool for capturing the subtleties of dream experience.

Even though you may think that you are relatively awake and compos mentis when you are mumbling your "notes" into the microphone, later you are likely to be amazed when you hear the different voices that have been captured in the middle of the night. Each of our "subpersonalities" tends to speak in a different and unique voice in the midst of sleep, and using a tape recorder to capture elusive dream memories often allows us to actually *hear* parts of ourselves that we were not consciously aware of. Most readers will probably remember the surprise they experienced the first time they heard their recorded voices played back; similar surprises and revelations await the dreamer who uses a tape recorder to record his/her dreams when the machine gives back the startlingly different, multiple voices of the subpersonalities that surfaced from deep sleep.

There are two possible drawbacks to using a tape recorder as the primary means of catching dream memories, however. First, if you share a sleeping place with others, speaking into a tape recorder in the middle of the night can be unforgivably annoying. It is also true that even if you use a tape recorder to catch your dreams initially, you still have to transcribe them into written form to make the most use of them. For many people, this is a cumbersome and time-consuming "extra" step that ends up making the tape recorder more of an annoyance than a help in recording dreams.

The people who settle on the tape recorder to catch their dreams are usually expert typists and, more often than not, they sleep alone. For skilled typists, the seemingly "extra" step of transcribing the initial tape-recorded notes is often the first exciting opening in their work with their dreams. The typewritten accounts flow effortlessly off their skilled fingertips, accompanied by wave after wave of exciting ahas about the multiple layers of meaning in the dream.

I strongly suspect that the usually strong initial rush of ahas that often accompany these skilled typists' transcriptions is the result of smooth translation of auditory stimuli into tactile/kinesthetic/visual expression. The more skilled and habitual the mechanical process of transcription, the less conscious attention needs to be focused on the physical task, and the more energy is available to observe the associations and resonances of memory that are awakened by the shift of the dream information from one limbic system to another.

Since the discovery of the ahas of insight is, at bottom, a process of *memory*, increasing the ability to recall the events and feelings of the dream is fundamentally related to grasping more of its many meanings. For this reason, techniques for improving dream recall also tend to increase comprehension as well.

Dream memory and comprehension seem to be enhanced by employing as many different modes of perception and expression as possible in the recording of the dream and in working with it later. The more the dream is recorded and explored in visual, verbal, auditory, tactile, kinesthetic, and other terms—involving all the physical senses as well as the mental/emotional responses in the process—the more likely it is that the dream will spontaneously offer up more of its gifts of insight and creative energy for conscious use.

Often, for example, a brief whiff of some particular odor, or some other seemingly trivial event, will stimulate vivid recall of a previously forgotten dream. When you spontaneously recall a previously forgotten dream, it is usually because the waking-life circumstance that triggered the memory (the smell of dust or decaying apples, the act of opening the car door or stepping into the shower, the momentary quality of light) is symbolically related to the central meaning and content of the dream it evokes. For this reason, it is always a good idea to note the circumstances in which the dream popped to mind, as well as the content of the memory.

One simple way to increase dream memory and subsequent under-standing is to get into the habit of *drawing sketches* of the visual memories of the dream. Working with dreams offers more proof of the old adage "A picture is worth a thousand words." The increase in sudden insights that often accompanies making even the crudest stick-figure sketch of a dream is directly related to the simultaneous activation of visual as well as verbal limbic systems of association and energy flow in the psyche.

Let me offer a concrete example. Several years ago I was awakened from a vivid dream of . . .

> an equestrian figure, a medieval knight in full armor astride an armored horse. Horse and rider are being carried steadily forward from left to right on a moving conveyer belt running down the middle of a torch-lit cave. The horse is shying and backing, obviously nervous and frightened at having the "ground" move beneath its feet, and the rider is having to work hard to keep his mount under control. As I watch, I see many dark-hooded little figures, like dwarfs or trolls, working along the sides of the moving "assembly line" belt. To my horror, I see that the horse and rider are being drawn forward into the maw of a gigantic stamping press. There are gutters around the base of the press, presumably to carry away the blood that I anticipate will flow when the knight and his steed are carried into the press. Sure enough, a moment later my worst fears are realized: the knight and the horse are crushed flat in the press as the upper plate comes smashing down. The force of the impact jolts me awake, but not before I notice with surprise that despite my fears, there was in fact no blood and gore in the gutters around the base of the machine.

I awoke and recorded this dream in my journal, experiencing my usual state of initial wonderment and confusion over the possible meanings of this curiously compelling and dramatic image. When I had writ-ten an account of the dream, it remained as mysterious as it had on first awakening. I decided to draw a quick sketch of the underground scene in my journal, right next to the written narrative.

As I drew the stamping press, I noted that the bottom plate of the press was not flat. Instead it formed a double "hump," which I had drawn with a single line made up of two mirror curves, much the way one might draw a sea gull in flight with a single line (‿︵‿). As I looked at the double-curved line I had drawn, I realized that this is also the way I would hastily sketch the pages of a book lying open.

The aha that accompanied this thought was physically palpable. I understood that, at one level at least, the dream was a "joke" about the "heroic" effort to remember and record dreams. The equestrian figure represented the dream itself, "smashed" and "flattened" into the written narrative on the pages of my dream journal. The dream, as always, spoke the truth. The quality of distortion and "flattening" that any dream goes through in the process of being remembered and recorded in words is analogous to the distortion and flattening and "killing" that the heroic knight and his horse suffer in the stamping press.

This dream, despite its seemingly gruesome imagery, ultimately reaffirmed the value of remembering the dreams and rendering them into sharable form. The knight struggling to hold the horse steady, as the two are moved slowly and inexorably toward the jaws of the press, is a figure embodying the important archetype of Willing Sacrifice. At this level, the dream is another clear example that death in the dream world is always deeply associated with the growth of personality and character. The knight struggles to hold his steed steady, overcoming fear, knowing they will both be squashed flat, but also knowing this is noble and necessary. That the knight and the horse are both in "full armor" implies that the "willing sacrificial act" is a conscious choice to overcome rigid and carefully crafted defenses.

The "willingly sacrificial" quality of the knight's behavior looks suicidal, but like most "suicides" in the dream world, it is a metaphor of conscious participation in growth and individuation. Obviously, if a dreamer is dealing with issues of an actual suicide in waking life (either his/her own or someone else's), then a dream image of suicide will refer directly to the waking situation as well. However, even in situations involving actual suicide, my experience is that a person's desire to "end it all" is often a response of *misplaced literalism* to the symbolism of the deep but frustrated archetypal desire for growth and fundamental change. In my experience, suicide is almost always a consequence of failure of imagination. The person contemplating suicide cannot even imagine, let alone actually accomplish, any way of living in accordance with his/her deepest character and beliefs, so death seems to be the only possibility for escaping the pain of "unrealizable" desire.

Since the "distortion" and "flattening" of the heroic equestrian in my dream is brought about in a "press" that looks like "an open book," another layer of ironic meaning concerns the increased vulnerability and openness to criticism and misunderstanding that is the inevitable result of "going to press" and publishing my work (involving as it does a certain amount of self-revelation and turning my life into "an open book"). When I encounter these fears in myself, I can only reaffirm my belief that the net result of publishing my ideas will be that some people will read and understand them and that those who "get it" will make a more positive difference in the world than those who don't.

This dream, like others, contains additional layers of meaning that would be worth exploring in their own right, but I offer it here primarily as an example of some of the possible benefits derived from regularly drawing and sketching one's dreams.

Because we regularly share the same bed and do not wish to disturb each other unnecessarily, my wife and I have both settled on the "light pen" to record our dreams. We both construct our own, using rigid ballpoint-pen refills taped to penlights. More streamlined, relatively inexpensive commercial light pens are readily available in stationery and specialty stores, but because of their limited ink reservoirs, and the difficulty in obtaining nonstandardized replacement parts, we have both settled on the less elegant but more easily maintained homemade versions. There is one advance in the consumer technology available for scribbling notes in the middle of the night that deserves mention. NiteNotes is an open-faced ergonomic plastic dispenser for three-by-five-inch cards or notepaper that also holds a write-at-any-angle ballpoint pen in the top. When the pen is withdrawn from its built-in holder, light-emitting diodes automatically come on and illuminate the page with just the right amount of light to write notes and draw little sketches in the dark. When the pen is returned to its holder, the light is automatically extinguished. It has proven to be a very handy, low-maintenance, high-performance gadget for catching dream memories.

We have both reached a level of comfort and ease with this method of capturing elusive initial dream memories where either of us can usually wake up multiple times at night and scribble notes without disturbing the other at all. We are able to make these notes on the paper by the bed with a minimum of movement. Moving around tends to dispel dream memories, so we keep motion to a minimum. Even when we do wake each other up, the other almost always remembers a dream and makes notes too. Using a light pen has become so smooth and relatively effortless over the past two decades, we both use it nightly, even when we are traveling and sleeping in unfamiliar surroundings.

More than half the dreams that I recall are first captured in the middle of the night with the light pen. I sometimes wake up in the morning with no dream memories, and no recollection of having awakened in the night to make notes, but there they are on the page, and when I read them over, they almost always trigger a much fuller recollection of the dream.

The converse is also true: some mornings I will wake with the thought "Oh, well, I can't remember what I was just dreaming, but I did wake up and catch a dream and make some notes in the middle of the night," but when I look at the page, it's blank. The technical name for such an experience is a "false awakening." It is a significant dream experience in itself. It is quite common, particularly among people who regularly record and work with their dreams.

Regardless of the specific method used, recording the dream experience in some fashion when it is first remembered is crucial, because no matter how vivid the memory seems to be on first awakening, it will usually disappear within an hour or so unless at least a few notes capture one or two of the strongest feelings and images.

Of course, almost everyone has one or two dreams, usually from childhood, sometimes recurrent, that he or she will never forget, even if they are never shared or recorded. Such dreams can easily be remembered years, even decades later, without their ever having been written down.

These spontaneously memorable dreams are particularly valuable to work with at many different times in your life. In my experience, such dreams are close "cousins" to recurrent dreams, because both embody particularly clear and poignant symbolic reflections of the dreamer's basic life issues. They are usually rich with subtle and multiple layers of intertwined meanings.

Such spontaneously memorable dreams can be viewed as particularly apt and elegant statements of the dreamer's fundamental "mythology"— the basic symbolic "story" that lends your life meaning, no matter how the external circumstances of your life may appear to change. Such dreams are so memorable and stay in our minds because they are relevant to our lives at every point. They stay close to our awareness over a life-time because their symbolism and imagery resonate continuously with our fundamental life actions and decisions.

However, these few usually memorable dreams are the exceptions. The rest of the tens of thousands of dreams that a person has in a lifetime, no matter how vivid and memorable at first, will simply disappear from memory if they are not soon recorded.

In their initial excitement and enthusiasm for the work, some people will try to record their dreams in detail every time they awaken. This can lead to a severe disruption of normal sleep patterns, and often results in an early "burnout" on paying attention to dreams. Brief notes on the most impressive elements in the dream are usually quite sufficient to recall a much richer and more complex memory of the dream later on when the notes are reviewed.

Occasionally, they will awaken directly from a dream so compelling that it demands to be written down in full, right then and there; often they will not be able to fall back to sleep until this has been accomplished. In my experience, such dreams are relatively few and far between, but they are quite recognizable when they appear, and we really have no choice but to wake up and perhaps sketch the images and write out a much fuller account. The vast majority of dreams, however, will be "satisfied" with the less-strenuous process of making notes and filling in the narrative more completely the following day.

The thoughts and feelings we casually entertain while falling asleep always exert a strong influence on the dreams that follow. In this important sense, we are always "incubating" what we will dream about, although most of the time we take no conscious notice of the process. The thoughts and feelings that twine spontaneously and "randomly" around our memories of the previous day's activities and experiences and our anticipations of tomorrow's events, as we drift off to sleep, always affect the themes and issues that will be woven together into that night's dreaming.

There is a more intentional way of incubating the content of our dreams. If we simply focus attention on the desire to remember dreams as our last intentional act before drifting off to sleep, and combine that with a gentle focusing on specific issues, problems, and situations that we wish to dream about, the dreams will usually oblige. This is the simplest dream-incubation exercise. The basic element of all incubation exercises and rituals is to focus the attention on the desired dream and to hold it until the dreaming mind responds.

The conscious practice of prayer, meditation, contemplation, yoga, and the like, focused on important life choices, will also lead to a richer, more vividly remembered and understood dream life. Dream-incubation exercises of this sort can even be extended to include focusing on the intention to become "lucid" in your dreams—that is, to become consciously aware that you are dreaming *while the dream is taking place*. You can even extend the incubation exercise to include the desire to practice your chosen meditative discipline(s) intentionally *in the dream state*. Athletes and martial artists have found this skill of immense value in improving their waking performance, and so might anyone. Mental rehearsal and intentional imaging have been shown to improve performance, and my experience is that these "mental rehearsals" are even more effective when undertaken in the dream than when awake. (See Chapter 8 for a more complete discussion of lucid dreaming and "dream yoga.")

It is best to write out fairly full accounts of the previous night's dreaming in the morning, just after waking up. The details and complexities of the dream are most clear and vivid then and available for translation into conscious terms. If you can't write out your dreams in full upon awakening, it is wise to make brief notes and to write out a more complete narrative at the earliest opportunity. My habit is to grab any free moments during the day to record the previous night's dreams, but sometimes I don't get to it until the last part of the evening before falling asleep. Occasionally, my schedule is so hectic and demanding that I simply don't get to it until the next day. Although this is far from ideal, my experience is that my notes will call up much of the dream detail even then. This will probably be less true for those new to the process, however.

The longer you wait to write down the dream memories, the more the details and subtleties tend to dissolve away and leave only the bones of the experience. However, no matter how long you wait, and no matter how much of the dream has been forgotten, what you *do* remember is always worth recording and pondering. Even the tiniest fugitive fragments (such as Mike's "maybe pastel colors") can yield dramatic energies and insights.

*Even the way we forget our dreams reveals their patterns of meaning and significance.* Like a pearl dissolving in a glass of vinegar, the dream's multiple layers of complex association and elaboration dissolve away, and we get closer and closer to its "reason for being," until we are left with the original grain of sand, the source of the "irritation" that caused the oyster to create the pearl in the first place. The dream fragment is like a little poem capturing the central theme and message of the much longer "novel." *Do not ignore your dream fragments.*

To summarize the three basic techniques for dream recall: (1) decide wholeheartedly that you want to remember and understand your dreams; (2) prepare the means by which you will record your dream memories when you awaken, and place the tools right next to your sleeping place; and (3) remind yourself as you drift off to sleep of your intention to recall and comprehend your dreams. It may not be necessary to do anything else to facilitate dream recall. In the absence of these three steps, it is unlikely that any of the other, more elaborate techniques for enhancing dream recall will have much effect, and with these three steps, more elaborate techniques may not be necessary.

When writing down your dreams, get into the habit of giving them vibrant, evocative *titles.* Then, at any point, you will be able to go back, review all the recorded dreams, and begin to get a view of the forest as a whole, instead of just the individual trees. Reviewing dreams in sequential series can be an important transition step between introductory dream work and intermediate or advanced dream work. Dealing with dreams in series, pursuing common themes and imagery through multiple dreams over time, is an excellent way to gain understanding of the overall evolution and glacial movement of one's deep interior life.

The titles should call up the experience of the dream, rather than some insight about its meaning, because a concrete image will be much more likely to bring the dream to mind. In other words, a title such as "Fleeing from the Burning Castle" will in the long run turn out to be much more useful than a more abstract title such as "Fear," or a more analytical title such as "Anger at My Family." Even though "fear" and "anger at my family" may both be elements embodied in the dream, the actual *experience* of the dream is much more likely to be called back into mind by "Fleeing from the Burning Castle."

If you want to capture an insight about one of the meanings of a dream in its title, put it into a subtitle. For instance, using the example above, I might center on a title such as "Fleeing from the Burning

Castle—Fear and Anger at My Family." Usually, when you have finished writing down and sketching a dream, a title will pop to mind spontaneously, springing from the same unconscious depths the dream sprang from initially. Often, the images that were first recorded in the dream notes turn out to make the best title.

If the title serves its purpose and allows me to recall the dream at a glance, then months and years later I may be able to glean new insights from it. For example, "Fleeing from the Burning Castle" may reveal layers of collective meaning I missed on first examination. Later, I may realize a collective level of meaning referring to the economic tribulations of the nation as a whole, or perhaps a reference to my physical health that I missed. In retrospect, viewed in the context of the dreams that followed, I may realize that it was precisely at the time when I had the dream that I really "let go" of some drama with my parents. Giving dreams evocative titles when you first record them is of great value for ongoing dream work.

It does sometimes happen that a person will take all three of the basic preparatory steps for dream recall and still not remember anything upon awakening. In such instances, a couple of things can be done.

Moving around in bed when you first wake up disrupts dream recall. As you find yourself waking up, hold still, reach back, and ask, "What have I been dreaming?" If you forget, or if the urge to move is too strong, the best thing to do after moving around and relieving the stiffness is to *return to the position you were in when you first awoke,* then ask yourself again, "What was I dreaming?" This will usually bring dream memories to mind when moments before it seemed that there was simply nothing there to be recalled.

We all have a series of body postures that we habitually roll through over the course of a night's sleep. Returning to each of these postures in turn is likely to release dream memories—presumably memories of dreams that occurred while the dreamer was lying in those positions. Even if one easily remembers a dream upon awakening, it is always a good idea—time and energy permitting—to roll back through *all* these habitual sleep positions to see what additional memories may be stimulated.

For millennia, occultists and followers of various Eastern religions all the way back to the ancient Egyptians have believed that the human psyche is made up of "multiple souls," all of which separate and have different experiences in sleep—experiences that we recall as "dreams" when we awaken. The different dreams that one often remembers when rolling through the habitual sleeping positions have been offered by these people as experiential evidence for the multiplicity of the "soul."

Sometimes people are not consciously aware of their habitual sleep positions. If you sleep with a partner, ask your bedmate what those positions are, and he or she is sure to be able to tell you. If you do not have a partner, just lie down as you would if you were getting ready to sleep, then feel into your body. What is the next position that feels right? The body itself will reveal its habits when asked, even if you aren't conscious of them beforehand.

Sometimes you might take all the suggested preliminary steps, awake with no dream memories, roll slowly through the habitual sleeping postures, and still not be able to remember anything from the previous night's dreaming. If this happens, don't give up—there is still one more exercise that regularly stimulates dream memories, even in this frustrating situation. Move slowly and meditatively through the set of habitual sleeping positions a second time, only this time, instead of asking the general question "What was I dreaming?" consciously focus on visualizing the faces of those people with whom you have the strongest emotional connections (positive or negative) in waking life.

These are the faces most likely to appear in your dreams. When you roll through the habitual sleep positions a second time and visualize these faces, a vision will often come of one of these faces set in a scene that is not being consciously imagined. This unexpected scene will almost always be a scene from a dream. Even if it is a memory of waking life, if it comes to you in this fashion, it is quite likely that you dreamed it again—emphasizing its symbolic importance—and even if you didn't dream it, since it appears spontaneously in this fashion while you are seeking dream memories, it is still worth treating as though it were a dream. Having succeeded in connecting with this one scene, it is almost always possible to "reel in" and record a much larger chunk of memory.

This technique will also produce positive results if you visualize other frequently dreamed images besides faces, such as your childhood home(s), specific qualities of light, windows and doorways, landscapes, pets, cars, and so on. As you become more familiar with the specific geography and seasons of your dream world, this list of regularly recurring images will fill itself in with other items as well.

The reasons why we remember or fail to remember our dreams at any given moment are multiple and complex. Natural "circadian rhythms" can be detected in the patterns of dream recall over time that seem to have little to do with the dreamer's will, focus of intent, or state of psychospiritual development, and everything to do with natural responses to the solar, lunar, and seasonal cycles. Every woman who keeps a regular dream record will soon discover a pattern of peaks and valleys of remembering and forgetting that tend to cluster around the rhythms of her menstrual cycle. Men, and women past menopause, will discover the same kind of 27-to-29-day pattern of recalling and forgetting, even though they have no obvious biorhythm to match it to. Diet, stress, and general physical and emotional health will also reveal themselves as factors in patterns of dream recall.

For many people, supplements of the complex of B vitamins appear to improve dream recall. Many different studies have been made of the correlation between B vitamins in the diet and the ability to remember dreams. Some of these studies developed elaborate double- and triple-blind protocols, where the participants in the studies do not even know what information the researchers are seeking, in order to prevent "self-fulfilling prophecies" and unconscious responses to suggestion. In many of these studies blind control groups took placebos while the blind experimental groups were given B vitamins in various doses and proportions. These studies regularly confirm that 75 to 80 percent of the subjects ingesting B-vitamin supplements will report a spontaneous increase in "dreaming" (i.e., remembering their dreams, where previously they did not), while over the same period the control groups report no such increase.

My own experience has confirmed this over and over; the closest thing to a legal "dream pill" is a standard B-complex vitamin supplement. Experience strongly suggests that taking the whole complex of B vitamins has the most reliable effect, although some studies have achieved almost the same results with vitamin $B_6$ alone. My own preference is for a total B-complex with added vitamin C. The C appears to help metabolize the B₃. I take my vitamin supplements before going to bed, so that they are digested and metabolized while I sleep.

Since the B vitamins are water soluble, the chance of overdosing on them is small. When more B vitamins enter the body than can be assimilated, they are flushed out through the urinary system and do not build up in the fatty tissues the way other, oil-soluble vitamins (such as vitamin A) sometimes do. If one takes too many B vitamins, the first symptom will be a noticeable increase in urination, sometimes accompanied by mild discomfort. The urine will also tend to be a much brighter yellow than usual, but increasing B vitamin intake at all, even within healthy limits, will tend to turn the urine bright yellow, so by itself this is not a cause for concern. B vitamins will build up in the body to toxic levels when taken in massive quantities. When this happens, the first symptom is increased urination, followed by a marked increase in the "tingling" and "going to sleep" of the extremities, and a progressive loss of sensation in the fingers and toes. As soon as the massive doses of B-complex are discontinued, the symptoms disappear completely, and full sensation returns to the affected areas. Since there is the possibility of uncomfortable side effects, you should consult your physician before making any radical alteration of your diet and vitamin intake.

And although I do not recommend these substances, it should also be noted that the National Institute of Mental Health has demonstrated conclusively that even infinitesimal doses of LSD and the natural "entheogens" (such as mescaline, peyote, ayahuasca, and ibogaine)— doses too small to create any observable alteration of waking perception or behavior—have the predictable effect of increasing dream recall dramatically.

Other mind-altering substances, particularly alcohol, marijuana, and the various coca derivatives, have precisely the opposite effect, and in even moderate doses they will make it difficult, if not impossible, to remember dreams. Barbiturates, "tranquilizers," and "muscle relaxants" have the same negative effect. Virtually all prescription and over-the-counter sleeping pills and "tension reducers" have a severely deleterious effect on people's ability to remember their dreams. In addition, many of the antipsychotic drugs will also have the unfortunate effect of reducing a person's ability to remember his or her dreams.

The loss of dream memories associated with many of the current antipsychotic medications is particularly tragic because it is often through dream work that profound mental and emotional disturbance can be effectively addressed. The drugs used for general anesthesia in major surgery also leave their "fingerprints" all over the dreams people have in the recovery room and later during convalescence. I have actually become fairly adept at "guessing" what anesthetic drugs people have been given from the characteristic images, stereotyped situations, and intense feelings they leave behind in the recovering patient's dreams. In my experience, even though many different legal and illegal drugs and medications regularly leave fairly recognizable traces on the surface of appearance in people's dreams, all those other multiple layers of meaning and significance that are always there in "ordinary," non-drug-induced dreams are still present; it is just that the dramatic "tracks" left by the chemicals often tend to obscure these other layers with their dramatic, emotionally charged overlays.

I worked as a senior therapist for many years in a Jungian-based residential treatment program for profoundly disturbed, schizophrenic and autistic, adolescents and young adults, doing regular dream work with the clients, and regular dream-work training with the staff. During my more than ten years of work and study at St. George Homes, Inc., in Berkeley, California, I was deeply impressed by how the dreams of even the most deeply troubled psychotic clients promoted health and wholeness. I was also deeply impressed with the tragedy of strong reliance on chemical treatment for this population in other institutions, precisely because it tends to separate them effectively from precisely those inner resources that are necessary for the effective transformation of their psychoses and their return to mutually meaningful social interaction and creative emotional life.

Systematic research has demonstrated that prolonged dream deprivation invariably leads to severe disorientation, agitation, hallucination, loss of small-motor abilities, and general disintegration of personality, even in otherwise healthy people. This has been demonstrated in the laboratory under carefully controlled conditions in multiple studies.

High levels of alcohol in the blood will also prevent a person from entering REM sleep and presumably also interfere with the dreams of non-REM sleep as well. This interruption of regular patterns and dreaming will tend to produce similar deleterious effects. Whenever an animal, human or otherwise, is prevented from dreaming, no matter what the cause, there is an immediate "bounce-back effect" where the dream-deprived individual will slip immediately into REM sleep at the earliest opportunity in an apparently spontaneous effort to "recoup" the lost dream experience.

The behavior of people in the grips of alcohol-produced delirium tremens (the d.t.'s) is virtually indistinguishable from the behavior of subjects systematically deprived of REM sleep in a laboratory setting. Prolonged dream deprivation leads to precisely the same kinds of deterioration in mental acuity, emotional stability, and motor function that severe alcoholism produces. This has led a number of researchers to conclude that the d.t.'s are actually a sleep disorder, a symptom of dream deprivation. They suggest that the severe alcoholic falls into an unconscious state, a state hardly worthy of the gentle name of sleep. The high levels of blood alcohol prevent the passed-out drunk from dreaming, but when he or she awakens, the levels of blood alcohol have fallen sufficiently for the individual to begin to "bounce back" and *dream while awake.* The attendant hallucinations are, in essence, dream images intruding upon the waking mind because they were prevented from appearing naturally in sleep.

By the same token, the "bad trips" of people ingesting psychedelic and entheogenic drugs are also essentially dream experiences that take place while they are awake. Those who have "bad trips" tend to report having had predominantly bad dreams (when they remember them at all) long before they experimented with drugs. Conversely, it is also true that people who experience entheogenic drugs as positive and profound almost uniformly report prior dream lives that were interesting and positive.

It appears that this class of chemicals lowers the barriers that ordinarily separate the unconscious (what Freud called "primary process") from the more logical and linear functions of the waking mind. The testimony of innumerable "psychonauts" is that different people can take precisely the same dosage of precisely the same drug, and some will have mystical experiences suggesting the felt-sense of the Divine, and others will fall into the depths of "hell" in "bad trips." The inevitable conclusion seems to be that it is not the chemical that causes the negative reaction, but rather the state of comfort and deep psychospiritual self-acceptance of the individual, and that ingesting the chemical is only a dramatic catalyst.

In the case of morphine, the issue is less clear. Many people have
reported terrible nightmares while on morphine, and it is difficult to tell
how much of this typical response is the result of their being in pretty
dire pain to begin with and how much can be ascribed to the drug itself,
but both factors appear to contribute to the nightmare effect.

In my experience, the individual's characteristic dream life is the
most reliable indicator of the likelihood of positive and vivid psychospiritual experience in serious prayer and meditation as well.

One of the most important things that separates "storming the gates"
of the deep unconscious through the use of drugs from approaching it
more gently through paying more careful attention to dreams is the difference in safety. If a person's dream life is essentially negative and scary,
it is more likely that he or she will experience a "mind-blowing bad trip"
with entheogenic drugs, brought about by opening too abruptly and violently to the upwelling, potentially overwhelming energies of the deep
unconscious. However, the chances of that same person's experiencing
a similar "mind blow" (psychotic break, schizophrenic episode, etc.)
through opening to the deep unconscious via the gentle, slower method
of increased attention to dreams is almost nil.

The dream process has a system of natural "checks and balances" that
all but precludes that kind of overwhelming negative experience. It is
precisely this system of protective checks and balances that is sometimes
short-circuited by the psychoactive strength of the powerful drugs.

The part of the dreaming psyche that Freud called "the censor" universally tends to suppress dream thoughts and memories that are too
challenging to the cherished beliefs and self-image of the waking ego.
Dreams that are too "radioactive" to be dealt with calmly by the waking
mind simply slip out of memory as soon as they are experienced. This
phenomenon is called repression, and it does account for a certain percentage of "lost dreams."

It seems fair to assume, for instance, that the majority of the dreams
that Mike undoubtedly had and did not remember during the semester
when he took the dream class were preconsciously *repressed* because they
challenged his most dearly cherished assumptions about his future as a
minister.

Note, however, that an unbroken continuum stretches from "repression" of material that is denied for essentially trivial reasons all the way to

those things that are mercifully rendered "unmemorable" because they are genuinely beyond the individual's ability to deal with in a creative or positive fashion. It may be the case that we dream about matters over which we have absolutely no influence, and which might destroy us if we saw them clearly, but that mercifully, we simply do not recall those dreams.

Sometimes, just as we awaken, there is a moment when we can almost remember what we were dreaming. It flits in and out, and then, more often than not, it disappears. This is usually all we see of the dim, preconscious struggle between the "censor" and the experience of the dream. The censor is attempting to "protect" our conscious view of our lives by repressing and rendering the disturbing and challenging dreams "unmemorable," while the dreaming unconscious is attempting to "wake us up" to the as-yet-unimagined creative but "dangerous" possibilities that lie unseen and ignored in the midst of even the most dismal of our life circumstances.

When the waking mind colludes with the preconscious "censor" and denies these possibilities and suppresses the dream, that is "repression," but when there is fundamental agreement between the unconscious forces that shape the dream and the conscious belief system that the material embodied in the dream really *is* more than the dreamer can handle, then the dream simply disappears from consciousness without a struggle, and we have no conscious or even preconscious awareness of this tug-of-war. In my view, losing dreams without any awareness of preconscious conflict simply cannot be classed as repression.

Experiences of severe trauma, particularly severe trauma experienced in childhood, often fall into this category; the memories of these terrible experiences, and the dreams that constellate around them, are lost to what we might call "healthy amnesia" rather than repression.

However, when this positive amnesia helps to suppress, say, childhood trauma, the individual continues to develop his or her emotional and mental strengths into maturity, uninhibited by the potentially overwhelming and paralyzing memory of the trauma. When this is the case, a time inevitably arrives when the unconscious determines that the mature person is *now* capable of facing consciously and creatively the memories that would indeed have once jeopardized the ability to survive and develop.

At this point the individual's dreams will inevitably begin to insinuate symbolic material related to the amnesic trauma into remembered dreams. Now, the healthy amnesia turns into repression, aided by the preconscious habits of a lifetime. The preconscious struggle between the habitual "censor" and the energy of the dream will become more and more visible, in which case the continued failure to remember and deal with the material that surfaced in the dreams *becomes* "repression," when before it was not.

It often happens that a person clearly remembers a dream that focuses on some life issue that he or she consciously *believes* is insoluble and to which there seems to be no positive response, but if the dream is remembered, then that is absolute proof that there *is* some creative response. Most often, this failure to perceive the creative possibility is born out of the reliance upon conventional thought and unexamined assumptions. The dream comes to awareness to attempt to draw the dreamer's conscious attention to the radical possibilities that have been ignored. Often these possibilities are new, the result of increased maturity, and were in fact not there before. (For a more complete discussion of this concept, illustrated with multiple examples, see Chapter 7.)

The "repression phenomenon" is sometimes demonstrated in working with dreams. A person will be working with a dream and have an aha of insight related to the dream, then suddenly remember another dream. Often, this "secondary dream memory" was not remembered at all when the dream first occurred. (If the dreamer has been keeping a fairly complete record of his/her dreams, then the question can be settled fairly easily by looking at the dream journals.) If the dream memory is "new," then it reliably indicates that the aha related to the dream is particularly important and has allowed previously repressed memories to rise to conscious awareness. Another "symptom" that often accompanies this process is a sudden surge of emotional and physical vitality and well-being, as the energy that was previously wasted on repressing the dream memories is released and surges back into the dreamer's awareness in a "free" form, available for conscious, purposeful allocation and creative use.

When work with a dream spontaneously calls up memories of other dreams, whether they were previously repressed or not, it indicates an aha of a fairly high order. The related dream memories will often resonate with one another, and when viewed together as a "matched set," they will reveal the depth and developmental course of the fundamental issue the dreams were each addressing at the times when they first appeared.

Although repression accounts for some forgotten dream material, in my experience it is responsible for much less than most people suppose. Most people invoke "repression" as the first and most likely explanation whenever there is an extended failure to recall dreams. However, even the most successful and dedicated dream recallers will only remember two or three dreams a night. Anyone who consistently remembers two or three dreams a night is doing well and can hardly be accused of cowardice or "repression." Yet the laboratory studies clearly indicate that everyone is dreaming five, six, or even seven times a night, so even the least "repressed" and most successful dream recallers are remembering only something like half, or less than half, of the dreams they actually experience.

The issue of whether we dream "in color" or "in black and white" is relevant here as well. My experience convinces me that everyone dreams in full color, but that some people tend to remember their dreams in black and white more than others.

Over and over again, statistical researchers conclude that "women dream in color more than men." Because the question can be studied with great ease, at minimal cost, the results have been replicated many times. *A direct archetypal correlation exists between the intensity of color in dreams and the perceived intensity of the dreamer's emotional life.* The more aware the dreamer is of the colors in his/her dreams, the more likely it is that the dreamer is consciously aware of his/her emotional life, and the emotional lives of others, when awake. This is one of the reasons why I believe that what these "color dreaming" studies actually show is the extent to which sexism has shaped the emotional lives of women and men.

Conventional child-rearing practices in this society systematically encourage little girls to pay close attention to their own and others' emotions, while at the same time discouraging little boys from taking their emotional lives seriously at all. To the extent that unexamined and oppressive sex-role stereotypes determine our conscious behavior, it is to be expected that "women dream in color more than men." However, the undistorted, natural predilection of healthy human beings is to lead rich, full emotional lives and to dream in full color. These two phenomena reflect and reinforce one another.

Not only do I find this analysis persuasive from a theoretical point of view, but the whole of my experience convinces me as well.

Over and over again, I have had people come to my dream work training sessions who say they "dream only in black and white." Over the years, many more men than women, proportionally, have told me this, confirming the more formal academic studies, but what is more interesting and important from my point of view is that, whether these "colorless rememberers" are men or women, they have uniformly impressed me as relatively emotionally repressed. The people who experience their dream lives "in black and white" tend to be in positions of direct authority over others and tend to believe that they "cannot afford to be sentimental" about their supervisory work or, indeed, about any aspect of their lives.

When people with generally negative attitudes toward the realm of emotion are drawn to dream work, it is often because they feel a vague dissatisfaction with their lives. Quite often, they describe themselves as "doing very well," professionally, financially, and sometimes even relationally, but despite these "successes," they feel there is "something missing" in their lives. When these seekers stay with dream work, it tends to take a predictable course.

At some point in the ongoing dream sharing and exploratory work, they report the sudden appearance of the color red. It is almost invariably red—the archetypal color of strongest passion and deepest feeling "in the heat of their blood"—that appears first. Often, the "black-and-white dreamer" will report seeing "a red car" or "red flowers" or some such, without even noticing consciously that the dreams are no longer presenting themselves to waking consciousness in shades of gray. Once red has appeared, all the other colors of the spectrum fill in the dream images quickly, until at the end of the scheduled set of meetings, he or she is "dreaming in color" like everyone else in the group.

In these repeated circumstances, I have been impressed in each instance by how the dreams appear to serve the dreamer's health and wholeness by drawing more and more conscious attention to the importance of emotional responses to waking events and by how the dreamer has actually become more and more aware of his/her feelings and emotions as a result. My theoretical conclusion is that the dreamer begins to *notice* the colors in the dreams, which were always there but were ignored, directly reflecting the way in which emotions were actually present but previously ignored in waking life.

It seems reasonable to suppose that as we liberate ourselves and our children from sex-role stereotypes, one result might be that the proportion of men and women who "only dream in black and white" would decrease in the population as a whole and that the disparity between the percentage of women and the percentage of men who remember their dreams in full color would disappear entirely. Studying these percentages might even be an "objective" means of assessing whether or not collective liberation from sex-role stereotypes is actually taking place.

The issue of "anger" in dreams, particularly in the dreams of men, also deserves mention here in connection with remembering dreams. Just as the sex-linked disparity in the ability of men and women to recall color in their dreams is directly symbolic of their relationships with emotional stimuli and experience in waking life, the actual emotions reported by the dreamer are also heavily influenced by the patterns induced by gender-linked child-raising practices. This is true of both men and women, and it is especially true with respect to the emotions and the ranges of emotional expression that are encouraged and accepted by parents and other adult influences on little boys.

In masculinist societies, boys in particular are most often discouraged from *feeling*, let alone expressing, any strong emotions *other than anger*. Even anger is not encouraged, only barely tolerated. "Boys will be boys," as the saying goes (often accompanied by the unspoken but very clear addendum "but we don't have to like it").

One tragic result of the consistent, gender-linked pattern of societally orchestrated repression and denial of strong emotion in males of all ages is that very often boys, and the men they grow to become, actually come to *experience internally a whole range of strong, complex emotion as indistinguishable from "anger."* When boys who have been shaped by this kind of child rearing grow to manhood, they *experience* grief as anger. They *experience* fear as anger. They experience both strong attraction and strong revulsion as anger. They experience frustration as anger. Many men are simply incapable of distinguishing between the emotions evoked by frustration and feelings of anger evoked by other situations (such as injustice, mockery, etc.). These are only a few of the most obvious examples; the phenomenon is fairly well known, pernicious, and very widespread.

One consequence of this collective distortion of natural emotional experience and response is that when "anger" is reported in dreams, particularly by boys and men (which statistically they do with much higher frequency than do girls and women), it is very often a "place holder" for other, more subtle and complex feelings. This often turns out to be true for women as well. *From a practical dream work point of view, it is always worth asking what other emotions may be "masked" and "carried" by "anger" in dreams.* This is also often a very good question to ask in waking life as well.

What is true of "anger" in dreams turns out to be true of the whole range of remembered emotions in dreams. *There is no more reason to take* **any** *of the emotions reported in a dream* **only literally** *than there is to take any of the other events or actions in a dream only literally.* The dreamer's report of his/her emotional responses to the experience(s) of any dream is always a very important piece of symbolic information, but in my experience, it cannot be taken as "a solid place to stand" to view the rest of the dream, any more than any of the other elements of a dream are to be seen as only literal and "off limits" to symbolic interpretation.

Over the years I have come to conclude that the primary reason why we all forget the majority of what we dream is that the dreams themselves are centered in the realm that Carl Jung called "the collective unconscious," rather than in the realm of our personal lives.

The realm of the collective is characterized by two things: it is "timeless," and the distinction between self and other ceases to exist. When dream experience is centered in this archetypal realm, it becomes difficult, if not impossible, to remember. This is because in the realm of the collective unconscious, everything happens at once. In the dream, there is no separate "I the dreamer" to whom things happen and who can remember and report them. In such a dream, "I" *am everything* in the dream. I experience everything simultaneously from multiple, overlapping, subjective viewpoints. Everything that "I" am happens *at once*, so that when I awaken from the dream, I cannot organize it into a sequential narrative. The totality of the experience is beyond my ability to put into concepts, words, or images and thus appears to be "gone" from my mind, even though I often have a frustrating recollection that *something* of great interest, energy, and importance was in fact happening just moments before.

When we awaken, the first two basic assumptions that we unquestioningly accept about the waking world are: (1) the linear flow of time (being awake is "now," sleeping was "then," and breakfast is "later"), and (2) the basic distinction between self and other (my body is "me," and everything else, from the warm bedclothes on out to the farthest reaches of the universe, is "not me"). However, these are precisely the assumptions that the experience of the dream centered in the collective unconscious does *not* make, so reacquiring these fundamental "sane" attitudes toward the nature of reality as the first preconscious act of awakening renders the dream experience centered in the collective realm totally beyond the purview of waking memory.

When a dream is centered in the collective unconscious, no matter how long the dream may seem to go on, the experience at any given moment is of the beginning, the middle, and the end all happening at once, so that in retrospect it is virtually impossible to separate events into a memory with a linear sequences. The experience of the dream centered in the collective unconscious is also one of simultaneous multiple personality: "I" experience "myself" simultaneously as everything and everyone in the dream, having all their subjective feelings and thoughts and experiences at the same time, so that there is no exclusive focus of awareness from which to organize the memory of the experience either. There is no "me" to whom things happen, only the complex, multiple, and subtle experience of everything happening at once to everyone and everything—all of which are "me" at the same time.

I am now regularly able to remember the experience in my dreams of being more than one person at once, and I recall multiple "story lines" going on simultaneously. When the number of "characters" who "share" my subjective awareness in the dream gets above three or four, I still find it virtually impossible to remember anything concrete about the "events." Awake, I try to imagine what the experience of being everyone and everything in the world would be like, and I come up with little that can be rendered into words, but I am convinced that each of us experiences dreams in this fashion to some extent every night.

To use traditional language, I believe that everyone "goes back to God" every night, dissolving away the boundaries of our ordinary ego personalities, our worries about the passage of time and the inevitable approach of death, and the sense of anxious separateness from our deeper unconscious selves, each other, and the Divine, but that this experience is so profound, so different from our habitual waking experience, that we simply fail to remember it when we wake up. I also suspect that these "dreams of the collective" are primarily responsible for the healing properties of sleep, even more than the dreams we are able to remember.

I think that other common dream experiences are also traceable to this phenomenon of "collective dreaming," beyond the conventions of time and waking ego awareness. Almost everyone has had the experience in dreams of having a conversation or listening to speech or reading a book, filled with excitement and pleasure at the information and insight being absorbed, only to discover upon awakening that the content of the communication has been completely lost, leaving only the ironic sense of pleasure and understanding. I believe that those dream experiences are indications that the "center of gravity" of the dream moved, at that point in the dream, away from the personal toward the collective and that the content of the "lost communication" is framed in an experience of "timeless communion with all," beyond the flow of sequential events and the distinction between self and other. I believe this is why portions of the dream that seem particularly interesting and luminous remain beyond one's ability to remember when awake.

I am convinced that this phenomenon of "collective dreaming" is also the primary reason for the common experience of being in the midst of a fascinating, pleasant, complex, and colorful dream, realizing that one is about to wake up, thinking with pleasure what a great dream this is—even sometimes having the clear thought "Wait till I tell my dream group about *this!*"—and then popping awake and having the whole thing disappear, leaving only the memory of the enthusiastic thought. It seems to me that the dreamer's immediate sense of profound significance and beauty is probably correct. The dream is so beautiful and profound, in fact, that it is beyond the ability of waking consciousness to frame in words or images. In such dreams, I believe, we look directly at the Divine, at the God Within, but as the mystics have testified throughout history, "Words can never soil it."

I also suspect that this "amnesic effect" that accompanies dreaming at collective depth is also the source of the common and surprising experience that habitual dream recallers often have when they first join an ongoing dream group. Sometimes, the very people who seem to be most interested and enthusiastic about the process of exploring their dreams in the company of others will suddenly cease to remember their dreams the moment they join a group. Often, these people will begin to accuse themselves of "secret," totally unconscious repression and self-deception. People in this uncomfortable position often become quite unhappy and filled with self-doubt as their usually prolific dream memories dwindle down to nothing. However, far more often than not, when questioned more closely about the actual experience of awakening and failing to recall their dreams, they will report the classic experience, already described, of feeling tremendous excitement and interest in the dream, only to have this followed immediately by the startling disappearance of the memory of what made them feel that way the moment they opened their eyes. The number of times that I have heard this same essential story from the people who are most interested in the work has led me to conclude that in the vast majority of instances, these people are the victims of their own initial enthusiasm. In the first flush of excitement over joining a dream group, they decide to focus even more attention on their dreams than they have in the past, and this, of necessity, takes them even deeper into the realms of the collective, where the profound and transcendent nature of the dream experiences puts them just beyond the grasp of waking memory.

In this sense, it is easy to understand that the dreams that we forget have just as much, or perhaps even more, to do with the preservation of our health and wholeness than the dreams that we are able to remember. I believe that there is an "invisible" layer of all dreams that partakes of this profound energy of the collective. This collective, archetypal layer of unconscious energy and experience is the "ground of being" in the dream (as well, I believe, as the ultimate ground of being in waking life). Even though we are simply not equipped to perceive it, it *is us* at our deepest core. To use traditional religious language once again, "the Kingdom of God is indeed within," and as Emerson says so succinctly and clearly, "Within is so great as to be Beyond."

Because of the subtle and pervasive archetypal energy that is the "ground" of even our most seemingly mundane dreams, they heal and promote wholeness largely whether we remember them or not. All dreams serve the ultimate needs of the organism (and the species and universe as a whole) through their very process, and remembering them and paying conscious attention to them is simply a means of enhancing that process and increasing the benefits that can be derived from it. Whether you remember your dreams or not, they are still performing their natural life-promoting and affirming tasks, in much the same fashion that the gastrointestinal system digests food and transforms it into vital energy, whether we pay conscious attention to it or not.

However, our dreams also regularly invite us to greater self-awareness and psychospiritual consciousness by remembering them more fully and inquiring more deeply into their multiple meanings. By increasing our capacity to remember and explore our dreams, we come progressively closer to this evolutionary potential.

*Chapter Five*

# DREAMS, NONVIOLENCE, AND SOCIAL CHANGE

*Asleep, we turn our attention to the reality of our interconnectedness as
members of a single species. In this sense, we may regard dreaming as
concerned with the issue of species interconnectedness. . . . Perhaps our
dreaming consciousness is primarily concerned with the survival of the
species and only secondarily with the individual. Were there any truth to
this speculation it would shed a radically different light on the importance
of dreams. It would make them deserving of higher priority in our culture
than they are now assigned.*

—MONTAGUE ULLMAN

The first piece of formal group dream work that I ever did was in 1969. I was part of a community organizing project dedicated to overcoming racism. The project was located in Emeryville, California, a tiny township nestled between Oakland and Berkeley, on the eastern shore of San Francisco Bay. At that time, I was fulfilling my obligation to perform two years of "alternate civilian service" as a conscientious objector to war. The East Bay project was sponsored by my denomination (Unitarian Universalist) through their world service committee. The project was directed by the Reverend George Johnson, an exceptionally gifted and able Methodist minister who had been hired by the U.U. Service Committee to set up grass-roots community organizations promoting self-empowerment and self-improvement in minority communities, particularly black communities, across the country.

The financial support for this innovative series of community organizing projects had come as part of a nationwide outpouring of grief and
anger in response to the racially motivated murder of a Unitarian Universalist seminary student, James Reeb. He had been walking in Dr. Martin
Luther King's March for Justice from Montgomery to Selma, Alabama,
when the marchers were brutally attacked in broad daylight by a mob of
angry white racists. James Reeb died as a result of the beating he received
at their hands, and in the wake of this tragedy, an unusual number of
cash donations came flooding into the denominational headquarters in
Boston to support programs aimed at confronting and overcoming the
racism and hatred that were the ultimate cause of James Reeb's death.

When I arrived at Unitarian Universalist Project East Bay (UUPEB),
I became the only white member of an otherwise all-black staff. As such,
it was immediately clear to me and to the other staff members that I was
neither the right color, nor the right class, to go out into the virtually
all-black, working- and under-class community of Emeryville and try to
motivate people to organize and change the direction of their individual
and community lives.

By default, I became the "office wife." I came in early and opened
the office, made the coffee, maintained the mailing list, answered the
phone, ran the printing press, and carried out a number of other necessary but mundane tasks. At staff meetings, when I raised the issue that my
skills and energies were underutilized, my dissatisfactions were greeted
with mostly sardonic, friendly amusement, but with little in the way of
new challenges or responsibilities.

Eventually, however, the Reverend Mr. Johnson took me aside and
told me a story about UUPEB before I had arrived on the scene. Months
earlier, a number of white volunteers had come into the community to
help set up the project. Many of these volunteers, although they had been
deeply committed at a conscious level to the eradication of racial prejudice and injustice in American society, had also exhibited unconscious,
condescending racist attitudes and behaviors, which had inflamed the
resentment of many local people, who had in turn "thrown the volunteers
out," with a good deal of stormy interaction and subsequent injured feelings on all sides.

Thus, these volunteers had disappeared, and their physical and financial support of UUPEB had dried up. As we discussed this sad history, the Reverend Mr. Johnson suggested to me that here at least was a situation that I *was* the right class and color to do something about, if I cared to give it a try. The problem, depressingly familiar, pushed me uncomfortably up against my own carefully suppressed "liberal" racism, but it also cried out for creative responses.

I accepted the assignment. In consultation with the Reverend Mr. Johnson and other concerned social activists in the San Francisco Bay area, particularly the Reverend Aaron Gilmartin, who was then the pastor of the U.U. congregation in Walnut Creek, we decided to offer a seminar, "Overcoming Racism," open to anyone who cared to come, and we specifically invited the disaffected volunteers to participate. The basic idea was that the former volunteers ought to have at least an opportunity to tell their individual stories to one another and perhaps begin to discharge and heal some of the injured feelings that had resulted. The hope was that we might create a "safe place" where these stories could be aired and reexamined in a larger context.

We put together a "curriculum" plan for the seminar, and the Reverend Mr. Gilmartin offered his church as a regular meeting place. We advertised the program generally in the community of Bay Area social activists. We also extended specific invitations to all the people in the area who had ever supported the project financially or volunteered there. The response to our announcements and invitations was gratifying. At our first meeting we had more than a dozen interested, committed participants. I started to move and gently find my role as the facilitator of the weekly group.

As we began to meet and to get to know one another better, a distressing pattern began to emerge. Although there appeared to be a good deal of immediate emotional relief expressed in sharing and reexamining the experiences of the early days at UUPEB, there was also a pervasive sense of pessimism and hopelessness about racism itself.

The impression that I was left with over and over again at the end of our meetings was: "We are the best and the brightest and the most deeply committed to radical, nonviolent social and political change. We have given it our best shot, and since we failed, it simply can't be done. Racism is like death and taxes; it's beyond anyone's ability to really do anything about!"

A tone of cynicism and bitter resignation began to dominate the group, and as a direct result, the participants began to be more and more antagonistic toward one another, focusing on their respective political and philosophical differences with increasing annoyance and forcing one another into the defensive positions of being "representative spokespersons" for their respective ideologies and conflicting points of view.

It was awful. I became more and more upset and depressed as the weeks went by. I finally decided about midway through the scheduled set of meetings that it would be better to cancel the remaining sessions and face the inevitable private and public shame of failure and admission of inadequacy than to continue with the meetings as they were. In my view, not only were we *not* "overcoming racism," we were making it *worse* by reinforcing the idea that it was an inevitable consequence of unchangeable human nature. Of course, canceling the remaining meetings would, in itself, reinforce the message that it was hopeless to try to confront and overcome racism. It was a terrible ironic double bind.

In desperation, I finally suggested at the end of a particularly frustrating meeting that at our next session, we not tell any more "war stories" about our disappointments in the streets attempting to promote nonviolent social change. "In fact," I said, "why don't we not talk about waking life at all next week, except as it relates to our *dreams*. Let's shift our attention to concentrate on telling dreams to one another, particularly those dreams that have overt racial feeling in them. In other words, next week why don't we tell one another those dreams that have scary, repugnant characters of other races in them as a way of maybe getting at the deeper psychological roots of racism."

So, that evening we agreed to change the format of the next meeting and concentrate on sharing dreams. I had been drawn to make this curious suggestion in large measure because of sharing dreams with my wife, Kathryn, a habit that we had fallen into during the early years of our relationship.

When we first got together, we used to argue ferociously with one another, mostly about the unexamined sexist assumptions of our behavior. In the effort to rid ourselves and our relationship of these attitudes, we argued and fought, and occasionally, in the heart of our passionate struggles, we even dragged our dreams into the discussions. "Why, last night, I even *dreamed* about what you keep doing to me!"

Over the years, we discovered that when we shared our dreams about our difficulties with one another, we tended to remember with relief and renewed good humor just why it was worth the immense emotional effort of working these issues out between us in the first place. Sharing our dreams, particularly those about the annoying, unconscious sexism we were both still heir to, seemed to help us stay actively and creatively committed to the often painful and difficult process of defining our evolving relationship. Sharing and talking about the dreams also seemed to help in the fundamentally related task of finding our respective places as individuals and as a couple in the larger society still dominated by sexism.

On the basis of this experience, it occurred to me that enough similarities existed between the individual emotions and larger social patterns associated with sexism, and the feelings and behavior associated with racism, that sharing and discussing dreams might well produce a similar positive effect in the seminar. The idea of relative strangers sharing some of their nastier dreams seemed more than a little crazy—even to me—but it was the only honest alternative I could think of. Just about anything, no matter how bizarre, seemed worth trying before we admitted defeat and gave up entirely.

The next week we gathered and began to tell dreams to one another. We shared many nightmares of being demeaned, menaced, pursued, and attacked by dark, scary people of other races. Despite the generally sinister and somber quality of the dreams, the tone of the group's interactions noticeably brightened and broadened. I had been hoping for something like this, but I was not expecting the extraordinary depth of the transformation that followed.

First of all, everyone in the group understood, without my having to belabor the point too much, that you can't *blame* anyone else for what you *dream*. Although our dreams often make clear reference to traumatic events in waking life, they generally transform those waking experiences so profoundly and mysteriously in a "strange sea change" that the dreamer has to take some sort of radical and personal (albeit not wholly conscious) responsibility for their quality and content.

The menacing gang of black youths prowling through my dreams presents a picture of things going on *inside* me, even more than it comments on external, waking events. This generally shared understanding meant that the cynicism and increasingly antagonistic debate that had been slowly and steadily escalating in the group since the first meeting disappeared abruptly and entirely at almost the moment the dream sharing began.

The next thing I noticed was that the dreams themselves were so interesting—they hinted at and actually revealed so much in a subtle and surprising and completely nonideological way—that I could practically hear the scales falling from my own and other people's eyes. Suddenly, the people in the seminar began to take notice of one another in a new and more personal and vulnerable way. No longer were people responding primarily with preprogrammed ideas about themselves and each other. The change of focus to dreams suddenly had the effect of awakening in us a much greater interest in one another as unique human beings. The exotic new symbolic material we were sharing caused us all to slow down and make fewer unquestioned assumptions about each other. By sharing our dreams, we began to inquire much more carefully about the deeper reasons why we each thought and felt and behaved as we did.

I was surprised, amazed, and overjoyed. At the end of that meeting, several of the seminar participants came up to me and said, in effect, "Jeremy, we are all pretty well-informed and experienced and sophisticated folks. Occasionally we pick up some useful little nugget of information from you that we didn't know before, but for the most part, all this history and sociology and economic and political theory is fairly well known to us—but this dream stuff! This is really new and interesting and different! Let's do more of this!"

Spurred on by such responses, we agreed to shift our emphasis in the weeks that followed from theories about racism, and telling our personal "war stories," to an open-ended exploration of the symbols of racial stereotypes and sentiments in our dreams.

It was during those first spontaneous group dream work sessions more than forty years ago that I began to search for ways of facilitating the exploration into what our dreams might mean, without asking anyone to relinquish their autonomy, and still encouraging everyone to stay actively and directly engaged the whole time.

It was here in the "Overcoming Racism" seminar that we first began to understand and acknowledge that even our most seemingly "objective" comments about each other's dreams were really projections of our own internal material. Out of this grew the "if it were my dream" form. We also quickly discovered the strength and reliability of the "tingle" of recognition when something true and on-the-case was said about someone's dream. We also began to understand that people could have perfectly valid and genuine ahas of insight for themselves from someone else's dream narrative, even if the dreamer didn't confirm them with his or her own "tingles."

The remaining weeks of the seminar sped by, and at the end of the last group meeting, I asked if anyone wanted to come down to Emeryville and volunteer for UUPEB's organizing activities. I did this with some trepidation, because I still had lingering doubts that what we had been doing might all turn out to be just another "displacement activity"—a sophisticated variation on "navel gazing"—an excuse to talk and intellectualize about our greatest collective challenges, without ever taking the next necessary risk of concrete action to promote real social change.

Much to my gratified surprise, almost all of the previously disaffected volunteers felt sufficiently reenergized and reenthused about the possibilities of direct nonviolent action to transform traditionally racist social institutions that they signed up for volunteer work with UUPEB.

My last fear was that the sad story of failed communication across race and class barriers might repeat itself when the volunteers actually began to work again. My fears proved to be unfounded. The renewed enthusiasm of the seminar participants carried forward without flagging into the actual work in the streets. The volunteers came into the neighborhood and began to work side by side with the residents who, with the help and support of UUPEB staff, were starting to organize around their most pressing community concerns.

As the seminar participants started to interact with the residents on a regular basis, we started to get a trickle of "unsolicited testimonials" from community people about the effectiveness of this newly trained group of volunteers. In fact, some of the Emeryville residents who had been the most adamant that certain volunteers *never* come back into the neighborhood started to drop by the office and tell us that the very people who had driven them crazy months earlier with their oppressive and condescending racist attitudes and behaviors were now among the most valued volunteers.

These reports became so numerous that the Reverend Mr. Johnson finally asked just what I had been doing out there in Walnut Creek all those weeks. I responded cautiously that the only change I had made in the initial plan was to persuade the participants to start sharing their dreams with one another.

A general outburst of hilarity and disbelief greeted this revelation, but eventually the Reverend Mr. Johnson quelled the laughter and the jokes with words to the effect of "You know, it sounds just as bizarre to me as it does to you, but we really ought to cut Jeremy a little slack on this one and give him the benefit of the doubt, because *look at the results!*"

It was not until the Reverend Mr. Johnson said it out loud, in just that way, that I actually allowed myself to have the clear thought "Yes, look at the *results!* If blundering around, simply sharing dreams with each other, without any clear idea of what we're doing, can have *this* effect—if it can begin to have a noticeable and independently verifiable impact on the deep, unconscious sources of *racism*—what *else* can it do?"

At that precise point, I made the conscious decision to explore the potential social and political value of dream work more fully and carefully. Now, more than thirty-five years later, I am still exploring the exciting, dramatic, creative, collective transformative possibilities of dream work, with no limit in sight. All I can say with certainty is that when people begin to share and explore their dreams together, overcoming the internalized oppressions and external behaviors of racism is just one of a number of profoundly positive things that regularly grow out of the work.

Since that first tentative experiment in group dream work, I have devoted a good deal of thought to what happened in those first meetings to produce such dramatic and startling results. I am now convinced that when we started to share those scary, repugnant dreams of being attacked and menaced by dark, sinister, hostile, and dangerous people of other races, we began to lift the repression of aspects of our own unconscious personalities that *had previously been denied and therefore projected onto people of other races in waking life.* The nasty characters in those dreams were, as they always are, reflections of those problematic parts of *ourselves* that we had been unable to accept. The "repression" of these elements through unconscious denial resulted in a deep emotional rejection of the people upon whose images these elements were projected, despite the veneer of "deference" and "politeness" that "disguised" it.

This repression/projection of selected elements of internal life is the deep, unconscious psychological mechanism of racism. By sharing our nasty "racist" dreams, we had begun to break this archetypal cycle of denial and rejection and to transform this basic process.

The fears and tensions we experienced in those dreams were, among other things, metaphors of the internal stresses created by this lack of self-acceptance. Having failed to accept aspects of ourselves, it became inevitable that we would project these "unacceptable" internal energies outward in a systematic pattern of unconscious "racist" distortion of what seemed like "objective" experiences and interactions in waking life. Subsequent experience has proven over and over that precisely this psychological dynamic of "repression and projection" is at the root of racism and, indeed, of all forms of collective prejudice and oppression.

In our own blundering way, in those first meetings of the "Overcoming Racism" seminar where we began to share our dreams, we rediscovered the basic understanding of Fritz Perls and the Gestalt school that "everyone and everything in my dreams is *me*." As the repressed, seemingly "negative" emotional energies that wore the masks of nasty people of other races in our dreams were admitted more into consciousness *in the simple act of sharing and talking about them*, the tendency to suppress and project those same energies onto others in waking life began to diminish.

As the dreams were shared and we continued to pay respectful attention to one another, it became possible to admit, in the words of Ram Dass, "I am that too." Since we did not immediately reject and pull away from one another when we heard these unconscious dream "confessions," each one of us was able, at least preconsciously, to grasp the startling and liberating truth: "These ugly, scary, dark, powerful, sexy, violent, irresponsible, dangerous dream figures *are vitally alive parts of my own authentic being*, and you know what—*they aren't so horrible after all*."

I have since proved to myself over and over that by increasing self-acceptance in this fashion, repressions are released, projections withdrawn, and even the most fundamental, ingrained, and habitual patterns of self-deception and destructive behavior are transformed.

Initially, we had the anxiety-reducing experience, in the seminar itself, of not being rejected or despised by the other participants as these denied aspects of our personalities and characters were revealed in our dream narratives. At that point of increasing self-awareness, self-acceptance, and release of fear, we also started to withdraw many of the projections we had been making on one another in the group meetings. In fact, I now see these two seemingly separate actions of increased self-acceptance and increased interest in and respect for each other as reflections of a single act of moral courage and creative imagination, invited into consciousness through the sharing of dreams.

Later, when the seminar participants returned to the community, the process continued. We began to recognize and relate to each person we worked with more as a unique human being rather than as a stereotype— an impersonal "screen" upon which we had previously been projecting disowned and despised parts of ourselves.

Not only did this change in perception and self-awareness make us all *feel* better, it altered our patterns of communication and interpersonal relating in subtle but profound ways. It gave us a much greater sense of our fundamental shared humanity. With the release of these neurotic self-deceptions came an exhilarating sense of renewed, concrete, creative possibilities for thinking and acting collectively—a feeling and an aware-ness of creative possibility that always derives from increased mutual respect and compassion. The experience of sharing the scary dreams changed how we related with one another in ways that were not only internally liberating and transformative but also immediately obvious to other people.

Authentic personal likes and dislikes began to replace ritual "polite-ness," blundering patronizing comments, and repressed fear. The energy that had previously been squandered counterproductively in maintaining the repression and projection suddenly came welling up into our feelings and awarenesses in a free form. These newly released psychological and emotional energies were experienced as spontaneous surges of vitality and well-being. Many people shared these renewed feelings of creative possibility and enthusiasm.

Increasing conscious self-awareness and self-acceptance through sharing dreams led to a release of neurotic "lock-and-key" dramas in the group. We no longer projected our own inadequacies onto those in the group who secretly believed they themselves were inadequate. The uncon-scious lock-and-key patterns of unproductive group communication were transformed into authentic encounters. Later, this liberation of authentic emotions and creative energies carried over into the interactions with the community people gathering to form Emeryville Citizens for Better Government (ECBG), the grassroots community organization that UUPEB helped to create and nurtured through its early years of development and struggle.

In ECBG, the people we were training and supporting began to feel enough confidence in themselves to assume more and more leadership in the community. The members of ECBG started organizing their neighbors in earnest and later went on to elect the first black people to public office in the history of the community, a community that, it is worth noting in passing, Earl Warren (when he was state attorney general, before his elevation to the U.S. Supreme Court) characterized as "the most corrupt community in California." It now appears, more than thirty-five years later, that the historical patterns of racial injustice and inequality in that part of the East Bay have been altered permanently.

Obviously, UUPEB and the "Overcoming Racism" seminar cannot take credit for the considerable transformations of community life, standards of justice, and expectations that have been brought about by ECBG, but I can state with assurance that we were there at the birth and performed some high-order midwifery. The experience also opened my eyes as perhaps nothing else could have to the potential of working with dreams as a tool for nonviolent political, social, and cultural change.

I am now completely convinced that the universal phenomenon of repression and projection is the root psychological cause of all racism. Indeed, I believe that this psychological phenomenon is demonstrably at the core of all forms of collective human oppression from racism and sexism, through the oppressions of age and social class, to the ancient ills of religious bigotry and linguistic intolerance.

All of these counterproductive behaviors have at their root our preconscious denial and rejection of the basic worth and humanity of unexplored aspects of our own unconscious makeup. Consequently, we project that "inhumanity" outward onto others. *Denying aspects of our own unconscious, natural human makeup makes denial of the humanity of others inevitable because we project those denied elements unconsciously.* By the same token, acceptance of those despised aspects of the deep unconscious self

can transform prejudiced feelings and perceptions, thus effectively relieving in a gentle, nonviolent way the collective, self-imposed oppressions
that plague us as a species.

My experience also convinces me that this same pattern of
preconscious self-rejection also lies at the root of our increasingly pressing
problems of planetary pollution and eco-cide. Fear and denial of the natural, spontaneous, "raw," "dirty," "untamed" quality of our unconscious
human emotional and psychological life *as a whole* leads to the projection
of that fear and negativity onto the "spontaneous" natural environment
*as a whole.*

This projection of preconscious internal anxiety is the source of
the impulse that says, "If it's green, pave it over!" To the person who is
unable to accept and embrace his/her deepest "natural/animal urges,"
all of nature, and the earth itself, is seen as "wild" and menacing and
destructive and in need of "taming." This is the unconscious archetypal
source of our suicidal destruction of the planet's ability to nurture and
sustain mammalian life. At a deep level it is a misplaced metaphorical
acting out of our own fear and hatred of disowned aspects of our own
unconscious collective humanity.

My experience has convinced me that *what heals these profoundly
destructive behaviors is awakening a sense of rapport with those same rejected and
despised aspects of the unconscious self.* In this way, the destructive projections onto waking reality can be withdrawn, and the basic creativity
and sympathetic humanity that is part of our common species heritage
can come to the fore. Working with dreams in nonauthoritarian groups,
using consciously projective language and techniques, is the single best
way to accomplish this end that I have yet discovered.

*The most effective tool of human oppression is the disparagement of native
imagination.* If someone is successful in convincing other people that the
playful and spontaneous products of their imaginations are "worthless"
or "trivial" or "substandard," then those people become slaves, regardless of any accompanying economic and political flourishes. Conversely,
if someone *fails* to persuade others that the spontaneous products of their
imaginative life are worthless or substandard, then no matter how much
physical, economic, social, or political oppression accompanies that failed
effort, those people will *never* be enslaved. People who are in touch with
the spontaneous archetypal creative/imaginative impulse are always in a

state of creative ferment and "revolution," whether they are intentionally "insubordinate" or not. Such people are always behaving spontaneously in new and unexpected ways that the oppressive authorities have not specifically prohibited because they have not thought of them.

For this reason, *the restoration of a positive, dynamic, spontaneous relationship with our imaginative life is an absolutely crucial part of any authentic and effective individual or collective liberation.* Once again, working with dreams on a regular basis with supportive friends is a most reliable way to achieve this revitalization of the life of the imagination.

It is always easier to see and point to the ways in which other people's imaginations are enslaved than it is to recognize how our own imaginative lives have been anesthetized. It is easy, for example, to see what horrid effects unimaginative standards of beauty and attractiveness have on people who do not fit those norms and who for that reason cannot imagine themselves as interesting and attractive. For example, hair straighteners, skin lighteners, lunatic diets, expensive and dangerous cosmetic surgery, etc., are all examples of how "other people" are enslaved by the internalized oppression of disparaged imagination.

However, to the extent that well-educated, responsible, "successful" working-, middle-, and upper-class people believe in their hearts that national and world events are determined by factors so vast and complex that they cannot even be grasped, let alone influenced and directed by personal or even cooperative effort, then they are "enslaved" by the conventional wisdom of the media and the establishment. The belief that we cannot even imagine ways of actually influencing and changing historical events keeps us depressed, immobilized, and alienated from our neighbors, and sure enough, we turn out to be "helpless" by virtue of our own inactivity.

The moment we begin to imagine that what we do just might possibly "make a difference," then our creative impulses are released and we begin to prove to ourselves that we can, in fact, directly influence not only the direction of our personal lives, but the fate of our communities, nations, and the species and the planet as a whole. Once again, paying attention to our dreams is the single best and most reliable way of opening to the imagination and the collective archetypal creative impulse that is so necessary for both our individual and collective liberation and self-determination.

It is interesting to note in this connection that the sacred texts of the world's major religions (and the "minor" ones too, for that matter) all proclaim the central importance of dreams and dreaming as a means of direct communication with the Divine. However, at the same time, the vast majority of those religions also frown on, or even forbid, actual attention to dreams in their contemporary practice.

I believe that this curious and paradoxical state of affairs is also a direct result of the fact that dreams come in the service of collective as well as individual health and wholeness. Our dreams always strive toward greater consciousness and a greater synthesis of knowledge, intuition, and creative vision than was previously possible. For this reason, the dream is the eternal enemy of dogmatism and premature closure in the search for meaning.

Whenever a religious intuition is frozen into inflexible dogma (even if the dogma was originally inspired by the deepest communion with the divine energy), then that religious vision becomes *prematurely closed*. Because of this arbitrary, dogmatic limitation placed on the development of spiritual intuition and possibility, dreams will inevitably come to criticize the partial and incomplete quality of the "Divine-revealed truth." The imagery and emotion in the dreams will begin to extend and expand the spiritual intuition beyond that false boundary of prematurely closed dogma. This implacable enmity toward premature closure wherever it appears makes dream work threatening to all forms of authoritarian human interaction, religious, political, academic, and economic. (For a particularly poignant example of such a dream, criticizing the prematurely closed dogma of the contemporary Roman Catholic Church, see the dream of Grace, the social-activist nun, discussed in Chapter 9.)

The sacred texts of all the world's religions proclaim the inherent and universal value of dreaming, usually by saying simply that "God speaks to us in our dreams." In a dream, Solomon asks God for the wisdom "to judge good and evil," and his wish is granted. An angel warns Joseph in a dream that Herod's storm troopers are on the way and tells him to take Mary and the baby and flee into Egypt. The emissary of God appears to Muhammad in a dream to prepare him for his epoch-making tour of the heavens. Black Elk sees the divine horses around the Tree of Life in his dream and proclaims a new way to his people. Queen Maya, the mother of the Buddha, sees the White Elephant with Six Tusks in her dream and knows that her child will be an "avatar," a divine incarnation in human form. Examples of this kind of divine communication in dreams from all the world's religious traditions are legion.

Religion tends to attribute the inherent value of dreaming to direct divine intervention, but at the same time, out of "administrative necessity," organized religion generally discourages the mass of people from paying any serious attention to their own dreams, because if they were to get directly in touch with this "divine" source of creative energy and transformative possibility, they would inevitably become difficult to direct and control. If it were generally understood that there is a divine component woven into every dream (another way of saying "all dreams come in the service of health and wholeness"), then the priest class would no longer have an exclusive right to interpret the "will of God" on behalf of the people. Their spiritual authority, to say nothing of their political power, social prestige, and economic security, would be in constant jeopardy from the spontaneous dream utterances of even the lowliest of their flocks.

The scriptural precedents for direct divine intervention in human communal affairs through the medium of dreams is so strong, and so firmly in place in the sacred texts, that it would be impossible for any merely local religious leader to exert control over people's beliefs and behaviors. Literally anyone, particularly people with minimal social standing and maximal zeal, would be free to speak up anytime and say, "I had a dream last night, and God told me to tell you . . ."

In the cases of Judaism, Christianity, and Islam, it is precisely because the sacred texts are so unambiguous about the regularity of divine communications in dreams (particularly when such dreams come to particularly scruffy and malcontent members of the community, who are then called "prophets") that the prohibitions against dream work become so "necessary" and inevitable. If the history of human communion with the Divine were not divided into two distinct phases in these traditions— the "primary" phase, when God does communicate directly with "His chosen people" in their dreams, and the "secondary" or "common" era, when these direct revelations no longer take place—then it would be impossible for any merely local authority to exercise pastoral control over any "flock."

Now, obviously, religious authority is always at risk from "schism" and "heresy" anyway, even without people paying attention to their dreams, but the problem would escalate a thousandfold if contemporary dream revelations were given the same sort of potential authority as the scriptural dreams of Jacob ben Abraham, Joseph ben Jacob, Joseph the Carpenter, and Bilal the Muezzin, and the rest. For this reason, as soon as Judaism, Christianity, and Islam became dogmatized, as soon as there were rabbis, bishops, and imams, it became an administrative imperative to outlaw "lay" dream work simply to "preserve order."

When the Protestants rebelled against what they considered to be the illegitimate authority of the corrupt medieval Catholic Church, they looked for a source of religious inspiration and authority that was "purer" and "closer to authentic Christian tradition" than the edicts of the Bishop of Rome. For a brief period, they embraced the direct revelations that came from dreams, but they were quickly "forced" into the same rejection of dream work that their Catholic forebears had adopted, and for essentially the same reasons. In order to prevent the fledgling Protestant movement from being fragmented into endless, competing, and ineffective splinters on the basis of the unlimited exercise of freedom of conscience, they too were "forced" to condemn and outlaw dream work, relegating it to the occultist fringes.

In fact, dream work has reentered the religious and spiritual dialogue in the Western world primarily because of the rediscovery of the value of dreams by clinical and academic psychology. It was only after secular psychologists clearly established that paying attention to dreams is a valuable means of diagnosing and healing neurosis and other psychological disorders that the Western Christian churches began once again tentatively to acknowledge the potential value of dreams as spiritual experiences. Even then, only in the last forty years or so has there been a nervous acceptance of lay people working with their dreams, and only then with the accompanying caveat that dreams should be used as a means of clearing away psychological impediments to spiritual exercise, rather than as a direct source of potential spiritual revelation.

Even in the realm of academic psychology and psychiatry, a similar nervousness about embracing the dream as a direct revelation of psychological reality can be discerned. Ever since Freud, Jung, and others set their theories about the nature of the unconscious in ideological concrete, the study of dreams as "the royal road to the unconscious," as well

as their practical use in analysis and therapy, has been on the decline.
This is because the dreams themselves do not conform as closely as it
appeared at first to the "laws" of structure and significance that the great
pioneers laid out.

Within the Freudian establishment particularly, there has been a general retreat from working with clients' dreams, usually on the grounds
that the dreams are "too rich" and provide "too much material." In the
name of "efficiency" and "service to the patient"—Freudians usually call
their clients "patients," after the traditional Western medical model—the
Freudians now seem to prefer "thematic apperception tests" and other,
more controllable, mechanical, and predictable methods of discerning
their client's abreactions to unconscious material.

However, my experience persuades me that the main reason for this
tendency to reject dream work as a primary therapeutic tool stems from
the fact that the dreams themselves regularly fail to look and behave the
way Freud said they would. Rather than revise the master's theoretical
formulations, many Freudians seem to find it easier and preferable to
deemphasize the work with dreams and instead focus on techniques of
diagnosis and intervention where the theory remains unchallenged, and
the "expert" therapist/analyst remains firmly in charge.

The Jungian movement, although less subject to this kind of ideological rigidity because of Jung's own many, unambiguous pronouncements on the stupidities and tyrannies of abstract theory, particularly
with regard to working with dreams, is nonetheless showing some signs
of suffering from some of the same sort of "hardening of the arteries"
with regard to dream work. Jung's more rigid pronouncements (particularly about the supposedly inevitable gender links in the archetypes
of the Shadow, and the Animus/Anima) are simply not confirmed by
the continuing, cumulative, direct study of contemporary dreams. For
this reason, the same dynamic of deemphasizing dream work in favor of
other, more technical therapeutic interventions seems to be at work in
the Jungian movement as well.

Besides the inherently "radical," getting-to-the-true-root-beyond-
mere-appearances quality of dreaming, there is a specific way in which
work with dreams contributes to the transformation of our cultural/
political circumstances. Dreams regularly offer specific creative inspiration for our collective struggles, in just the same fashion that they provide

creative ideas and energy for our other deeply felt individual creative activities.

A story from the life of Mohandas Gandhi may serve to illustrate.

At the close of the First World War, it was assumed throughout the British Empire that the traditional political rights and responsibilities of Empire citizenship that had been suspended by the Emergency War Powers Act would be restored. Among the most important of these traditional British political values were freedom of the press, freedom of assembly, and the right to have a voice in the appointment of local officials, particularly judges and magistrates. After all, the British and their allies had won, and what had the whole conflict been about, if not the preservation of the system that nurtured and honored these traditional values?

The British government sent a legal expert named Rowlett to India to survey the situation and to advise the Colonial Council on the most orderly and effective way to return that country to legal normalcy now that hostilities had ended. Rowlett was conservative and a racist, and when he arrived in India, he looked around and saw the trains running on time, the opposition press silent, labor unions in disarray, corporate profits at an all-time high. He liked what he saw, and so he decided to advise the Colonial Council simply to install the provisions of the Emergency War Powers Act as the new law of the land in peacetime.

The colonial authorities accepted Rowlett's recommendations and adopted the now infamous "Rowlett Acts" as the new framework for postwar legal and political life. When the provisions of the Rowlett Acts were made public, India erupted into violent protest.

Readers who saw Richard Attenborough's film biography of Gandhi may recall the scene where the angry crowd sets fire to the police station, then slaughters the policemen as they flee from the burning building. That was a dramatic reenactment of just one incident among many during the horrible "Rowlett Act riots," which broke out all over the Indian subcontinent.

During the civil unrest, Gandhi attempted to speak against the violence and in favor of restraint at public meetings, but he was consistently shouted down and prevented from addressing the angry crowds. He wrote passionately articulate letters to newspapers in both India and Great Britain, but the papers refused to publish them. He felt himself increasingly isolated and ineffective in his efforts to promote nonviolence in the struggle for national self-determination.

In deep frustration, he retired with a small group of his closest associates to the summer home of his old friend and supporter Chakravarti Rajagopalachari (who later became governor-general of free India) and began to fast and pray, seeking inspiration for a nonviolent solution to his nation's terrible agony. His biographers tell us that he had been praying and fasting for more than a week when he awakened one morning after a compelling dream.

He went immediately to tell Nehru and the others that it had come to him in a dream what they should do. They should "call upon all the religious sects in India to practice *hartal* at once. *Hartal* is a Sanskrit word meaning "public prayer and celebration." Gandhi had dreamed that the Congress Party organizers should call upon the leaders of the many diverse and warring religious groups in India—Hindu and Moslem, Parsi and Jain, Buddhist and Sikh—to abandon their respective traditional calendars for public ritual gathering and practice their respective festivals of prayer and public procession *at the same time*.

It is reported that this idea was greeted with disbelief and even derision by Nehru and the rest of Gandhi's supporters, but Gandhi was adamant and retired to his quarters to handwrite the letters calling for simultaneous *hartal*.

In retrospect, one may speculate that it was in large measure because the invitations came in Gandhi's own spidery handwriting, instead of as typewritten communications from his secretaries, that his appeal had such unexpected success. His dream-inspired proposal of simultaneous *hartal* was accepted by virtually every religious leader who received it, and as a result, followers of Vishnu and Shiva, Brahma and Durga, Mohammad and Buddha, Guru Nanak, Mahavira, Baha Ullah, and others took to the streets in great numbers, not to protest the imposition of the Rowlett Acts directly, but to worship and pray and seek solace and inspiration from their respective gods and goddesses.

As a result, the violence was greatly reduced, and India was totally paralyzed by her first successful general strike. The colonial government attempted to "restore order" and keep basic services operating with military coercion and direct employment of troops to run the railways and telephone exchanges, but they failed. In a matter of days, the Colonial

Council was forced to reconvene in extraordinary session and rescind the Rowlett Acts, moving at the same time to restore all the traditional rights and responsibilities of British Empire citizenship, particularly the rights of freedom of assembly, freedom of the press, and participation in the election and appointment of local officials, particularly judges and magistrates.

Anyone who has given that matter any serious thought will be forced to conclude, I believe, that the religiously inspired general strike is perhaps the single most powerful instrument of collective, nonviolent social change that we have yet devised, and it is no accident that the inspiration came to Gandhi in a dream. Just as Elias Howe was truly and wholeheartedly focused on inventing a machine that would sew, and just as Niels Bohr was truly and wholeheartedly focused on understanding the dynamics of atomic structure, so Gandhi was passionately focused on discovering a nonviolent strategy for social change that would both free his nation from foreign rule and cultivate the best indigenous leadership for the postcolonial state.

Working with dreams invariably releases the deep archetypal creative impulse, focused on whatever the dreamer is truly and wholeheartedly involved with in his/her waking life. In this way we are always "incubating" our dreams, whether we realize it consciously or not.

This release of the archetypal creative impulse in dreams in direct proportion to the depth and sincerity of the dreamer's waking efforts is also one of the reasons why I believe that *wholeheartedness* is the most important psychospiritual dynamic in developing consciousness, "individuating," and living. I have come to see that wholeheartedness and genuine enthusiasm and involvement with the people and activities of one's life make the most difference in evolution and individuation—much more even than what one is wholehearted about. Enthusiastic, wholehearted involvement in even the most seemingly trivial affairs will promote authentic psychospiritual development, while even the most clever and superficially skillful participation in the most profoundly important activities, if undertaken with interior divisions and withheld feelings and energies, will not.

This is as true of working with dreams as it is of anything else. The cleverest and most perceptive dream work undertaken with secret internal cynicism and disrespect for others will be counterproductive, while the most naive and blundering work with dreams, undertaken with wholeheartedness and openness, will be profoundly useful.

As Jung said about children—and I believe it applies just as accurately to adults—"Children learn from who we *are*, rather than what we *say*, and to believe otherwise is a disease of the mind." In fact, to believe otherwise is, to quote T. S. Eliot, to "long for systems so perfect, no one will have to be good." There are no systems that absolve us from individually evolving our self-awareness and moral expression.

Since the initial evolution of human consciousness all those millions of years ago, the collective unconscious and the divine energies within it have served the evolving psychospiritual needs of the human species through our dreams, whether we remembered them or not. In exactly the same fashion, the physical environment—Mother Nature—has nurtured our individual and collective evolution spontaneously and naturally, without any conscious effort on our part. However, as human consciousness has developed, we have used our increasing self-awareness to interfere with the natural rhythms and balance of the biosphere, changing them by our activities, just as the spontaneous "incubation" of our nightly dreams is being influenced more and more by the artifacts and experiences of our complex culture.

Since "the beginning of time," or at least since the development of human awareness of time, the earth could be relied upon to heal herself of the wounds we inflicted on her without any help from us. Since "always" we have been able to dump our noxious garbage into the streams, rivers, and oceans because they would purify themselves "naturally." In the same fashion, we have always been able to rely on our dreams to heal and help our psyches grow, despite whatever psychospiritual blunders we might make, whether we paid any conscious attention or not.

However, we have now reached a point in the absolutely linked development of the planetary ecosystem and our collective human consciousness where this is no longer the case. (When I wrote the first draft of this chapter, in haste I typed the word *ecosystem* as "echosystem"—a slip that now seems to me to be an even better way of spelling it to evoke its deeper meaning and the fundamental relationship between psyche and cosmos.)

We can no longer simply rely on the earth to go on cleaning up our human messes without further conscious thought or responsible action from us, because the physical "echosystem" itself is reverberating with our mistakes, calling us to greater consciousness and responsibility. Our evolving individual and collective consciousness is so inextricably inter-twined with the development of the "echosystem" that we can no longer afford to be unconscious of the consequences of our technological devel-opments or of the nature of the energies that motivate our deepest cre-ative/destructive potential. Working with dreams (or other activities that bring us to deeper understanding of our collective unconscious patterns, energies, and possibilities) is no longer just a playful voluntary activity for creative people; it has become an absolute necessity, a requirement for planetary survival.

The crisis in the planetary environment is growing daily. The pro-portion of hydrocarbons in the atmosphere has drastically increased over the two centuries since the invention of the steam engine and our first large-scale industrial use of fossil fuels. This "unnatural" worldwide increase in combustion has shifted the pH of rain radically toward acid. Over the years, this technological development has heated the entire envelope of atmosphere several degrees with the carbon dioxide of the unceasing hot exhausts of all our insatiable burning. Thousands of spe-cies are now extinct because of our predatory activities and our uncon-scious "carelessness."

Since the development of nuclear weapons, and the continuing release of atomic radiation into the air, water, and soil through weapons testing and atomic industrial "accidents" and planning failures, the total "background" radiation all over the planet has risen by several hundred percent. Since background radiation is directly related to natural muta-tion, the dramatic increase in recent decades is undoubtedly increasing mutations in all species.

The increasing number of unauthorized releases into the environment of previously unimagined microscopic life-forms created by the manipu-lation of genetic material in the laboratory makes the point clearly. These and other blundering interventions of human consciousness and technol-ogy have radically altered the "echosystem" and are ongoing and have progressively greater and greater impacts. Even the bitter conviction of many that AIDS was purposely designed as a weapon of genocide is *sym-bolic* of what we all know: our increasingly sophisticated technology is killing us. As a result of our own increasingly sophisticated intervention in the natural world, our survival as a species is profoundly at risk. *We can no longer afford simply to "let things develop" without an active, conscious effort to understand our own unconscious nature more fully.*

Our sorcerer's apprenticeship in conscious self-awareness, science, and manipulation of the environment in contemporary times has brought about a radical change in our deepest relationship to the collective unconscious. Let me offer one small-scale example that reveals even more of the irony in the evolving nature of our collective psychospiritual problem.

An active but dwindling commercial fishing fleet made up primarily of men who learned their ancient trade from their fathers and grandfathers, and of emigrants from Europe and most recently Southeast Asia, operates out of San Francisco Bay. Although their boats are now sophisticated and highly mechanized, the attitudes and assumptions of these fisherfolk (one or two women now skipper their own boats) are basically unchanged from those of their great-grandfathers. Their deeply stoic and grimly individualistic values are those that traditional fisherfolk have held for millennia. They resent, and some simply ignore, the new and seemingly biased and capricious rulings of Fish and Game officials about when and where they may fish and how big their catches can be, because of the ancient assumption that the fisheries are inexhaustible, that, to use traditional, archetypal language, "there are always more fish in the sea!"

For as long as human beings have been catching and eating fish (which, from the archaeological evidence, appears to be "since always"), this basic understanding has been true. In fact, this archetypal association between fish and inexhaustible (masculine) fertility is so deeply ingrained in our collective psyche that the fish has been an image of the deeply hidden, inexhaustible masculine divinity ever since the formulation of the myth of the great fish-headed Creator God, Ea, who climbed out of the alluvial mud to found the first settled human civilization in Mesopotamia almost nine thousand years ago. The association of fish and divine, inexhaustible, masculine "Willing Sacrifice" (offering up its own life that others may live) was inexpressibly ancient long before the Greek word for "fish," *ichthys* recommended itself to the early Christians as an acronym for what translates to "Jesus Christ, God and Savior." But "suddenly" (from the perspective of the unconscious), within the memory of living people, the ancient wisdom no longer appears true. It appears that, in fact, there may *not* "always be more fish in the sea!" To even think such a thought, to the traditional mind, is idiotic and verges on sacrilege.

"Tradition" always implies a deep relationship with the archetypes of the collective unconscious—a relationship that has aided individual and collective survival for the whole procession of our ancestors, back into the dimmest recesses of time. *Unconscious traditional assumptions about the nature of reality can be changed only by acts of great individual courage and by acceptance of tremendous psychospiritual danger and risk.* It is this kind of deep unconscious motivation that causes many of the traditional-minded fisherfolk of San Francisco Bay (and elsewhere around the world, I can only assume) to regularly ignore and flout the Fish and Game regulations and to continue to hang on to the dying trade (taking grim satisfaction from the demise of their competitors), because they have all seen "bad years" before, and they believe "in their bones" that "the fish will come back."

It has *always* been so, for the strong, who stick to the trade through the hard times and don't give up. Why should they believe the young, overeducated, short-on-real-experience-at-sea men and women from Fish and Game when they (often arrogantly and insensitively) try to tell them how to pursue their ancient craft?

The tragedy is that while the psychology of the recalcitrant fisherfolk can be understood, the sad fact remains that by clinging to their ancient, archetypal views about the inexhaustible fertility of the sea, they *will* destroy the fisheries and drive even the most numerous species of fish into extinction. The archetypal image of the inexhaustible fertility of the ocean, the cradle of all life on the planet, is deeply ingrained in all of us, but we ourselves have brought an end to that in the latter half of the twentieth century.

What has changed, within living memory, is nothing less than the very *nature* of the problem. Our voracious technology, *created and driven by our own deep unconscious,* has reached a point where we no longer have the luxury of allowing evolution to take its own way without our increasingly conscious, creative, and responsible participation. Just like the Sausalito and San Francisco commercial fishers, we must change our cherished habits and worldviews to reflect this new reality, or *our old, unexamined, unconscious habits of mind and heart will destroy us.* What is easy to see and condemn in the ecologically unsound practices of commercial fishing (logging, farming, mining, military conflict, ethnic bigotry, etc.—one may "fill in the blank" almost endlessly) is, in fact, a manifestation of our own unexamined unconscious habits of mind and heart.

The dynamics of the tragic situation of San Francisco Bay fisherfolk reflect similar struggles at all levels of global society and culture. *Our application of increasingly sophisticated technology to physically exploit the natural environment has far outstripped the development of our individual and collective self-awareness.*

At this level, our shared psychospiritual problem is the same as it has always been since the very beginning of human consciousness: how to become more truly self-aware. At the more conscious level, the task has always been how to overcome greed, stupidity, denial, and self-deception. At the less conscious level, the task has always been to look long enough without flinching into the magic mirror that never lies to see beyond the ugliness to the divine depths beneath and within.

In contemporary times, the dramatic increase in the scope of our technological power has made the consequences of our ancient human failings far greater than ever before. The consequences of our repression and projection of internal realities once menaced only individual societies and local environments; now our ignorance of our deeper collective humanity threatens the whole planet. At one time, we may have had the luxury of separating ourselves from other people and societies and pursuing "our own interests" or "our own salvation" in isolation. We could afford natural, slow, unconscious evolution of awareness past narrow, prematurely closed definitions of interdependence and community. Today, because of our technological sophistication, we no longer have that dubious luxury.

The economic, political, educational, and religious institutions we have inherited from that simpler time are no longer adequate to define the possibilities and collective tasks of our age. *The problems we have created for ourselves will not stop "by themselves," nor can we continue to rely on the "echosystem" to heal itself and us "naturally," without our more conscious, creative, and morally self-aware participation.*

We human beings have picked up the fire of consciousness and technology. We have been burned by it, but it has become part of us. We cannot put it down and pretend it never happened. Our only viable choice is to move forward to develop a more comprehensive, honest, and practical understanding of our own unconscious natures that begins to match our understanding of the mechanics of the physical universe.

Perhaps the most important way of understanding the current crisis of planetary civilization is that it has been brought about by the disparity between our tremendous and rapidly growing knowledge of the mechanics of physical reality, and our pitifully underdeveloped understanding of our own unconscious depths. In a filmed interview with Carl Jung toward the end of his life conducted by John Freeman of the BBC, Jung expressed it this way: "Man himself is the source of all coming evil, and we know nothing of man—we are woefully ignorant!"

The disparity between our external power and our internal ignorance will destroy us if we do not immediately undertake to learn as much about our own individual and collective unconscious lives, about our fundamental shared psychospiritual nature as human beings, as we have learned about the heart of the atom and the fabric of the stars.

Searching for the aha of self-understanding that comes from remembering and understanding more about our dreams is not the only way to accomplish the crucially important task, but it is the most universally available, and in my experience the most reliable, means to increase dramatically this self-knowledge and to release the creative energies necessary to transform our individual *and collective* circumstances. If we do not accomplish this radical increase in self-awareness, the destruction of the human species, and in all likelihood the entire biosphere and its countless other species as well, is all but inevitable. Confucius ("Master Fu of the clan K'ung," K'ung Fu-tsu) said it simply some 2,500 years ago: "If we do not change our direction, we will end up where we are headed."

# Chapter Six

# WORKING WITH
# DREAMS IN GROUPS

*Dreams can and should be universally accessible. There are skills that can be developed to extend dream work effectively beyond the confines of the consulting room to the interested public at large. Although the dream is a very private communication, it requires a social context for its fullest realization. That is not to say that helpful work cannot be done by an individual working alone, but, rather, that a social context is a more powerful instrument for the type of healing that can take place through dream work.*

—MONTAGUE ULLMAN

Even relatively sophisticated people share a general prejudice that working with dreams is so "personal," so intimate, so "dangerous" and fraught with psychological and emotional risk and vulnerability, that exploring dreams should only be undertaken as a solitary exercise, or with one other person, at most, in the carefully protected setting of the therapist's office. My experience is, however, that working with dreams in groups is a far superior method of raising to consciousness and releasing the multiple creative energies, increased understandings, and gifts for living that dreams invariably bring.

We are, in fact, much stronger and more resilient beings than these fears, politenesses, and taboos about emotional risk and self-revelation would have us believe. Social norms that limit self-revelation, emotional risk-taking, and intimacy are oppressive handicaps to growth and creative expression. The common fears that dream work may "unlock demons" and bring to light unacceptable, or merely embarrassing, truths that will cause other people to turn away from and shun the dreamer out of anxiety or disgust are simply not borne out in practice.

Working with dreams in a group does require a certain amount of courage, good humor, emotional honesty, and trust, but virtually all human beings are easily capable of the creative openness and risk required. People working in dream groups generally do not find the revelations of their own or other people's dreams "too horrible" to bear. On the contrary, the vast majority of people are strengthened, liberated, revitalized, and deeply supported and affirmed by their experiences in dream groups. Group work with dreams regularly generates ongoing relationships that become sources of deep emotional and psychological support of tremendous benefit to all involved.

The gradual discovery in working in a group that you are not as fragile and at risk as you had always supposed is, in itself, a tremendous gift. The pains and joys, the ancient wounds and dramatic new possibilities, of the other dream group members always end up reflecting your own habitual fears and hopeful intuitions. Recognition of these archetypal feelings and ideas grows from a deep common ground of unconscious shared humanity. Working in a group almost always brings a liberation of spirit and creative energy of a high order.

## SPECIAL SITUATIONS IN GROUP DREAM WORK

On rare occasions, a person may show up at a dream group meeting with psychotic or prepsychotic tendencies. In such a circumstance dream group members should be prepared to offer friendly and firm support to the troubled person in finding appropriate ongoing help. In a group open to all comers, the organizers should have a list of mental health professionals available for referrals.

Remember that *all* dreams come in the service of health and wholeness—even the dreams of severely disturbed people. The appearance of even the most grotesquely disturbing dream material means, in fact, that the dreamer *is capable* of dealing creatively with the issues surfaced by the dream(s). Whether or not a person *will* actually deal courageously with the issues and energies that surface in dreams is always a matter of the dreamer's mood and choice, but people in a dream group may rest assured that if the dream is remembered at all, then such creative resolution is *possible*.

The problems that "ordinary people" have—even the disturbingly common experience of surfacing buried memories of childhood emotional, physical, and sexual abuse—in working with dreams are not beyond the scope of the supportive circle of trust and intimacy that is usually generated by an ongoing dream group. (For a much more complete discussion of this particular issue, see Chapter 7.)

## DREAM GROUPS PROVIDE MULTIPLE INSIGHTS

Dream groups regularly create supportive communities that help people through even the most dramatic difficulties and growth in their lives. Another reason why group dream work is so beneficial is that there is no such thing as a dream with only one meaning. Because all dreams have multiple layers of significance, the chances of a dreamer actually reaching something approaching the full range of meanings in any given dream are much greater working with the multiple suggestions and projections of a group than working in solitude, or even working one to one with a highly skilled, sensitive dream worker.

## SOME DRAWBACKS OF WORKING
## WITH YOUR DREAMS BY YOURSELF

Working on one's dreams in solitude is difficult and heroic. It can be done, but overcoming our inherent tendency toward selective blindness and self-deception requires tremendous effort.

It is a monument to Freud's genius that he was able to unlock so many of the basic secrets of the unconscious by working with his own dreams *in solitude*. Without help he overcame the universal human stumbling blocks to self-understanding. If Freud's formulations are sometimes overly rigid and prematurely closed, that in no way diminishes the astonishing scope and significance of his accomplishment. His groundbreaking book *The Interpretation of Dreams* (released in 1899 but bearing a publication date of 1900 in honor of the new century) almost single-handedly reopened the gateway to the unconscious and to serious work with dreams. No one today can undertake any honest examination of his/her dreams without at least referring to the maps of the dreamworld first drawn up by Freud, even if some of these charts have to be modified or even discarded later on as a result of further exploration. (For a list of specific techniques to overcome the inherent tendency toward selective perception and self-deception in solitary work with your own dreams, see Appendix II.)

## DREAMS NEVER COME JUST TO TELL YOU WHAT YOU ALREADY KNOW

Dreams always come to reveal new information and promote health and wholeness through further development. The greatest temptation in working with your own dreams in solitude is to focus on and see only the multiple ways in which the dream confirms what you are already aware of. These initial ahas of insight never tell the whole story.

The dream always refers to the dreamer's current state of conscious self-awareness, but only to help extend the boundaries of waking self-knowledge into the next area of growth. A reasonably well-functioning dream group will always help the dreamer past these layers of "obvious" understanding to the more problematic and challenging areas of his/her growth—the very areas that are the easiest to miss, ignore, and undervalue when working alone.

## SOME POTENTIAL PITFALLS OF GROUP DREAM WORK

Now, having said this, I must note that one of the inherent, ever-present pitfalls of group dream work is that people of "like minds" (for which read "similar patterns of repression, denial, and self-deception") can sometimes join together in a group and end up colluding to avoid and suppress the more challenging and problematic messages in one another's dreams. Even relatively well-functioning dream groups, made up of a healthy diversity of individuals with contrasting ideas and worldviews, can develop ritualized and somewhat predictable patterns of communication. If and when such a pattern of repressive preconscious group collusion occurs, it can be difficult to overcome.

Often, simply having old members drop out as their life needs change and replacing them with new members who do not share the same history and experience will enliven the group and break down any unconscious collusions to avoid particular issues or areas. However, groups that are more deeply and neurotically locked into preconscious collusion seldom welcome new members unless they show a willingness to "go along with" the group's established patterns of emphasis and acceptable discourse.

Another way of addressing the issue is for every ongoing dream group to reach out from time to time and invite "guest facilitators" to instruct the group in new techniques of dream work. Often, the guest leader's new insights and energies will expose previous unspoken agreements and reveal collective patterns of avoidance more clearly to waking consciousness.

## FURTHER ADVANTAGES OF GROUP WORK

Another advantage of working with a group and employing the "if it were my dream" format is that the suggestions regarding the possible meanings of someone else's dream will always be of use to the person who offers them, and to other members of the group, *whether they are confirmed by the original dreamer or not.* Indeed, a person will often come to a clearer understanding of his/her own unconscious symbolic material by working with and projecting on another person's dream than by working on a dream of his/her own.

The dreamer's own dream is always precisely and exquisitely aligned with the serpentine boundaries of his/her unique pattern of waking self-awareness. For this reason, that person may not see the meanings in his/her own dream with any clarity. Someone else's dream, focused on essentially the same archetypal drama, may offer images and metaphors that are just far enough away from the original person's selective blind spots so that he or she can see the significance without difficulty. As Carl Jung said, "The limit of our ability to work with dreams is for me to share my dream about your dream," to which he added: "It is fortunate that something good almost always comes of it." Because the language of the dream is universal, the mutual projections in a dream group almost invariably produce valuable insights for all involved.

As Jung says in "Marriage as a Psychological Relationship" (on

p. 324 of volume 17 of the Princeton *Collected Works*), "Anyone who wishes to interpret a dream must himself be on approximately the same level as the dream, for nowhere can he see anything more than what he is himself." He says essentially the same thing again in *Analytical Psychology: Its Theory and Practice* (on p. 122 of volume 18): "Dreams are as simple or as complicated as the dreamer is himself, only they are always a little bit ahead of the dreamer's consciousness. I do not understand my own dreams any better than any of you, for they are always somewhat beyond my grasp and I have the same trouble with them as anyone who knows nothing about dream interpretation. Knowledge is no advantage when it is a matter of one's own dreams."

The projections of group members are of immense help, not only to the dreamer, but also to all the group members who are exploring their own unconscious issues through the medium of their imagined versions of the original dreamer's narrative.

## THE IMPORTANCE OF ACKNOWLEDGING PROJECTIONS

All efforts to understand dreams more fully are generated out of and through projection, whether undertaken in voluntary groups by amateurs or one-to-one in consulting offices by professionals. For this reason, all dream work is ultimately confession. No one has any ideas about the possible meanings in someone else's dream without imagining and enlivening it with his or her own versions of the emotions and images the dreamer reports. For this reason, *anything* that is said about the possible meanings in someone else's dream is *always a projection,* a reflection of the interior life and symbol dramas of the person making the comment, more than it is a reflection of the possible "objective" significance of the dream itself. As Orpheus says to the frustrated painter in Cocteau's famous film of the same name, "When are you artists going to realize that you are not capable of anything but self-portraiture?"

When working in a group, the "confessional" quality of the "if it were my dream" format constantly reminds everyone of the potential value of every suggestion for *themselves and each other,* as well as for the original dreamer.

People who stay with the same dream group for any length of time begin to see more and more clearly how the comments and projections of particular members of the group always reflect the most important issues and evolving dramas of the people offering the comments. The patterns vary, but usually someone in the group is particularly skilled at detecting dream puns, and another finds issues of power and dominance/submission most important; another person focuses on meanings about social acceptance, while someone else is particularly attuned to creative expression. Others may focus on issues of psychospiritual evolution and development; usually at least one person is particularly sensitive to the "Freudian" layers that resonate with physical sexuality and emotional relationship, while another is particularly sensitive to layers of metaphor reflecting physical health.

Far from hindering the work, these more or less predictable patterns of interpretation from various group members almost always wind up being "endearing," ensuring that those particular layers of potential significance that the particular group members are most sensitive to are never forgotten or ignored in the work with anyone else's dream.

The universal tendency to project our own symbolic material into the meanings we see in other people's dreams is invariably accompanied by a certain degree of blindness toward those same issues as they appear in our own dreams and waking lives. Thus, group dream work reflects back to us our consistent patterns of projection as revealed in the work with other people's dreams.

For example, in one ongoing group a woman named "Zoe" always saw metaphors of social acceptance and struggles with external authority in the dreams of other people. However, she was not consciously aware that this was an area of central concern in her own life until the others in her group began to remark on her always seeing this pattern in their dreams. Zoe's realization that she herself needed to break free of the domination of her husband and the unquestioned values of her parents, and her fear that if she did so, she would be seen as "unacceptable," was very poignant.

## THE VALUE OF THE "NEGATIVE AHA"

Occasionally, a person in a dream group will suggest a meaning for a dream, and the dreamer will respond with a "negative aha" that says, in effect, "No, that's totally wrong, but it's so far from the mark that it makes me realize what *is* true!" Seldom in human communication do totally erroneous and fallacious comments lead to a discovery of deeper truth, yet it happens all the time when people work together in groups to discover the meanings in their dreams.

## THE ROLE OF THE GROUP FACILITATOR

Dream work groups can be leaderless or led by nonprofessional or professional facilitators, with equal success. The inherent advantages of working in a group, outlined above, will manifest themselves regardless of their leadership.

The universal human tendency toward self-deception and selective blindness always makes solitary work with your own dreams particularly problematic. To overcome this tendency has always been a primary reason for entering into ongoing professional therapeutic relationships. However, even when one works a dream one to one with an experienced dream worker, only two trains of thought can be followed at the same time—the dreamer's and the dream worker's—whereas in a group, as many trains of association are present as there are members. Therefore, group work with dreams regularly reveals more of their multiple meanings than does solitary work, or even one-to-one work with a skilled dream worker.

Sadly, one of the greatest and least-acknowledged problems in professional one-to-one analysis is the "countertransference" of the professional's own unconscious material in projected form onto the work with the client. Undergoing a "training analysis" in preparation for a career as a professional raises the trainee's consciousness about this tendency to see reflections and projections of his/her own issues in the client's life struggles and dreams. Unfortunately, such professional training does *not* prevent this countertransference in subsequent practice. Some projection of the therapist's own unconscious material onto the client is, in fact, *inescapable,* and no amount of training and experience in bringing one's own issues to consciousness can prevent it. One-to-one work with a professional therapist, analyst, pastoral counselor, spiritual director, or the like can be, and regularly is, of immense value, but the claims of "objectivity" made by so many professionals in these fields are simply pompous exaggerations. In my experience, the more adamant the claim, the more rampant the self-deception that usually accompanies it.

No matter how much work is done, no matter how sensitive and self-aware one becomes of the inevitable tendency to project, *the contents of the unconscious are without apparent end.* Whatever issues and symbolic material are in the process of surfacing in the dream worker's own life and psyche will inevitably color his/her judgment, perception, and efforts to be "objective." As Jung says, ". . . to believe otherwise is a disease of the mind."

"Objectivity" is a shining ideal that should inspire a dream worker to greater and greater self-awareness, openness, and sensitivity to others, but like so many other ideals, it is a vision of perfection that can be approached but is ultimately unattainable in practice. The belief that one has actually achieved an "objective view" of one's own dreams, or anyone else's, is in itself a doorway to self-deception. In my experience, the best and easiest way to avoid this potential pitfall is to work on one's own dreams with a group on a regular basis.

For this reason, I always share a descriptive title of one of my own recent dreams at each meeting of any group I work with, and I also work with at least one of my dreams in depth at least once in the course of an ongoing dream group. This work is in addition to the regular sharing and working with my dreams that I do in the twice-a-month "family dream group" to which my wife and I belong.

Not only is this work with my own dreams in various groups of immense use to me personally, but it also demonstrates clearly on each occasion that I'm as selectively blind about my own symbolic material as are the rest of the group members about theirs.

The ability of a group I have trained to bring me to new insights regarding the multiple meanings in my own dreams is also the single best and most nearly "objective" means at my disposal for evaluating the success of my teaching.

I usually wait to explore one of my own dreams in depth until toward the end of the semester, or until one of the last regularly scheduled meetings of a private group, because I believe that all the group members should have an opportunity to explore the process, work with at least one of their own dreams in some depth, and get comfortable with the emotional risks and group communication dynamics before they undertake intensive work with the facilitator's dreams.

This general principle for facilitating honest, successful group dream work can be phrased: "Don't ask anyone to do anything—to share anything or take any emotional risk of self-revelation—that you're not demonstrably willing to do and to model yourself in relation to your own dreams." In other words, group dream work is, or should be, a "contact sport," not a "spectator sport," even for the group facilitator. Adequate dream work can be done by leaders who hold themselves aloof from the process, refusing to share or work with their own dreams in the group, but in my experience the long-term effects of this lack of participation are usually distinctly counterproductive. A group leader who withholds sharing and working with his/her own dreams tends to foster elitism and dependence in the members of the group, who will tend to look to the leader as a "guru."

The lack of full participation in the group by the leader will also tend to reinforce whatever ideological rigidity and self-deception he or she may harbor. In addition, it is a shame for the facilitator to miss receiving the insights and emotional gifts that invariably come from other people's projections.

The only regular exception I would offer to this general principle of *full* participation in the work by the facilitator is when the work is with groups in institutional settings, such as prisons, hospitals, residential treatment centers, and the like. Most often, the people in hospital, prison, and other institutional dream groups can not honestly be viewed as "fully consenting adults." Overly generous or premature self-revelation on the part of the group leader may be viewed by some of the participants as naïveté, arrogance, or simply stupidity. Whether these client perceptions of weakness and inadequacy in the facilitator are accurate or not, they can invite inappropriate struggles for power over who will set the ongoing *tone* of the group's proceedings. Such power struggles, no matter how subtle, are almost always counterproductive and can best be avoided by limiting the leader/facilitator's own self-revelation simply to sharing his/her dreams without comment at the same time as everyone else's initial dream sharing before the exploratory work begins.

However, even in these highly charged and essentially involuntary institutional settings, if the requisite levels of trust, mutual respect, and understanding can be established, working with my own dreams has proven to be tremendously valuable, not only to me but by all appearances to the other people in the group(s) as well. So, even this exception to the "rule" of full participation must be carried lightly and even discarded occasionally in actual practice.

## GROUP DREAM WORK WITH INSTITUTIONALIZED POPULATIONS: SAN QUENTIN, A CASE IN POINT

Dream work with institutionalized populations can be very reward-ing for everyone involved. Because of their shared circumstances and their enforced isolation from society at large, people in institutions often are much more willing and able to learn from one another than they are from the "visitors" from the "outside world."

Several years ago, I ran a "drop-in" dream group inside San Quen-tin prison. We met every Wednesday night, except when the whole prison was "locked down" in response to riots, murders, and attempted escapes. The dream group met every week, with only these unpredict-able interruptions, for more than a year. (All this took place before the maximum-security facility at Pelican Bay was built.)

Initially, I proposed that the dream group be open to both inmates and staff, but the warden's office refused even to consider it. Ironically, regulations required that I be accompanied at all times by an armed, uniformed corrections officer, so the dream group ended up including guards and prisoners together on a regular basis anyway, but without any official acknowledgment that the process might be beneficial for the guards as well. It was a "drop-in" group because it was impossible to assure any continuity in attendance, given the way the prison population was administered, the general understaffing, and the ambivalence of the inmates.

Thus, attendance at the San Quentin dream group varied dramati-cally from week to week. The smallest meeting I ever held included a guard and three inmates. The largest single meeting involved more than twenty men. Usually the group involved eight to ten inmates, most of whom were looking forward to possible release within the next year or two, either through parole or through completion of their sentences.

Every Wednesday night, I would drive over to the prison, identify myself at the gate, and submit to an extensive search. Then I would meet the uniformed officer assigned to the group that night. The officer and I would then move through the first three successive perimeters of security and proceed to the chapel, a cinder-block room about thirty by sixty feet with a low ceiling, harsh overhead lights, and a bare concrete floor. The room was furnished with metal folding chairs. A single fire door opened directly onto the main exercise yard.

From week to week, any given prisoner's ability to come to the meeting depended on a complex and seemingly capricious and arbitrary series of decisions made by different prison officials at various levels. These decisions regarding "eligibility" were influenced by such factors as the security status of the prison as a whole, the status of the particular division and cellblock where the inmate resided, and the changing assessments of the individual inmate's "ability to benefit from the program." A number of other "unofficial" considerations were only hinted at in my presence, such as personal, racial, and gang relationships and enmities among inmates, inmates and guards, and among the guards and administrators themselves. The inmates who wished to come and were judged "eligible" that week would come out through the next two successive security perimeters from deeper inside the prison, then across the main exercise yard to the chapel.

San Quentin prison itself is a monstrosity. A "maximum security facility," it is architecturally and administratively designed not only to contain and isolate the most dangerous convicted criminals in the state of California but also to be a punishment in and of itself, depriving the inmates of sun and sky, privacy, and any sense of expansiveness or possibility. The prison was, and still is, *terribly* overcrowded. The tiny, windowless, claustrophobic, and oppressive cells designed to be occupied by no more than two inmates now often house four to six men. Inmates assigned to San Quentin tend to respond to even the casual events of their lives with grim, habitual dishonesty, mistrust, and explosive violence.

Every Wednesday night, I entered the threatening environment of the prison with great fear and apprehension. To call up the energy to proceed, I regularly had to remind myself that doing group dream work with the prisoners and guards was a *really* good idea.

So, each week I would dress in the restrictive "uniform" of my "preacher's suit" and make my way over to the prison. I would control my misgivings and stifle my desire to bolt and run each time another set of iron doors closed behind me and I found myself in another dimly lit, claustrophobic hallway. At the end of each evening, when I was outside the walls under the beautiful night sky again, I was always glad that I had forced myself to go through with it, despite my initial trepidation, but I also knew that I would have to work to overcome my anxiety and dread all over again the following week.

Among the uniformed officers, the assignment to monitor the dream group was generally considered an onerous detail—almost a punishment—and week after week, my first task, after overcoming my own fear and repugnance, would usually be to try to lessen the prejudices and hostilities of the guard assigned to the group that week, so that he or she did not actively disrupt or sabotage the process. Whenever I was able to win a uniformed officer over to the process, so that he or she subsequently requested the dream group assignment, the request would always be refused, and I would be assigned yet another new guard who had no respect for dreams.

More often than not, when I met the guard assigned to protect the group that evening, I would be greeted with a bitter and hostile speech about how the guard had "better things to do" than "protect your bullshit dream group," how the prisoners were "all just a bunch of animals" who couldn't possibly benefit from any "candy-ass 'therapy,'" and how "dreams are all crap and don't mean a damn thing anyway!"

More often than not, I was able to establish some minimal rapport with the new guard as we talked and passed together through the succession of corridors, gates, checkpoints, and "air locks." I would always try to explain briefly the social and psychological basis of the work. Sometimes I was able to get the guard to tell me a dream as we walked and waited and walked. When that happened, I could sometimes then do a quick bit of nonthreatening "if it were my dream" work on it, until he/she experienced an aha. When this happened, the officer often had his/her negative opinion of dream work changed, or at least shaken and called into question, by the emotional impact of the unexpected insight.

Sometimes, however, I would fail in this initial effort, and the guard, with both words and body language, would indicate to me and the inmates that the group was all "bullshit," at least until we moved further into the evening's activities.

One night, I was assigned a particularly annoyed and hostile guard who left me in no doubt about his feelings regarding "coddling hardened criminals with liberal-crap rehabilitation programs." His annoyance was compounded because he was being forced to miss a major televised

sporting event "to hold my hand." His complaints were so vociferous
that he and I proceeded through the successive checkpoints and opened
the chapel without my having an opportunity to say much of anything.

I set up a few chairs in a circle, and we moved back outside to wait
for the inmates. We stood by the door, and as I watched the prisoners
cross the yard in the early-evening light, it became clear, even from a
considerable distance away, that tonight I was in for even bigger problems than usual.

A giant of a man, perhaps seven feet tall and weighing probably over
three hundred pounds, came across the yard, more or less in the midst of
the widely spaced group of inmates, all of whom were clearly trying to
avoid him. The giant man was "laughing" boisterously and darting back
and forth with surprising speed and agility, grabbing at the nine or ten
other men coming to the dream group with him.

When his selected target was too slow to avoid capture, the big man
would grab him around the neck with his huge forearm under the man's
chin. He would then lift the man up off his feet and carry him along a
few steps, shaking him and swinging him around with his legs flailing.
Then the big man would drop the prisoner he had been "playing" with
and go darting after someone else. From a distance, this all appeared to
be "in fun," but it also had an obviously dangerous, perhaps even lethal
edge to it, lurking just below the "playful" surface (as indeed did almost
every interaction I witnessed or participated in while I was inside the
prison).

This man's extraordinary physical size and strength clearly allowed
him to behave in ways that would not have been tolerated from a
normal-sized man. It was also obvious that he had chosen to play the role
of "the overgrown child," "the unpredictable strong one," acting out of
self-indulgent emotional volatility and mitigating his threatening behavior with mercurial mood swings and a short attention span. The socio-
gram displayed by the prisoners as they approached us across the yard was
both clear and distinctly unpromising. I asked the guard about the big
man, and he told me his name—I will call him Frank.

As the group came closer to the door of the chapel, Frank dashed
ahead and stationed himself right by the entrance so he could grab anyone who tried to enter. Clearly, none of the other men would even try
to enter until Frank either moved further away from the door or went

inside. The guard, as near as I could tell, seemed grimly amused at my predicament.

I decided to concentrate on getting Frank to come inside. He was "showing off" and had succeeded in making himself the undeniable center of everyone's attention. Approaching him, I asked him in a loud voice whether or not he really wanted to work with his dreams. I told him we were there "to work with dreams," and if he didn't want to do what the group was scheduled to do, then he'd have to go back to the cellblock.

Actually sending a prisoner back to the cells was a virtual impossibility, requiring phone calls, the declaration of a low-order "official emergency," and the assignment of another overworked and almost certainly unwilling off-duty uniformed officer to supervise the transfer. All of that would amount to an official admission on my part that I couldn't handle the group. All of us—the other inmates, Frank and I, and particularly the guard—were well aware that sending a prisoner back from an assigned activity usually meant the end of that volunteer's work in the prison, as well the end of that prisoner's accrued privileges, but the willingness to risk it appeared to be a necessary ritual opening gambit.

I finally managed to get Frank through the door by talking at him loudly, nonstop, about "how interesting" it is to work with dreams and how we only had "a certain amount of time" to do it, and "crowding" him with my body without actually touching him while I talked. Once inside, we dispersed around the circle of chairs I had set up, and I got them all to sit down and to tell their names. No one would sit close to Frank, and twice during the initial introductions, Frank leaped up and knocked his chair over backward in response to some supposed slight from one of the other men. Each time the noise of the metal chair's crashing on the bare concrete in the low-ceilinged room was deafening. The guard standing in the corner jumped nervously and unsnapped the strap on his holster, and I became increasingly apprehensive.

Once all the names had been shared, I started my brief orientation about how everyone dreams and how all dreams come to "help the dreamer get his life together." Because of the drop-in nature of the group, I had to start from scratch every week, repeating my introductory remarks for the new members and yet keeping the rap lively enough, and brief enough, to hold the interest of the few men who returned week after week. Frank was not interested and interrupted constantly with lewd remarks and laughter.

Eventually, we got to the centering exercise where I asked them all to stand and hold hands and breathe silently together visualizing light. On even the best of evenings, it was difficult to get them to do this, but that night it was almost impossible. None of the other inmates was willing to hold Frank's hand, and it took all the "ministerial" presence I could muster to get the rest of them to take each other's hands. I took Frank's hand on one side, and we managed an opening circle with a "hole" in it on Frank's other side. We held the silence for the agreed twelve breaths, although Frank did snicker and mutter quietly to himself.

When we sat down again to start the work, Frank did not want to let anyone else tell a dream. His interruptions made it impossible to get around the circle and hear a dream from everyone before we started work, so I decided to see what we could do working just with Frank's dreams.

He did not want to tell any recent dreams but started immediately "bragging" about how all his boyhood dreams involved "giants" who were "out to get him" yet whom he was able to evade with relative ease. When he had told three or four such dreams, I repeated that all we could do was imagine the dream stories as if they had happened to us, then guess about what they might mean.

I started off by saying, "If it were my dream . . ." At one level, the giants in my childhood nightmares—and I believe, in the dreams of most children—would be mirror images of the adults around me, who always seem "big, like giants" from the small child's physical and emotional point of view. I went on to suggest that the same is usually true about the "big, slow giants" in fairy tales as well, and to offer the image of the "giant" as one example of how myths, dreams, and fairy tales all speak the same symbolic language.

I also suggested that death in dreams is always, at some level or another, a way the dream has of showing growth and change. "It's as though the person I imagine I am has to die before the person I'm growing into can have a place to exist. For that reason, when I get attacked and harassed and chased around in my dreams by people or monsters or giants who want to kill me, and I manage to dodge around and get away from them, it usually means that I'm not allowing myself to grow and change—that I'm 'escaping' from the inner promptings that it's time to let go of some idea about myself, or some way of being, or some set of outdated emotions or feelings, and get on with my life."

Frank was obviously annoyed. His boyhood dream "triumphs" were being questioned and cast in a new and different and less flattering light, and yet he was also obviously having an aha, as his next remark clearly showed. He scowled angrily and leaned forward into my face.

"Wait a minute! You saying I never grew up!"

I was pleased, despite the surge of physical fear I experienced as he suddenly lunged toward me. He was giving the insight back, in his own words, with what appeared to be real feeling.

"I wouldn't have put it quite that way, but yes, if it were my dream, that's certainly one of the things it would mean to me!"

Frank uttered a really foul expletive in a tone of surprise, then sat back, speechless, withdrawing into himself—a sure sign, in my experience, that some kind of important aha is being felt and integrated. It crossed my mind to wonder, in that moment, how many times this same suggestion might have been made to him by others, but in a more coercive and authoritarian context, where he had not been prepared to hear or internalize it, as he appeared to be doing now.

I decided to take advantage of this momentary lull in Frank's aggressive and manipulative behavior to finish the aborted go-round of initial dream sharing. The other men seemed quite surprised by this turn of events, and with Frank's initial dream work setting the tone, they all started to share dreams and nightmares from childhood, particularly dreams of being attacked and abused by "giants."

It was fairly clear that my suggestion to Frank about the "giants" in his dreams being metaphoric of the adults around him in childhood, and the connection of the dream experience of death with psychological and emotional growth, had provoked ahas in many of the men. Frank came back to himself when we had progressed about halfway around the circle and started interrupting again. This time, he started blurting out interpretive comments, refusing to wait until everyone had shared a dream, or even to use the "if it were my dream" form, despite my repeated efforts to get him to do so.

As we continued sharing dreams around the circle, he intruded his ideas and interpretations spontaneously, and I was repeatedly struck by how accurate and on-the-case his remarks seemed to be, despite his aggressively crude and insulting language. My opinion seemed to be shared by most of the other men. Even the body language of the previously hostile guard changed and he moved in closer, apparently trying to hear better and to get a better view.

"Shit! That dog in your dream is just some feeling that you're afraid of. . . . Why, man, that's just a dream about thinkin' you can't cut it!"

"Yeah, all those birds—that's religious stuff. You're always tryin' to get right with God. That's what that's all about."

Frank appeared to have an intuitive hit on almost every dream shared. Other men started to offer comments and interpretations as well. Occasionally, one of the men would try to use the "if it were my dream" form, but they soon dropped even the pretense of doing the work with each other's dreams in the formal and "approved" way and just went at it.

The overall tone of the meeting had changed from negatively tense to something very different—a more positive tension born of focused interest and surprised curiosity. Everyone, including the guard, who had by now pulled up a chair and sat down and joined the circle, leaned forward and pulled in closer. The men's voices were getting lower and lower and softer and softer as the dream narratives and attendant stories of being abused and beaten in childhood were shared at greater and greater emotional depth. The stories were depressingly similar, usually involving physical abuse in the name of "corporal punishment" and "discipline," carried out by adult authorities who were often drunk. The abusive adult disciplinarians were usually male, but stories about being beaten at very young ages by women were also common.

Initially, the men greatly resisted *feeling* the full impact of the dreams and the memories evoked by them. Frank himself had started off by bragging about the ferocity of the beatings he'd received from his father and his mother's brothers (until he grew to his gargantuan size and could defend himself, at which time he was placed in a juvenile facility). Other men also "talked tough" about how the beatings they had received as boys had only "made them strong," but slowly the emotional and psychological truths of the dreams began to make themselves felt. The cumulative tone of misery, and the false brittleness of the denials, eventually became quietly obvious. The tone of aggressive bravado disappeared. Longer and longer silences began to punctuate the dreams and the comments about them as the men appeared to settle into feeling the remembered pains and sadnesses of their abused boyhoods and to find the strength to face them more consciously and courageously in this shared moment of their revelation.

In the midst of this work, I knew a major hurdle had been crossed when the guard took his pack of cigarettes out of his breast pocket, shook one out for himself, put it in his mouth, then looked around at the other men before lighting it. I watched him pause, make the decision, and then pass the pack around. Each man took a cigarette until the pack came back around to the guard almost empty. We shared the silent "communion" of smoke (designed to dull the emotions being evoked by the dreams) and moved ahead.

As we worked, I made the point over and over again that when the aha of recognition comes in working with a dream, it means not only that some of the dream's message is "getting through" to consciousness but also that the dreamer is changing inside at that moment, as the psychological and emotional energies get reorganized and smoothed out in the work with the dream. A great deal of grief and pain was reexperienced that night as the dreams and the boyhood stories came out. Eventually, the guard himself shared a dream, a recurrent nightmare of fleeing from a menacing male giant down dark streets that got narrower and narrower, and he shared some stories of being beaten by his drunken father.

At the end of the meeting, everyone appeared surprised that the time had gone by so quickly. When we rose again to hold hands at the end, there wasn't a rustle of protest. This time, only the guard seemed to find the exercise difficult, and then only because regulations prevented him from physically touching the inmates in any casual or friendly way. He came and stood close beside me and put his hand on my shoulder, while I held Frank's hand on one side and someone else held his other hand.

As the men began to file out through the door and back across the yard, they didn't avoid Frank, as they had so dramatically a couple of hours earlier. The dozen or so of them all passed through the chapel door together and started back across the floodlit exercise yard in a tight little group. As they passed by me, I overheard comments that made me think that some real changes might indeed have taken place that night.

"Shit! Did you *hear* that man? I always thought he was a dummy. A big, fuckin', stupid dummy! Shit! The man's no dummy. Did you hear what he said about my dream? Damn!"

One of the most difficult things to do in an institutional setting is to assess accurately the value and effectiveness of any therapeutic/rehabilitation effort. In my experience, it is almost impossible to separate with any certainty the "games" that are "run" for the benefit of "the visiting preacher," the "shuckin' an' jivin'," from genuine alterations in feeling and behavior. In an effort to "get a second opinion" as to the effectiveness of the group dream work at San Quentin (and in the two other prisons I have worked in, the Federal Correctional Facility at Pleasanton, and the California Medical Facility at Vacaville), I have always kept in fairly close and regular contact with people in the chaplains' and psychological counseling offices who have access to regular reports on inmates' behavior.

In the particular instance of the work with Frank and the others that night at San Quentin, members of the prison staff confirmed to me that Frank's behavior changed fairly radically after the night of dream work. Although none of them were willing to credit the dream work per se, they reported that Frank was suddenly much less volatile and more able to control himself. Even more dramatic, from my point of view, was the report that the rest of the inmates appeared to treat Frank differently after that night.

Prior to that Wednesday night, one of the most difficult things about having Frank in prison—one of the reasons why he had been transferred to the maximum-security facility at San Quentin, though his convictions were of the sort that had put him in a medium-security facility initially— had been that he was regularly manipulated by his fellow prisoners into creating disturbances whenever they wanted. Before that night, if a prisoner made a provocative joke or remark to Frank, he would explode into his "big, strong, uncontrollable child" routine, drawing the staff's attention to him, thus creating a momentary "bubble" of distraction so clandestine activities could be carried out under the very noses of corrections officers. After that night, not only was Frank much less volatile, but apparently the other inmates stopped attempting to provoke him and "use" him as before. In fact, the transformations in Frank's behavior, and the behavior he evoked in others, were so marked and consistent, he was eventually transferred back to a medium-security facility.

Now, I grant that even consistent reports from psychiatrists and chaplains do not constitute firm "evidence" of psychological growth. Possibly the whole thing was an elaborate charade put on to con me and the guard and the people in the chaplains' and psychiatric services offices—conceivably, the guard could even have been "in on it" too—but I don't think so. If it was all theater and confidence tricks, everyone involved deserves an Oscar for both their individual and ensemble performances!

In addition, I don't believe that the kind of smooth, sophisticated, conscious *cooperation* that would have been required to make everyone in that room work as convincingly together as they did—particularly across racial and class barriers that were obviously present—was possible for that group of men. At no time during the whole evening did I detect any side glance or smiles or slight body gestures that led me to suspect that any con was being run. I have had the sense that cons were being run by individuals and small cliques in institutional dream groups on other occasions, so I do think I have some skill in recognizing when it's happening. Although I cannot prove "beyond a doubt" that this was a genuine transformation of individual and collective consciousness as a result of group dream work, I still believe it was.

I believe that we began that evening as a group of men with stereotyped ideas about how "the others" were "just animals." As a result of sharing and working with some of our more painful and emotionally charged dreams, we experienced an unexpected recognition of essential common humanity that changed how we thought, felt, and behaved toward each other, even after the meeting was over. I believe that these transformations of self-awareness and attitude toward others were achieved as a direct consequence of working in a group.

The initial confusion and tension at the beginning of the meeting seems to have created a fresh, less stereotyped situation and relaxed habitual responses, defenses, and denials. I believe the recognition of common humanity that followed, and the reinforcement of the changed feelings and behavior that resulted from that startling recognition, required the presence of the group and could not have been achieved in the same fashion or degree even with extensive one-to-one work.

What was true for those inmates in that horrible prison on that cool autumn night is true for us all. We grow and change most authentically and deeply in the company of, and with the support and energy of, other human beings. Exploring the multiple meanings of dreams in the company of others in a nonauthoritarian setting regularly leads to a positive transformation of thought, feeling, and behavior.

The primary objection that other professional dream workers usually raise to the kind of group process described throughout this book is that the insights generated are often "too rich," "too complex," or "too ambiguous and multivalent." They fear the dreamer will be "flooded" with potential understandings of his/her dreams, so many that he/she can not easily internalize or make practical use of any. While this kind of "overstimulation" does occur in some instances, I consider it an advantage, not a disadvantage. In group dream work, *the cumulative insights of all the group members are most important, not just the insights the individual dreamer is aware of at the time.*

## GROUP DREAM WORK WITH INTROVERTS AND EXTROVERTS

As the example of Barbara's "silent basement party" dream, discussed in detail in Chapter 2, clearly indicates, a dreamer may often have important preconscious ahas that will not percolate up to full conscious awareness until later on. In fact, the more introverted the dreamer is, the more likely that he or she may *not* experience any ahas consciously during the group meeting, simply because other people are present.

When I first began group dream work on a regular basis more than thirty-five years ago, I would sometimes experience what felt like a "failure." After working with someone's dream for the usual thirty-five to forty minutes, I would think that we had come up with a number of good ideas and insights, but the dreamer seemed to have no aha reaction. The dreamer would often say words to the effect of, "Well, thank you all for all your attention and energy and cleverness, but no. . . . In fact, nothing that anyone said tonight has evoked the slightest aha in me."

I used to leave such meetings with a deep sense of frustration and confusion. "Where did we go wrong?" I would wonder to myself. "What didn't we get to? The suggestions were all interesting, and some of them certainly gave *me* ahas. What did we miss that would have caused the *dreamer* to feel some aha of recognition?"

Eventually, I began to notice a distinct pattern in the "touch-ins" at succeeding meetings. The dreamer who had worked the previous week and experienced no discernible ahas at the time would say something like "You know, I was sitting in the bathtub the other night, thinking about what the group had said about my dream, and I remembered what Louise had said about it, and I had an aha! And then I realized, well, if that's true, then what Jack said has to be true too, and then I realized that this other thing that nobody said at the time is true too!" We would then be treated to an elaborate account of multiple layers of increased conscious understanding of the dream, understandings that were all clearly generated out of the work we had done together in the group but that had surfaced in the dreamer's mind only afterward, when he or she had gone over and considered the experience in solitude.

After watching this essential pattern repeat, I realized that the more introverted the person working on the dream appeared to be, the more the ahas of insight would tend to come only afterward, in solitude. When the results of this solitary reflection were included in the overall assessment of the success and worth of any given group meeting, it became clear that the individual dreamer's not having any ahas during the meeting was an unreliable criterion of evaluation.

What I now know is that introverts *require solitude* to evaluate the value, meaning, and even the *reality* of their experiences. A deeply introverted person will take in all experiences had in company with others and "hold them in suspension" until he or she can get away and "evaluate" them—that is, really experience them fully—in solitude. This is why introverts periodically have to break off even the most interesting and positive interactions with others in order to spend time alone. It is not, as so many extroverts suppose, that they are "fickle" or "cold and unfeeling," but rather that they require a regular amount of solitude to invest even the most positive and heartfelt experiences with full emotional *reality*.

A deeply extroverted person, on the other hand, will feel fully alive and real only in the company of others. Extreme extroverts will feel themselves "disappearing" and "turning into phantoms" when they are alone, and they will be driven to seek out the company of others to come back to life.

Whether you are primarily introverted or extroverted, the task of maturing emotionally and intellectually, which Carl Jung called "individuation," requires a development of the seemingly "opposite" (actually complementary), underdeveloped, unconscious potential. Dreams come to us to tell us what we don't know. They serve the dreamer's evolving individuation. For this reason, the dreams of introverts often point to deeper and more intense and sustained interaction with others, while the dreams of extroverts tend to point consistently to more solitary intro-spection and self-analysis.

Group work with dreams has the added benefit of bringing together both introverts and extroverts in an ideal meeting ground for people who might in other settings find each other totally incomprehensible or even repulsive. Romantic couples will often be of opposite "types," and work-ing together in dream groups can bring them to a much fuller apprecia-tion of each other's basic psychology.

In my experience, the people who are initially most attracted to dream work tend to be introverts, but as they proceed, the natural ten-dency toward wholeness in the dreams usually leads them to discover the pleasures of "extroverted" interactions with others in the dream group. Conversely, group dream work tends to have a comparable balancing effect for extroverts drawn to the group aspect of the work; they will tend to find the insights generated so pleasantly and easily in the group setting beginning to occupy their minds and hearts while they are alone, helping them feel real and vital and alive, even in solitude.

## LOSING THE INSIGHTS

Group dream work usually generates solid insights into the multiple meanings in dreams, but this feeling of solidity can be deceptive because the insights themselves initially come from the same place that the dreams do: the unconscious. I blush to admit how many times work on a dream of mine has seemed rewarding at the moment of insight, but later I have found the specific insights have slipped back into unconsciousness again, just like a dream that I thought I would "never forget" but that disap-peared from my mind because I didn't record it.

To compensate for this tendency of the insights to disappear, group members will sometimes agree to serve as "recorders" for others when they are working their dreams. The recorders write down important suggestions made during the group's work with the dream, then give this record to the dreamer. This helps the dreamer recall the specific ahas of the initial work, and it often helps him/her to gain further insights that were not immediately apparent.

If meetings are tape-recorded, the dreamer can later replay the work with his/her dream and pick up many of the suggestions missed the first time around. Each dreamer should have a tape to put into the machine to record just the work on his or her dream, so anonymity and confidentiality can be maintained.

In practice, I do not recommend tape-recording the group's comments and suggestions until after the group has met for a while. Developing the unconscious as well as conscious trust and bonding that a group needs to function well takes time. If the idea of tape-recording the sessions is introduced too soon, the enthusiasm and openness with which people participate may be "chilled," despite whatever conscious understanding they may have of "what a good idea it is" to record the sessions.

## ORGANIZING A GROUP

As mentioned earlier, probably the best way to begin working with dreams in a group setting is to invite your friends who are interested to join together and experiment with the conscious projective technique of "if it were my dream." If you don't have five or six interested friends, the next best thing may be to advertise the formation of an introductory dream group in your church, support community, local paper, or what have you.

One caveat: a group can certainly be made up of colleagues in the workplace, but this may be problematic. Work with dreams, if honestly undertaken, tends to undercut the seemingly necessary formalities, unspoken protocols, and hierarchies of most work environments. This can be an important tool for social change in the workplace, but there should be clear agreement at the outset that such a goal is desirable. Dream work's enlivening and socially equalizing effect can be very beneficial, releasing previously unimagined creativity, but it requires a flexibility and a concern for emotions and deeper human values that are not often honored in the workplace.

One basic principle of group dream work that should be borne in mind while organizing a group is that *everyone in the group should have at least one chance to work with one or more of his/her dreams in some depth during the initially agreed-on set of meetings.* With this in mind, the ideal size of a dream group can best be estimated by striking a balance between the frequency of meetings and the number of people who regularly attend. A group meets for two to three hours once every week or so, and workable numbers of participants run from four or five up to about ten, with an ideal size of six to eight. If not everyone can attend regularly, then a slightly larger number can be accommodated, because the chances of having more than seven or eight people at any given meeting is not that great, and when it does happen, it will not be too hard to handle.

Obviously, the larger the group, the less time there will be for any one person to work with his/her dreams or to express ideas about other people's dreams. At the same time, however, the larger the group, the more diverse and useful the suggestions and projections are likely to be.

When I do introductory weekend workshops, we always work with a couple of dreams in the whole group to demonstrate the process and the benefits of the "if it were my dream" technique with concrete examples and experience. Then we break up into smaller work groups. Invariably, the larger the group, the more diverse and dramatically useful the work, although, of course, only two or three individuals have a chance to work on their own dreams in the full group, regardless of the number of people in attendance.

In general, an ongoing dream group should have regularly scheduled meetings once a week or, failing that, once every two weeks. Less frequent meetings tend to be less productive, since the intervening time becomes so great that touch-in tends to expand dramatically to allow everyone to "catch up" with one another's life. Another problem with meeting less frequently than once a week or so, particularly for introductory groups, is that the basic issues of trust and bonding may have to be addressed "from scratch" again at each successive meeting.

At the outset, agree on a specific number of meetings for the official life or "cycle" of any given group. Since each group member should have a clear opportunity to work with his or her own dreams at least once a cycle, the more people there are in the group, the more meetings should be scheduled in any given cycle. If a group of relative beginners has agreed to meet once a week for three hours and has eight members, it should probably schedule an initial cycle of six to eight meetings.

The initial organizing meeting of either a leaderless or a facilitated group is usually taken up with discussion and theoretical orientation, and the group will probably work with only one person's dream as a demonstration of the process. For a group of six to eight people, it is reasonable to suppose that at subsequent meetings, touch-in, occasional discussion of theory and ongoing group process, centering, and dream sharing will leave time for work with only one or possibly two people's dreams per meeting.

## THE BASIC ELEMENTS
## OF A DREAM GROUP MEETING

Individual groups inevitably develop their own rhythms and patterns of work over time. To begin with, I would recommend a pattern consisting of: (1) touch-in, (2) centering, (3) dream sharing, (4) intensive work with particular dreams, and (5) closing with a repetition of the centering exercise. Each of these elements will be discussed in more detail presently.

If a group begins in this fashion, it will be easy to branch out into more exotic and dramatic ways of work later on, when the group's trust, intimacy, and comfort level have been clearly established. The most productive way to branch out into other methods of work, in my experience, is to invite a "guest facilitator" with experience in the particular technique(s) the group is interested in to attend a specific number of meetings. For example, a group that has become familiar and comfortable with the "sitting and talking" techniques presented here may wish to invite a facilitator experienced in Gestalt techniques, dream theater, dream body work, mask making, etc.

Once every group member has had a chance to work with one or more of his/her own dreams in some depth, it is usually a good idea to allow that cycle of regularly scheduled group meetings to come to an official end. It is always possible to set up another round of meetings if people are still interested and enthusiastic about the work. Most groups have found it easier and less emotionally draining to go on to the next cycle with more or less the same membership rather than disbanding and calling for all new members. In this way, many groups will continue for years, even decades, renewing themselves periodically with new members, and making spaces for older members to exit or "take breaks" from the group, without any feelings of frustration or rejection.

It is usually best to begin each meeting relatively promptly at a predetermined time. Laxness about time agreements and commitments often leads to an atmosphere of disrespect for one another's subtle needs. Rigidity is certainly not a desirable tone to set, but conscious care for time agreements promotes good dream work.

## TOUCH-IN

Touch-in (some people prefer to call it a "check-in")—a period set aside for brief statements about how and what each group member is *feeling* and what he or she knows consciously about *why* he or she is feeling that way—is the best way to begin each meeting. Unfortunately, touch-in tends to expand and fill up all available time. One reason for this is that we live in a culture where we seldom have the opportunity to share our emotional lives at any depth, so when a regular opportunity does arise, we each try to make it serve the pent-up needs for emotional community and for understanding and support that we bring from all other areas of our lives. Be that as it may, it is a good idea to agree at the outset that each person will have a specific amount of time for his/her touch-in.

Once again, rigidity in these matters is counterproductive. Allowing each group member to say something about his/her feelings in the moment and his/her emotional life since the last meeting is important. The information shared and gathered at touch-in is often extremely useful when the group works with that individual's dreams. Often, someone will say, "Your dream sounds just like your touch-in"—a seemingly "obvious" correlation that was completely obscure to the dreamer. Corrier and Hart suggest "the dream is a picture of a feeling"; at one or more levels, this is always true. Regular, ongoing familiarity with the emotional lives of the people in one's dream group is one of the most important elements in good dream work, and touch-in deserves a regular place of honor at the beginning of every meeting.

Depending on the needs and tastes of the group, somewhere between one and four minutes per person is usually sufficient. Many groups deal with the inherent problem of "ever-expanding touch-ins" by actually timing people as they speak. I believe this is essentially a good idea—it's one of the only things that actually *works* to keep touch-in under control—but having a particular person serve as "timekeeper" often leads to unnecessary emotional tensions and unconscious resentments toward the person in that role. The best solution, in my experience, is a mechanical device; a simple kitchen timer, reset to four minutes each time a new speaker begins, works very well. (I have a digital watch with an elapsed-time beeper that I count as one of my professional tools for facilitating group dream work.)

Sometimes people will become very moved or upset during touch-in and will need more time to express themselves and feel understood and "seen." One of the most difficult emotional problems in dream group arises when a particular person *always* requires more time for his or her touch-in than anyone else in the group. The group may feel that such people manipulate and dominate the group through their vulnerability and neediness. No one wants to be the one to say "stop it," but unless someone does say it, the resentment and unhappiness of everyone else in the group builds until the work and pleasure of the group itself is jeopardized.

In a leaderless group, this problem can sometimes be solved by one or more people speaking up and voicing their feelings in a gentle and non-coercive fashion. Sometimes, the dreams of group members will begin to depict this problem, and the conversation can be initiated naturally in exploring the dreams.

One of the clear tasks of a group dream facilitator is to step gently into such situations and raise consciousness about the unconsciously manipulative behavior. In such a situation the leader/facilitator has a responsibility to invite other members of the group to express themselves, while at the same time protecting the "needy" one from becoming the object of negative group projection, emotional coercion, and scapegoating. This may be more easily said than done, but when such behavior is detected, it is necessary to confront it consciously.

This is one of those situations where it is imperative to extend the "if it were my dream . . ." form into the "if it were me / my needs / my behavior . . ." form. Consciously owning projections while making "process commentary" is just as important as, if not more important than, using some language form that consciously acknowledges projection in commenting on dreams themselves.

## THE CRUCIAL ISSUE OF SETTING TONE

As a general rule, more dream groups "turn sour" and collapse because of the accumulated weight of "politeness" and unacknowledged, unspoken feelings than are jeopardized by blunt talk and by stepping past the seeming bounds of propriety.

The answer to this problem is to set a strong, gentle, and unambiguous *tone*—a tone of serious interest and curiosity, mutual respect, emotional candor, good humor, and nonjudgmental support. All leadership, in the final analysis, is effective to the precise extent that the leader is able to *set and sustain a positive and productive tone*.

The facilitator's ability to set and maintain such a tone grows directly out of his/her intellectual and communication abilities, knowledge, life experience, and emotional maturity. Formal professional training may be useful in acquiring and developing these skills, but everyone has them to some degree or another, and professional training is by no means necessary to facilitate an effective dream group. In a so-called "leaderless" group, the task of setting and maintaining a productive tone will be shared more or less equally among all, but the basic issues of setting tone will remain the same.

The person who sets the tone *is* the leader, no matter what it says on the flow chart, or what the uniforms and the insignia suggest. If you can persuade others to operate with the tone you wish, you are a leader. Good leaders set a good tone, and crummy leaders set crummy tone, no matter what their other competencies or failings may be. A "leaderless" group is enhanced by the willingness of participants to discuss and share openly in setting a positive and affirming tone.

## THE CENTERING EXERCISE

Once everyone has had an opportunity to touch in, it is valuable for everyone to share a "centering exercise" before further dream sharing. There are several reasons for doing this.

Psychologically, it is valuable to mark in an obvious and formal way the transition from "ordinary talking" to the more emotionally charged and intellectually ambiguous sharing of dreams. This will help group members "clear their minds" and relax the habitual patterns of narrow awareness with which we all live, to some extent, throughout our waking lives. The centering exercise speaks simultaneously to the mind, the body, and the spirit, saying clearly and unambiguously, "What comes next is *different*."

An effective centering exercise will quiet the internal monologue that most people live with on a preconscious level most of their waking lives, the part of consciousness that Buddhists have called "monkey mind." Group centering creates a shared, relaxed awareness where intuition is freer to rise into waking consciousness. The intuitive function links our waking awareness with the deeper layers of our unconscious. It is the most useful faculty we have for working with dreams. Without some kind of centering exercise, the quiet voice of intuition is likely to be "drowned out" by the chatter of habitual consciousness.

The centering exercise I like best, and use regularly in the groups I facilitate, goes like this:

Hold hands in a circle. If the people in the circle hold their hands out in front of them with the left palm up and the right palm down, with both thumbs pointing to the left, then when the group joins hands, each person will "receive" with the left hand and "give" with the right. Hold hands while either standing or seated. The particular needs and comforts of any physically handicapped members of the group should always be borne in mind here, and in all the physical arrangements of the group's meeting place and process.

For the space of twelve in-and-out breaths the group holds hands in silence, breathing easily and deeply. What anyone does inside his/ her own head is always their own business, but what I always recommend is this:

Visualize light entering your body on the in breath, so that as you continue to breathe and hold hands, you see yourself more and more vividly in your mind's eye becoming filled with light, from the soles of your feet all the way to your scalp and the tips of your hair, with the light flowing in and out of your hands to the other members of the group.

If you find your mind wandering during the course of this exercise, extend the visualization to include all the other group members in the circle as clearly and vividly as possible. If your imaginative powers are still not fully utilized in this process, extend the visualization of internal illumination to include any group members who may be absent, other absent friends and loved ones, anyone who may be in need of healing, etc. A particularly valuable and spiritually athletic extension of this exercise is to imagine particular people whom you consider to be your "enemies" and visualize them being filled with the same healing, transforming light.

## INITIAL DREAM SHARING

After the centering exercise is complete, each person simply shares a dream or two, more or less without comment. Usually, this sharing can best be accomplished by offering a "headline"-style title or two. Using titles instead of whole narratives leaves more time for the actual exploration of the dreams themselves. If this dream sharing is left until the end of the meeting, there often isn't time for it. Even if the conscious mind accepts this state of affairs as "unfortunate but unavoidable," the unconscious is likely to "take offense" and cause the dream memories to dry up in subsequent weeks in "protest" over the failure to be acknowledged. To ensure this does not happen, make sure everyone has a chance to share a dream, or at least a dream title, at the beginning of the meeting. This usually takes no more time than touch-in.

The sharing of dreams around the circle at the beginning has two important effects: (1) it reinforces the trust and bonding in the group by confirming in actual practice that everyone present is taking the same risk of self-revelation; and (2) it builds up an ever-increasing backlog of unconscious knowledge about the deep interior lives and symbol dramas of the other group members.

As a dream group continues to meet over time, there is a marked tendency for the work with the dreams to get more and more useful and insightful. This is due to the fact that people become more skilled at calling up their intuition and intellectual powers of symbolic analysis and that if they have been regularly sharing dreams from *everyone* in the group at every meeting, they have also been building up a store of pre-verbal knowledge of and insight into the deeper structures of each other's unconscious life.

## INITIATING AND CLOSING GROUP EXPLORATION OF SPECIFIC DREAMS

When everyone has had a chance to share a dream, or an evocative dream title, the floor is open for the people who want to work their dreams in more depth. Deciding "whose turn it is" and who might best be the focus of the group's attention is also facilitated by having everyone share a dream at the beginning. The person who is most in need of the group's attention, insight, and support does not necessarily put his or her dream forward for attention first. After a regular touch-in, and dream sharing from each person in the group, it is often much easier to decide whose dream is best to work on. As the facilitator of several ongoing groups at any given time, I find it invaluable to hear the emotional information conveyed at touch-in, and the dreams of all the group members, before suggesting to a particular person that he or she might be the best one to work that meeting. In a leaderless group, deciding who will work is informed by the same basic understanding of fairness and emotional need.

After determining which person will work his/her dream(s) in more depth, the next step is to share those dream(s) in their entirety, even if they were shared during the first dream go-round, so that the dream material will be vivid and fresh in everyone's mind as the work begins. From here on, the only two limits to the work that can be done are the natural limit of the group's imagination (which is the collective sum of the imaginative powers and emotional boldness of each of the members) and the limit of the group's collective sense of propriety, whatever that may be. Within those two natural boundaries of imagination and propriety, quite literally, anything goes.

However, at the outset, if people need to ask clarifying questions, it is better to begin with these questions and answers than to jump in with "if it were my dream" projections and comments about the archetypal/mythological associations awakened by hearing the dream. The question-and-answer process keeps the work grounded in the dreamer's reality and specific dream images as the members of the group project and intuit and imagine their own versions of the dream.

When the "if it were my dream" suggestions begin to flow, and the exciting discoveries of the ahas of insight are off and running, the poking around and exploring and projecting on the dream should be allowed to continue for as long as seems generally productive, then brought to a close. Here there is an important point to be understood: *all endings in dream work are arbitrary.*

Over the years, I have developed four questions that I ask myself to help determine when to make the inevitably arbitrary break in the work on someone's dream(s) and move on. The first is: Has my own understanding of the dream been illuminated and deepened by the discussion? In other words: Have I experienced any ahas myself with regard to my own version of the dream? If I have found anything at all to say about the dream, then the answer to this question has to be yes.

The more satisfying my own projected understanding of the dream, the more reason there is to move on to the second question: Have most other people in the group also had ahas in exploring the dream? Again, the extent and quality of the projections made are fairly good indicators of the number and quality of other group members' ahas, since no one can even come up with an idea about the possible meanings in a dream without feeling some tingle of intuitive/emotional/intellectual possibility.

You can also fairly accurately assess the answer to this question for the people who haven't spoken by staying aware of their facial expressions and body language. Once again, success in group work with a dream has much more to do with the discovery by some or all the group members of at least some of the possible meanings of the dream than with just the ahas of recognition of the original dreamer.

The third question is: Has the dreamer experienced any ahas in the course of the work? Often, dreamers will generously express their ahas as they occur, but even when they do not, the impact of the work can usually be assessed with a fair degree of accuracy from the dreamer's facial expressions and body language. Remember, the more introverted the dreamer, the less likely that he or she will experience ahas on the spot. So, even if the dreamer seems not to have gained any insight from the group's exploration of the dream, it does not necessarily mean that the work has failed to touch any of the dream's meanings.

The final criterion for ending a piece of work on a dream is simple clock time. If the group has an agreement about when the meeting will begin and end (and I strongly recommend that such agreements be made and honored), then when closing time approaches, the work with the dream must be brought to an end, even if there is a shared sense that working on it a little more would produce many more insights. If there is an agreement to work on two or three (or even more) different people's dreams each time the group meets, then simple fairness demands that the time available be divided more or less evenly and the transition from one piece of work to another be determined in large measure by the clock.

As with touch-in, I strongly recommend using a kitchen timer or some similar device to keep track of the time, to ensure that each person who works a dream has more or less equal time. In this way, all the people in the group can devote full attention to working with the dreams without one person's being distracted by having to keep an eye on the clock.

Once I have asked and answered these four questions for myself, in order to make the inevitably arbitrary ending to the work a little less abrupt and arbitrary, I always like to ask two more "ritual questions." The first question is to the group as a whole: Does anyone have any additional thoughts, feelings, ideas, projections on the dream, or the work with the dream—particularly any ideas that are "on a different case" or propose yet a different way of looking at the dream?

For instance, if the work with the dream has focused on emotional issues, then it may be wise to consider what the dream may be suggesting with regard to the dreamer's physical health, spiritual life, search for right livelihood or creative solution to specific technical problems, etc., in addition to the layers of meaning already touched on.

At this juncture I always encourage people to say any "obvious" things they may have thought but not said. (As Arthur Conan Doyle said, "It requires an unusual mind to undertake an analysis of the obvious.") If the work has progressed to the point of asking these "last" questions, and these "obvious" points have not yet been made, then it is almost certain that what seems "obvious" is not so obvious to anyone else and therefore needs to be said. At this stage, I also ask people who have been silent if they have anything to say, either about the dream(s) or the process. Often, this last little spurt of thoughts and projections released by this final question turns out to be as productive of insight as all the earlier work put together.

The second and final "ritual question" is directed to the dreamer: Are there any other places in the dream(s), or elements in the dream(s), that you would like to explore a little more before we end this work with your dream? Usually, the answer is no, but sometimes the dreamer will be drawn back to some element of central importance that the group overlooked, or did not address as fully as the dreamer desired, in their initial explorations and work with the dream.

Depending on the habits and patterns of group activity (which will make themselves increasingly clear over time), this process of closing down the work with any particular dream(s) should allow sufficient time to explore whatever new elements are brought to the surface by these last two questions. Flexibility is absolutely necessary. A balance is always being sought between efficient and responsible use of time, and the free-ranging, spontaneous following of the ahas and trains of thought, association, and implication wherever they may lead.

It has occurred to me that if the result of sharing and working with a dream were a "blinding," shared mystical experience of total oneness with all things, past, present, and future, then one might be able to say that closure had been achieved, that the dream had been worked and understood completely, that there was no further work to be done with it. However, any understanding of a dream or series of dreams that falls short of that complete, cosmic harmonization of thought, feeling, intuition, and physical sensation of all the people present is going to be partial and incomplete, because that fantasy of shared mystical revelation is a metaphoric suggestion of the kind of universal "health and wholeness" out of which the dream is born, and back toward which all dreams are striving.

Group work with dreams may never reach that profound, cosmic level, but it does regularly move us toward that kind of "being at home" with our deepest selves and the external cosmos at the same time. Like "objectivity" and "love" and "acceptance without judgment"—all of which may indeed be different ways of talking about the same thing—this kind of shared cosmic aha of insight and understanding of the multiple layers of meaning in every dream is a shining, inspiring ideal toward which to strive, rather than a perfectionistic "ideal" we should seek to achieve. Working with our dreams in company, in a group setting, brings us ever closer to that ideal, even though we may never achieve it.

# Chapter Seven

# RECURRENT DREAMS AND RECOVERING MEMORIES OF CHILDHOOD TRAUMA IN THE DREAMS OF ADULTHOOD

*The child is the potential future. Hence the occurrence of the child motif in the psychology of the individual signifies as a rule an anticipation of future developments, even though at first sight it may seem like a retrospective configuration.*

—C. G. JUNG

A woman repeatedly dreams the same single, brief, static image:

A disembodied close-up view of a wooden surface painted white. The paint is just beginning to blister and bubble.

Each time she dreams it, in the fleeting instant she catches sight of the slight bulges in the white-painted surface, she is assaulted by feelings of despair and anguish and terror—feelings far more intense than any similar emotions she experiences in waking life.

Invariably when the dream occurs, she jerks awake feeling misery and terror clinging to her even on into wakefulness. As these feelings slowly ebb, anger, confusion, and frustration replace them: "What possible reason could there be for such a seemingly innocucus dream to be so *horrible! Why* do I keep dreaming it, over and over again, all my life?"

This woman, I will call her Mary, told this dream at the initial orientation meeting of a dream group I was leading some years ago. She offered it early on as a specific challenge to my assertion that *all* dreams come in the service of health and wholeness. She told the group that she regularly remembered many of her other dreams also, and that she knew from working with them that most did indeed have many valuable gifts of creative energy and insight to offer. But this particular dream was the bane of her life and seemed to her to be "totally meaningless and pointless."

Seeing no other adequate way to continue, I said I could only respond to her dream, and to the larger theoretical question she was raising in sharing it, by attempting some work with the dream, right then and there, if she was willing. She agreed to have the group explore her dream, although she made it quite clear that she did not hold out any hope at all of discovering any "health or wholeness" in it.

I skipped through the remainder of my opening presentation, then we launched into an exploration of Mary's dream as a concrete introductory example of how to apply the projective "if it were my dream" technique.

In response to questions, Mary said she'd had this dream, in more or less this exact form, for as long as she could remember, several times a year, most recently only a few days earlier. She also said that she couldn't detect any waking experiences that seemed to relate in any way to the dream.

In dealing with recurrent dreams such as this, and with dreams in general, several points are worth keeping in mind.

First, a dream is a wholly natural phenomenon, and like all natural phenomena, it conforms to certain basic principles, which in turn give rise to a dazzling diversity of specific instances and events. In this way, the dream is like water, always seeking its own level by the easiest path it can find, given its inherent fluid properties, the temperature, the force of gravity, and the obstacles in its path. As Carl Jung says, "[The dream] harbors no desire to distort or hide, any more than a flower or stone . . ." In this important sense, every dream that a person remembers is a "best fit"—*the best possible dream* for that person to have had at that particular moment.

Just as one can examine a flower or a stone with a naturalist's eye and reasonably deduce many of the broader, more "hidden" environmental and ecological influences that determined its structure and condition, so can one also examine the form and content of a dream with an educated intuitive/psychological eye and come to understandings of the more "hidden" multiple meanings its specific shape and structure embody and reflect.

Although dreams appear to be constrained to speak only the truth, they also appear to be totally unfettered as to how those truths can be hinted at and revealed. In that sense, they appear to be totally free to create *any* image or experience. Dreams can "do anything they want." Since imagery in dreams is not limited by rationality, logic, or the laws of physics, or even by the waking constraint to "come in under budget," it is reasonable to suppose that anything that any given dream actually does end up doing is in some way "the best possible thing" it could do, given the complex demands of the multiple layers of meaning it has to convey. If a dream *could* "do it better" or "say it better," while still remaining true to its multiple layers of significance, it *would*.

For this reason, one can always be sure that the more complex and "bizarre" a dream image is, the more it diverges from the naturalistic expectations and assumptions of waking life; such dreams might use images such as water running uphill, human beings flying without mechanical aids, people and objects changing shape before the dreamer's eyes, etc. *The more the image takes that particular "dreamlike" form, the more layers of meaning it has to convey.*

When a particular dream repeats itself unchanged again and again, it is safe to say not only that it is the best possible dream the dreamer could come up with the first time it occurred but also it continues to be the best possible dream to make the point. If there were a better dream to be had, the dreamer would have had it. The repetition of a specific dream or dream image means, in theory, that this particular dream serves the dreamer's evolving health and wholeness better than any other possible dream that person could have had in that moment, each time it occurs.

The ritually "frozen" quality of a repetitive dream experience suggests strongly that something of overriding importance in the dreamer's life is essentially the same as it was the last time the dream occurred, despite whatever changes the dreamer has made. A recurrent dream draws the dreamer's attention to the aspect(s) of his/her life and character that remain unchanged in the midst of all the other, more obvious developments he or she is aware of.

To put it another way, recurrent dreams tend to be about the deeper layers of the dreamer's personal "myth"—that essential, archetypal, symbolic story that a person tends to act out, over and over again in various forms, over the course of his or her entire life. Recurrent dreams, particularly recurrent dreams with particularly strong affect, such as Mary's dream of the "blistering paint," often turn out to be concise metaphoric statements of as-yet-unfulfilled aspects of the dreamer's fundamental "life task," or the "deepest value conflict" in his/her life, not just in the moment, but over the entire span of time during which the dream has been recurring.

In the dream work with Mary, I shared a specific projection on her dream: "If this were my dream, each time I had it, at one important level it would be about my having grown up in a particularly repressed middle-class home where the spontaneous expression of authentic feeling and emotion was strictly tabooed—'covered up' with metaphoric, socially acceptable 'white paint.' Having grown up this way, each time I picked up any indication in my current waking life that this habitual facade, or veneer of 'politeness' and repression, was in danger of 'blistering' and peeling away, for whatever reason, then I can easily imagine myself having this dream.

"In my version of the dream, the 'paint blistering' is an evocative picture of the 'bubbling up' of emotional 'heat' and 'moisture' that has been 'trapped below the cosmetic surface' of the collective, for-public-consumption story about my family of origin, and/or my current life as an adult. I imagine that each time I have the dream, I briefly touch *all* the pent-up fear and misery and frustration that I have not allowed myself to feel consciously, from my earliest childhood right up through a few days ago. If it were my dream, it would be about the revenge of these unlived, unexpressed emotions that I have habitually repressed since childhood."

Mary experienced a substantial, visible aha with this suggestion. At the same time, but unknown to the group then, she was also suddenly flooded with previously suppressed memories of specific incidents of physical abuse and emotional trauma from her childhood—memories that until that very moment had been completely forgotten.

As suggested earlier, one of the surest and most "objective" measures of the accuracy and success of a piece of work with a dream is this kind of spontaneous surfacing of previously forgotten and repressed material, whether it is previously unremembered dreams or recollections of waking events.

Several other people in the group also experienced ahas; they shared family backgrounds and personal histories sufficiently similar to Mary's so that the suggestions about "blistering white paint" and repressed emotions struck a chord.

Mary was distressed by her sudden recollections. Her distress was particularly poignant because, as the metaphor of "white paint" suggests so clearly, one of her strongest reactions to childhood traumas had been to attach immense importance to social respectability. Mary had also internalized an equally intense and complementary fear of social stigma and rejection. In fact, the deeply held value of social acceptability had been one of the primary, preconscious motivations for repressing the "unacceptable" memories of the traumatic events in the first place, for "whitewashing" them.

Part of the successful coping strategy Mary had developed as a girl had been to accept and internalize the adult fears that the family's social status would be ruined if anyone learned the family's private, guilty, abusive "secrets." She had also internalized the belief that any family member who let the terrible secrets "out of the bag" would be particularly "shamed" and "stigmatized"—more so even than the actual perpetrators of the abuse.

This kind of "exaggerated" sensitivity to shame and exposure is common in abuse victims, particularly where amnesia protects the individual from painful memories. In some sense, it appears to be a compensation for the lack of appropriate shame and sensitivity exhibited by the perpetrators of abuse in the original family drama. It is almost as though the compensatory sensitivity of the victim has an impersonal, shared, archetypal quality to it. In addition to serving as a personal protection, the extreme sensitivity of the victim also appears to be a means of preserving a kind of collective balance and sanity in the family as a whole, in spite of, and in direct proportion to, the lack of appropriate feelings and actions in other family members.

Even though Mary did not share any of the details of the terrible memories that welled up in her, the mere fact that other people were present when her lifelong amnesia started to lift was threatening and distressing for her.

On the face of it, it might seem that the upsetting result of the initial work with the dream did not serve Mary's "health and wholeness," but a deeper examination suggests that these repressed memories of childhood trauma were spontaneously pushing to come through into conscious awareness *precisely because she had grown and matured to a point where now she could face and successfully integrate and deal with this previously repressed material.* Each time the recurrent nightmare fragment of the blistering white paint came, part of its purpose was to bring her to a greater state of self-awareness, and in doing so, to release the mental-emotional energies that were being wasted in maintaining the repression.

In that sense, her lifelong history of the recurrent nightmare is a clear affirmation of Mary's inherent strength of mind and character; she had been capable of facing the terrible truths about her family, and her childhood experience, each time she had the dream.

Mary's original childhood strategy of banishing the specific abusive, painful incidents from her conscious memory was, I believe, an absolutely necessary and healthy act *at the time.* Without the amnesia, she might, in fact, have suffered dire consequences ranging from mental illness to death in the effort to escape the pain and desolation of her experiences. Severely traumatized and brutalized children who do not go amnesic often become ill or have "accidents." Sadly, my experience convinces me that many of the serious and fatal illnesses and accidents in childhood are often unrecognized forms of suicide and attempted suicide.

Amnesia regularly protects the traumatized child from such dire solutions. It allows the character and personality to continue to develop with at least a degree of health and normalcy, albeit with the "frozen" and "tabooed" areas of amnesic memory embedded like a cyst in the matrix of the developing personality.

However, the coping mechanism of amnesia can become a problem in adulthood. What began in childhood as a heroic and effective survival strategy becomes neurotic repression once the personality has developed adult strengths and capabilities. The very fact that it does become a problem demonstrates that the amnesia has served its protective purpose: the developing personality has, in fact, been shielded from the horribly disruptive and crippling memories and emotions of the traumatic experiences, maturing in a relatively healthy fashion.

To achieve their protective goals, the amnesia and repression have to remain unconscious and become habitual. To solve the subsequent developmental problem, when the formerly abused child has in fact matured to a point where he or she *can* "face the facts" without being crippled or overwhelmed, the dreams, in the service of health and wholeness, will always begin to offer increasingly dramatic and emotionally compelling metaphors of the repressed material. The dreams embodying the previously repressed material become memorable, clear, and often recurrent at precisely this juncture.

In general, my experience convinces me that recurrent dreams, particularly recurrent nightmares, come as much to affirm the dreamer's essential health, potential strength, and fundamental stability as they do to point to specific unresolved psychospiritual and developmental issues.

Sadly, this drama of recovering previously amnesic memories of childhood abuse in the dreams of adulthood is *very* common, even in the dreams of "normal" people. I am devoting this amount of space to a discussion of dreams that embody this theme because the likelihood of a person or a group coming across this archetypal drama in even the most casual examination of dreams is, alas, very great.

Emotional, psychological, physical, and sexual abuse of children is rampant and has been throughout history. Much of the time, when the stories of molestation and abuse come to light, the abusers were consuming alcohol and/or other psychoactive substances. In almost every instance, it also turns out that the abusers were themselves abused as children. The terrible cycle is perpetuated by the emotional scars of the former victims, and by the general belief that corporal punishment is a necessary and appropriate element in bringing up children, coupled with a blind conviction that children are "property" and "should respect their elders," no matter how those elders behave.

Violence, fear, and coercion through inflicting physical pain, and withdrawal of love, affection, and respect, are *always* counterproductive strategies in human relations. When these miserable coercions are inflicted on little, emotionally immature, physically weak people by big, strong, supposedly mature people—who are usually self-righteously angry or self-indulgently sexual at the time—they are *abominable*. They leave scars that incline the victims to become perpetrators of abuse themselves in later life or that drive them to self-destructive repression, madness, or suicide.

I hope to make it clear that even though surfacing amnesic memories of physical and emotional abuse and sexual molestation always warrant serious concern (and may even call for supportive urgings and referrals for further therapeutic work with a trained professional), they are also appallingly common. Because the dreams themselves are a reliable, self-regulating, and self-protecting phenomenon, the material and the memories that the dreams so often bring to consciousness can be explored with positive and profound results within the bounds of imagination and propriety in a lay-led or leaderless dream group, always provided the work is undertaken with a modicum of emotional sensitivity, basic intelligence, and authentic goodwill. In such situations, making use of the "if it were my dream" technique is even more important. For example, admitting that such a dream might be mine, even if only hypothetically, would allow the dreamer to consider the subject of his own dream indirectly, thus engendering in him a stronger chance at understanding it.

In Mary's case, the unexpected appearance of the repressed memories of childhood abuse led her to intensify the professional therapy she had already undertaken. She did not need to explore this further in the dream group. Eventually, she talked more candidly with her adult siblings.

It turned out that each one had been abused separately and had suffered in solitude and silence, supposing that the disturbing dreams and occasional flashes of horrible memories were "made up" or that he or she "had been the only one." When Mary found the courage to speak with her siblings (energy born directly out of her work with her dream in the group), they all experienced tremendous relief, along with shock, grief, sadness, and anger. Their darkest and most confused memories and intuitions were acknowledged and confirmed by other family members.

With these shared revelations, lifelong patterns of confused relating and neurotic avoidance of commitment and intimacy in Mary and other members of her family suddenly began to make more sense. As the amnesia and the denials were lifted through honest talk, the patterns of neurotic behavior in the whole family began to change.

This tendency of recurrent dreams to focus on deep life issues—the unconscious archetypal symbol-dramas, or "myths," we tend to live out, from childhood through to old age—is also demonstrated by the following disturbing recurrent dream:

> I am fleeing in absolute terror, running through a barren landscape, pursued by something so horrible I cannot bring myself even to look back and see who or what it is. I run flat out through the sand and rocks with the horrible pursuer right behind me until I come to a big, deep chasm that blocks my path of escape. A frail-looking rope suspension bridge hangs across the chasm. I plunge onto the swaying rope bridge with the thought that if I can just make it to the other side, I may be able to grab a quick look back and get a glimpse of who or what is pursuing me. But before I can get across to the other side, the rope bridge snaps, and I end up falling through space. This falling always wakes me up in terror, my heart pounding.

The dreamer, a man approaching middle age, whom I will call Harold, reported that this dream had come to him many times, at seemingly random intervals, throughout his life. His earliest recollection of the dream was from when he was about five years old, and the most recent was only a month or so old.

The dream group, made up of people drawn together by a strong shared concern for spiritual awareness and development, began by asking questions for clarification. During this initial phase of the group work, Harold said that he had been raised Catholic and had been particularly devout as a child, imagining that he would grow up to be a priest. When asked why he had not done so, he said he had become "disillusioned" with the prospect, largely because he doubted the spiritual validity of certain church dogmas and practices. When questioned further, he said that he would place the original disillusionment "at about five years old." He was surprised to realize this coincided with the first occurrence of the dream.

As the group began to explore the possible connection between the dream and Harold's evolving spiritual search, he noted that throughout his life, he had been seeking authentic religious experience. In particular, he had been searching unsuccessfully for a church or other religious institution to which he could devote himself with the same fervor and wholeheartedness that he had originally devoted his child self to the God of Catholicism. Each of his experimental forays into different religions and spiritual traditions had ended in new disillusionment as he became more intimately acquainted with the dogma and liturgy of the religious community and with the personal failings and hypocrisies of its leaders.

This account led several people in the group to the same projection at the same time. "If it were their recurrent dream," it might be a picture of the dreamer's life of religious search, with the "broken rope bridge" embodying the feelings of despair and desperation that attended each successive disillusionment. Harold's aha was dramatic. He was visibly excited and moved by these suggestions. Suddenly, the apparently "horrible" and "meaningless" nightmare that had plagued him since childhood began to reveal itself as a moving metaphor of the depth of the religious impulse in his life.

Both Harold's and the group's tingles and ahas started coming thick and fast. Suddenly, the horrible "unknown pursuer" began to take on the quality of Francis Thompson's "Hound of Heaven." The frail rope bridge revealed itself as the "suspension of disbelief"—all puns unconsciously intended—with which he entered into each new exploratory religious encounter. The "snapping" of the bridge became, at one level, the moment when his experimental suspension of disbelief could no longer be maintained. The dream revealed itself as an affirmation of both the depth and the pain of his unrealized religious longings.

The feelings in the dream mirrored the emotions of misery and despair that he felt each time the prematurely closed dogmatic systems of belief of each successive religious "franchise" failed to "sustain the weight" of his inquiring mind and search for reliable religious truth. What had seemed like a single feeling of "pure terror" now began to differentiate itself in Harold's internal experience. He began to detect multiple feelings simultaneously in his reliving of the dream. In addition to the raw fear and terror, he now became aware of longing, disappointment, misery, resignation, anger, bitterness, and even a shred of pride. These emotions had always been there but had been masked by the more dramatic "nightmare" feelings.

The trail of suggestions and aha's led Harold to an understanding that the roots of his complex feelings of misery and terror lay in child-hood at the time of his first exposure to the concept of "eternal damna-tion." This idea had shocked and disoriented him because it contradicted the deep and vibrant intuition of his childhood that God is loving and all-embracing.

As we worked, Harold came to see that the dream affirmed (by its recurrent nature as well as by its content) that his search for religious truth and commitment really was at the center of his life, no matter what other concerns and desires might take precedence from time to time. He suddenly grasped that in a deep sense, he chose to suffer the frightening emotions of the dream because of his unwillingness to give up his most deeply held spiritual intuitions and principles, even in exchange for the longed-for comfort of being accepted and embraced by an active and vital religious community promising sure "salvation."

Harold's emotional relief at this new understanding of his dream was profound and dramatically visible to all the rest of us in the changes in his facial expressions and body posture.

With this level of meaning verified so clearly by Harold's ahas, sev-eral people in the group began to explore the dream further, and to focus on the "desert" quality of the landscape through which the pursuit took place. Suggestions flowed about the possible connection between the "desert" setting of the dream and the "desert spirituality" of the early church fathers.

A large part of the legacy of "desert spirituality" in the patriarchal, Christian tradition has always been a refusal to grant full spiritual and social equality to women, a rejection of the physical world as "sinful" and "fallen," and a prohibition against spontaneous, pleasurable sexual expression. In contrast, the ancient "fertility religions" have always focused on intuitions of the Divine in feminine form, celebrated women's role in liturgy and worship, and offered physical sexual expression as an exalted pathway to the consciously felt sense of the presence of the Divine.

Several people in the group already shared a growing interest in these "Goddess traditions." Some of them began to suggest ways in which fem-inist theology, and the contemporary "rediscovery" of the Goddess and the feminine aspects of the Divine, might offer real alternatives to the "barren, rocky desert" of exclusively masculinist approaches to religious life that the overall background of the dream seemed to imply.

Many of the group members began to have ahas for themselves around the idea that the "barren and rocky" background of the dream might depict the preconscious assumption of patriarchal "spirit/body dualism." Some suggested that "if it were their dream," an implication embedded in the background of the dream would be that "finding water in the desert"—that is, opening to and embracing the more feminine/emotional aspects of the psyche—might profoundly alter Harold's spiritual dilemma.

For many of those in the group who shared this feminist theological perspective, accepting "the feminine" and the sensual experience of the physical body as full and equal partners in the intellectual search for religious truth was a mute but compelling implication of the dream as a whole. Following this train of thought, some suggested that the "unknown pursuer" might even be a woman, "invisible" because she has been rejected and despised by the official, patriarchal church and by Harold, who had unconsciously internalized this idea from an early age. Although Harold seemed to find these projections intriguing, he did not report any ahas.

As work continued, a few people started to focus on the repeated phrase "the other side" in Harold's narrative. It was suggested that what seemed at first glance like the most upsetting aspect of the dream—the suspension bridge's snapping and then Harold's "falling into the abyss"—might in fact be a metaphor for "not getting to 'the other side,'" that is, of remaining alive and *not* dying. Harold again experienced a strong confirming aha.

At this level, "falling into the abyss" turned out to be a metaphor for Harold of his ongoing existential uncertainty. For Harold, as for many in our culture, the unpredictability of life had produced anxiety equivalent to falling into the abyss. At that level, "catching sight of the pursuer" after "crossing over to the other side" was a metaphor for Harold's secret (preconscious) conviction that the dead are offered the opportunity to "see God" when they die, at least to the degree that they cultivated their spirituality while they were alive.

Right in the moment of working with the dream, Harold realized consciously that holding this belief did make him "long for death" from time to time, not just as a release from the pain and uncertainty of living, but as a way of satisfying his deep longing for spiritual certainty. Once again, many members of the group shared ahas of recognition at this suggestion.

There is a profound clue here, I believe, to the deeper, archetypal nature of the so-called death wish, which Freud called Thanatos. I believe it is a real element of the collective psyche, and that at one important level, it is an inevitable "shadow side" of authentic spiritual intuition and longing.

This dream is also another specific example of the archetypal truth that *in dreams, no matter how it appears, death is always associated with the growth and development of personality and character.* In this particular instance, the "death" that would result from actually being caught by the "unseen pursuer" reflects the death of old attitudes and preconscious assumptions about religious and spiritual possibilities. Such a dream "death" is the necessary precursor of rebirth into "new life"—in this instance, a richer, deeper, and more satisfying spiritual life in which the feminine and the physical are welcomed as spiritual guides and supports, rather than feared as enemies and stumbling blocks.

All of these interlocking layers of insight into the spiritual implications of dreams were strongly confirmed by Harold's own ahas. However, there remains at least one more major layer of implication in the dream that evoked major ahas in me, although at the time not in Harold.

I suggested to Harold that if it were my dream (and my life) the dream might be showing me that I had been severely abused, possibly even sexually molested, in childhood, probably beginning around the age of five, by someone in religious authority, possibly a priest or a nun.

In my version of Harold's dream, the endless fleeing and the fear that prevents me from "looking back to see who or what is chasing me" are both poignant metaphors of adult repression and amnesia of childhood molestation and abuse.

I suggested that Harold's repeatedly frustrated search for religious belief and community, characterized by "feeling betrayed" by the hypocrisy of religious communities and their leaders, might be a symbolic repetition of "betrayal" at the hands of childhood abuser(s). I act out the same drama again and again, in the vain, preconscious effort to "make it come out right," but without allowing myself to be fully aware of the traumatic sources of my compelling desire.

The deep emotions hidden from conscious self-awareness by my continuing amnesia about the abuse, but still active in my most important internal archetypal "myth," would be a major factor in my (hyper?) sensitivity to "betrayal" by adult institutional religions. To the extent that I remain unconscious of the full nature of my original abuse and "betrayal," I am unable to satisfactorily resolve my strong, repetitive, negative feelings about "betrayal of religious trust" in adult life. Unless I become more consciously aware of the amnesic childhood experiences that give symbolic shape to this "myth" that I am continually acting out, I am "doomed" to repeat it over and over again.

In the name of health and wholeness, I suggested, my dream comes repeatedly, in exactly the same form, to help me understand that there are crucially important unconscious aspects of this life theme that *have remained unchanged.*

In my version, the recurrent dream presents a poignant picture both of the amnesia and the emotional nature of the traumatic event(s) being forgotten. The question of "who or *what* is chasing me" adds a suggestion of a monstrous and inhuman (as well as divine) quality of my pursuer/ (abuser). The "religious" quality of the unknown pursuer—strongly confirmed by Harold's own ahas—also suggests people in religious authority (priests and/or nuns) to me. However, if my mother and/or father were particularly or neurotically pious and devout and were a primary source of my unusually intense religious ideas and feelings as a boy, then the dream image of the "unknown pursuer" would point directly to them as suspected abusers.

Ultimately, however, as the successive layers are peeled back, "my unknown pursuer" becomes an intimation of my own deepest unknown self, the part of my archetypal being that I have "forgotten," the answer to the famous Zen query "What was your face before you were born?" At this level, the "unknown pursuer" is linked not only to all the specific persons and traumatic events I have lost in my conscious memory but also to the crucial question What is my life's deepest purpose and meaning now?

In my version of Harold's dream it is the link between these two aspects of my ultimate wholeness that makes the repetitive dream, and the repetitive waking drama of the unfulfilled religious search, so all-consuming and compelling. One aspect of my potentially whole self has been "sacrificed" to the amnesia, and another remains unknown because it is my deepest, as-yet-unconscious and unrealized spiritual self. To become truly *whole*, I must become more aware of both of these. Each unconscious aspect (the repressed, "downward," amnesic, unique, and personal aspect, and the collective, transcendent, "upward" divine element) *requires* the other for me to achieve an authentic spiritual experience of the divine wholeness of my life. What began as a necessary protection, like the cocoon in which the caterpillar metamorphoses into the butterfly, becomes a terrible trap if I cannot break out of it and leave at the appropriate time. The more pervasive, extended, and nasty the childhood abuse, the stronger the cocoon of amnesia needed, and the more poignant and tragic if I fail to break free of it as an adult when I have developed the ability to "fly."

As suggested earlier with regard to Mike's dream of the "pastel colors," even if this projection of "hidden" meaning onto Harold's recurrent dream is nothing more than a reflection of my own as-yet-unsolved life issues, it still serves as a specific, confessional example of just how *impossible* it is to avoid projecting one's own symbolic material into the work with other people's dreams. Since Harold did not confirm any of these last suggestions with his own ahas, this discussion remains speculation. Even if being molested as a young boy by some person(s) in religious authority is not part of Harold's deep, hidden, unconscious "myth," it is still worth noting that such a history is likely to manifest itself in just such a fashion, both in dreams and in the recurring symbolic patterns of waking life.

Profound childhood traumas invariably exert a deep and lasting effect on the formulation of the child's "myth," his/her basic worldview, and overall emotional attitude. Since mind and body are intertwined, childhood traumas are regularly reflected in mental and emotional tensions, and in physical health and development. If a person's basic worldview and underlying emotional attitude are stunted, the body will tend to reflect those traumatic "deformations." In the name of health and wholeness, dreams that surface memories of childhood trauma will also regularly refer to the dreamer's physical condition and body image. As an individual develops emotionally and physically, his or her dreams will work toward healing and reframing both body and worldview.

The following dream, shared by a woman in her mid-forties is a dramatic case in point:

I am riding on a bus, sitting in the back. A big, dark, hairy man sitting in front of me turns around and starts to paw at me and touch me. Frightened and angry, I pull away from him and get up and go to the front of the bus to complain and ask the bus driver for help. The driver seems to be "on my side," but doesn't do much to protect me. I sit down on a strange little seat just behind and to the right of the driver. It faces off to the right, not straight ahead the way all the rest of the regular seats do.

When I sit down, I notice a couple, an older man and woman, sitting in the seat right behind the driver. The man is collapsed asleep with his head lolling back against the seat and his mouth hanging open. The woman sitting next to him is nodding and dozing and "out of it."

I also notice that I am now sitting on a bunch of old dresses on wire hangers. They are all in the style of the forties and fifties. I somehow know that they belong to the older woman who's dozing. They are making me uncomfortable, so I pick them up and try to hold them on my lap, but they keep falling off the hangers. Eventually, I become so annoyed by them that I stand up and dump them over a strange sort of "motor housing"—like the tubular canvas canopy that comes up over the cars in the old "caterpillar" amusement-park ride—that has now appeared running down the middle of the bus all the way to the back. The dresses slip down behind the housing so I can't see them anymore, and I sit down again.

As the dreamer, I will call her Sally, began to work with the dream, she had an aha that identified the "big, dark, hairy man" with her stepfather, a man who had in fact molested her repeatedly. This identification led Sally immediately to an identification of the "old couple" as her mother and natural father. Sally said that the old man's "passed-out condition" reminded her strongly of her natural father's particular "style" of alcoholism, and the "befuddled and out-of-it" state of the woman reminded her of her mother's denials and preconscious, co-alcoholic refusal to notice or acknowledge her first husband's alcoholism and, later, the abuse that her second husband was inflicting on her daughter.

These ahas clearly located one primary level of the dream in the psychological landscape of childhood abuse and recovery. Sally has been consciously dealing with her childhood abuse, and her own alcoholism, for some years. In that sense, poignant though the dream and her initial ahas were, they didn't seem to offer any new information or understandings. Sally and the other members of the group were already quite familiar with the abusive stepfather, the passed-out father, and the unconscious, denial-filled mother.

This apparent lack of new information led us all to look further, since no dream ever comes just to tell the dreamer what he or she already knows, particularly if that knowledge is already being acted upon, as was the case with Sally. Occasionally a dream will come to reiterate information the dreamer is already aware of, but only if he or she has forgotten it or is failing to take some necessary step from conscious awareness to concrete action.

Initially, the group focused on the old-style dresses in the odd little seat. Since they belonged to the "out-of-it" woman, an image of Sally's weak and codependent mother, then the "clothes in the style of the forties and fifties" might be metaphors for the conventional, passive sex-role stereotypes her mother embodied and attempted to "pass on" to her daughter.

Sally's confirming aha left no doubt about just how "uncomfortable" she was in the dream "trying to sit on the dresses." Conventional feminine sex-roles made her uncomfortable, and she refused to "sit on" her discomfort. Sally had consciously rejected passive, "feminine" behaviors a long time ago, in large measure because she had come to see how her mother and she had been victimized repeatedly by conventional ideas about "how a good woman is supposed to behave to support her man."

There was a brief exploration of whether the "coat hangers" possibly referred to abortion, and to the multiple connections between abortion and the paradoxes of the conventional, oppressive sex-roles of women in the forties and fifties. The work then moved on to the strange "canopy" that appeared in the middle of the bus, and the moment of dumping the offending dresses over to the other side of it, "out of sight and out of mind."

Sally had a visible aha that, at one level, the "canopy" might be a metaphor for the spinal column. Suddenly, a number of elements of the dream slipped into place, since Sally suffers from chronic, recurring lower-back pain. The work with the dream led to a series of spectacular ahas about the deep, preconscious relationship between this physical problem and the psychological/emotional scars from her being molested and abused.

In response to the abuse from her stepfather, and to the failure of her mother and natural father to come to her aid, Sally had "retreated into her head." In the dream, this is suggested metaphorically by her "retreat up the aisle" to just behind "the driver's seat." There, in the little crosswise jump seat, she adopts an alert and fearful stance, which Sally associated with her relatively bleak, suspicious, aloof, and cynical emotional outlook in waking life, and also with the way she habitually carried her body.

Working with this dream, Sally realized that her perpetually vigilant, slightly off-center, tense, and ultimately fearful *bodily* stance was a primary source of her chronic back pain. Corresponding to her slightly withdrawn and suspicious emotional stance—depicted in the dream as "sitting sideways, just behind the driver"—was the defensive/aggressive way she habitually held her neck and shoulders tense and off-center. The compensatory twist in her lower spine contributed dramatically to her chronic lower-back problems.

Suddenly the "dresses falling off the wire hangers" revealed another layer of meaning. The dresses "fell off" because the tension in her neck and shoulders (another layer of meaning embodied in the "wire(d) hangers") resulted in her habitually holding them "crooked." In "dumping" the oppressive feminine sex-role "styles of the forties and fifties," Sally had also shifted her physical center of awareness "to one side" (of her spinal column), favoring the right-hand, the conscious and vigilant, side over the left-hand, "weaker" and "more feminine," side. At one level, the dresses "kept falling off the hangers" because they were *supposed* to. She had rejected them and now held her body so that those "styles" could find no way to "hang on her."

All this was manifested in the habitual tilt of her head and shoulders—a bodily posture that, as a result of working with the dream, *suddenly came back into her conscious kinesthetic awareness, and consequently, back under conscious control.* Like Barbara's dream of "the silent basement party" (see Chapter 2), Sally's dream pointed simultaneously to physical health problems and to the deeper psychological reasons underlying them.

This dream and the work with it vividly demonstrates the intimate connection between mind and body; *the body and the dream are one,* and together they serve as the repository of *all* memory, whether it is recalled consciously or not.

In Sally's case, the ongoing task is to *remain consciously aware of* the way she has habitually held her head and shoulders, so that the ingrained habits of a lifetime do not simply reassert themselves unconsciously. Once the insight has been gained, the irritating back pain can serve as a reminder that the emotions are being repressed. In fact, there is theoretical reason to suppose that the emotional pain is "somaticized" in large measure to ensure that the pathway back to health and wholeness (through lifting the emotional repression and denial) will not be lost or forgotten. The back pain can trigger feelings of self-confidence and self-worth, and these new, adult feelings of self-worth can reinforce and be reinforced by the reduction of pain that accompanies the new kinesthetic awareness.

At another weekend workshop, another woman, I will call her Celeste, shared a dream that on the surface did not appear to have any dire childhood-abuse implications:

I'm with a bunch of other people in a field. I'm watching while they try to ride funny great big balloon animals. You know, like the ones people make at fairs and carnivals by twisting up those long, skinny balloons, only big—big as ponies—big enough to ride around on. The problem is they are all half filled up with water or something, so when you try to ride them, the water sloshes around inside, and they flop all over the place and don't go anywhere. It's funny. There's a split-rail fence right next to them all. I see it's all full of big splinters, and I'm afraid that if the people bump the balloon animals against the fence, they'll burst.

Celeste offered this dream toward the end of an emotionally and intellectually strenuous day when we had worked with several other people's dreams in the "talking circle." She said that she wanted to work with her dream using some of the "dream theater" techniques that I had mentioned during my introduction.

In this way of working in a group, all the characters, objects, and actions in the dream are divided up into "roles" and acted out by members of the group, under the direction of the dreamer. The dreamer can participate directly as a character—either as the "dream ego," embodying the perspective from which the dream was first experienced, or as one of the other figures in the dream—or can simply coach the action from the sidelines.

In this instance, Celeste had been a relatively passive observer in the dream, so she simultaneously "played herself" and directed from the sidelines, telling the others how to behave as the figures in her dream. Some people squatted down and joined hands to become "splintery fence rails," creating a boundary on the left side of the "stage," while the rest were divided into equal groups of boisterous "riders" and comically floppy "big balloon animals."

In such an exercise, the feelings and intuitions developed by the other group members as they enact the dreamer's scenario are as important to the work as the dreamer's own thoughts and feelings. Often, the deeper layers of meaning in the dream are unlocked by the feelings and ideas of the others.

As we began to act out the scene in playful good spirits, the tone slowly became ominous and somber. Our hilarity melted into surprised silence as it became increasingly clear to us all that we were acting out a rape scene in which the helpless "balloon animals" were the passively resisting victims being mounted and molested by boisterous (drunken?) sexual attackers. Celeste began to weep.

She confessed that she had thought the dream was playful and cheerful and thus "safe" and "not about that." Now that she saw it acted out, she realized that she had inadvertently invited us all into her "shameful" secret of having been repeatedly molested by male relatives on the ranch where she had grown up.

We returned to the circle and began to explore the dream again with the somewhat more gentle and less physical "if it were my dream" projective method. It became clear that the "water" sloshing around inside the balloon animals had at least two distinct levels of meaning. At one level, the "water" was a poignant metaphor for the unshed tears and other unexpressed feelings of rage, sorrow, and despair that were "sloshing around" inside Celeste herself, making it impossible for her to "get anywhere" in her waking life and relationships. At another level, the water represented the semen that had been released into her body during the incestuous rape(s). The number of "balloon animals" in the dream also turned out to be an accurate count of the number of times she had been molested.

At one level, the "splintery fence" was revealed as a metaphor of her abusers' warnings to her to remain silent. She had been threatened with

death and "worse" if she ever dared to speak. As a child she had internalized the fear that she would be "utterly destroyed" by the revelation of
these terrible events. In the dream, this took the form of the "balloon
animals" bursting, leaving only "a wet spot" and the tiniest, unidentifi-
able shreds behind. At another level, the "dangerous boundary" marked
by the "splintery fence" was also a metaphor of the habitual and preconscious prohibitions against trust and intimacy that Celeste had internalized and was continuing to place on herself and her actions and emotions
long after these events were over.

Many people in the group were frightened and upset by the sudden, unexpected turn of our work with Celeste's dream. I had to remind
everyone gently and firmly that in my experience, if we had not all coop-
erated to create a "safe and sacred space" where Celeste really felt secure
and respected, her unconscious would never have allowed her to expose
herself "accidentally" in this fashion. I suggested that it was important for
us all to live up to the promise of that trust, and no matter how upsetting
the material Celeste might share with us, we were in fact fully capable
of responding to it with strength and intelligence and sensitivity. At
Celeste's request we pushed ahead with the work on her dream.

The continuing *tone* of the group's work with Celeste and her dream
was of utmost importance. Celeste's dream brought the members of the
group closer to the deep wellspring of compassion and shared communal feeling that always lies just below the surface of even the most dismal and distressing situations. My experience is that these feelings are
always there to be called upon when needed. In a facilitated group, it is
clearly the group leader's responsibility in such moments to remind participants of their shared strength and compassion, but even in a leaderless
group, the healing energy of everyone's empathy and support will have
its positive effect, even if initially people are tongue-tied with surprise
and shock. That afternoon, we all took a metaphoric deep breath and ral-
lied to Celeste's support and gently continued to explore the dream.

The "dehumanized" image of the "balloon animals" as rape victims was particularly poignant to all of us as we explored it further. As
a child, Celeste had felt powerless and fragile. She had internalized this
vulnerability and the sense that she was worthless and "disposable." Both
of these internalized oppressions were given metaphoric shape in the
big, fragile, silly "balloon animals." At another level, the way in which

"balloon animals" are created—by being held and twisted into shapes that they then hold until they burst or deflate—was also painfully meta-phoric of both the physical brutality of her rape(s) and the "frozen" qual-ity of her emotions and her body after the fact. "Balloon animals" were also a poignant picture of the ways in which she had been "manipulated" into assuming that frozen, hopeless position.

As we continued to explore Celeste's dream, emotions in the room overflowed, and two other people consciously realized they had been abused and molested as children. These people too were upset, creating further strain on the group, but we managed to open the circle of caring attention and support to include them as well.

That evening when I finally got back to my motel room, I was momentarily overwhelmed with the thought that Freud must have been right. This kind of horrible sexual abuse of children simply *couldn't* be as appallingly commonplace as these increasingly frequent and dramatic experiences in dream groups suggested. Freud discovered repressed memories of sexual molestation and abuse so often that he concluded that it must be a universal childhood *fantasy*, later mistaken for an actual waking memory in adult life. Freud made it a foundation stone of psy-choanalysis that such memories were merely symbolic symptoms and confirmations of the "Oedipal drama" and did not indicate any actual physical abuse or trauma.

That evening, lying exhausted in my bed, I could understand emo-tionally why Freud had come to this conclusion. The personal and col-lective consequences of accepting that this destructive and cruel behavior is as common as the evidence suggests are pretty grim. But alas, it is the case, and I believe that we must face up to the emotions it evokes and to the work we must still do to expose and transform it.

Although a few hysterical people may wind up imagining that they were physically abused and molested, the confirming evidence—from other family members, social workers, alcohol and drug rehabilitation counselors, et al.—that the vast majority of such reports are authentic is overwhelming. Sadly, it now appears that this kind of abuse of children is so common as to be considered the norm rather than the exception.

Even where it is possible that the reports may be hysterical fanta-sies, the emotional urgency of the "delusions" indicates the dreamer did experience psychological abuse. Thus, even if one suspects that there may be an element of "hysterical fantasy" in the report(s) of molestation and abuse, the dream group, dream worker, or other helping professional(s) must still take the emotional cry for help as seriously as if the physical events were confirmed.

Recent work in the Freud Archives (Masson, 1988; Malcomb, 1989; etc.) strongly suggests that even Freud himself had deep misgivings about whether or not his clients were merely "misremembering" their childhood Oedipal fantasies as fact, and that he chose to make the assertion that they were because of his "broader" political and cultural (to say nothing of economic) concerns. All these concerns clearly reflected his fear that the infant science of psychoanalysis would be rejected and despised and ultimately crushed if it also had to take up the task of proclaiming just how pervasive child sexual abuse was as a fact of middle- and upper-class life.

The magic mirror of the dream does not lie, and the innumerable times that dreams have brought to the surface previously repressed memories of abuse and sexual molestation in childhood lead me to the sad conclusion that this is a terrible "fact of collective life." I also believe that the slow evolution of our collective social and psychospiritual development is actually addressing the problem, and that the increased incidence of surfacing memories may in fact be a collective indication of increasing health in our culture.

Just as we have succeeded in the past century in reducing the economic exploitation of women and children by establishing more equitable laws and labor practices, we are also starting to diminish the physical, emotional, and sexual exploitation of women and children in the home by increasing conscious awareness of domestic violence and child abuse.

The connections between domestic violence, child abuse, and the oppressions of sexism and ageism are multiple and obvious. I believe that dream work has a potentially crucial role to play in this collective transformation of society, as well as in healing the personal wounds and traumas of formerly abused children and abusing adults. Dreams regularly bring to greater awareness the crippling and counterproductive consequences of these preconscious attitudes and beliefs, both in individual experience and in society as a whole. As we understand more how these collective oppressions limit our awareness of the creative energies and possibilities of our own lives, our attitudes and behaviors change, and the collective oppressions themselves are altered.

The dream of a woman attending a weekend dream workshop, held in a convent for both professional religious and lay people may serve as a final example.

The first night of the workshop, the woman, whom I will call Julia, slept in the convent dormitory and had the following dream:

> I am standing in front of a closet. I see a black bug on a pretty, multicolored sweater. It is chewing holes in the fabric. I brush it off the sweater and it falls to the floor. At that point there is suddenly another woman standing next to me.
>
> She says to me, 'You know, that's not a bug, it's a *snake*—and if you keep watching, you ll see it turn into a snake."
>
> Sure enough, as I stand there looking at the black bug, it starts to grow and turns into a big snake with shiny scales. As the bug grows into the snake, the woman standing next to me starts to shrink down and turns into a pretty little girl.
>
> I know that the snake is out to get us, so I grab the little girl, and we dash into the bathroom and shut the door to get away, but as soon as we get inside, I realize that even the bathroom isn't safe, because the snake can crawl under the door.
>
> No sooner do I have this thought than the snake does crawl under the door and into the bathroom. I jump up onto a little stool to get away from it, but there isn't any place for the little girl to get away, and the snake slithers up to her and rears up and bites her.
>
> I see this happening, and I jump down and start to beat the snake off the little girl, so that it falls to the floor.

The following afternoon, Julia shared this dream with her small group, and before anyone else could ask her anything, she said she knew it was about having been sexually molested when she was a little girl—a new piece of information to her. She said that when she awakened, the meaning was clear, and that as she ate breakfast, and throughout the day, a number of previously repressed memories had surfaced one after another.

She also said she understood that spending the night in the convent had triggered the dream and the memory, because she now remembered that she had been sexually molested by a priest while she had been attending a Catholic boarding school. Sleeping in the similar surroundings and atmosphere of the convent with its attached girls' boarding school had brought it all back.

As we started to work with her dream, she also realized that a number of things "bugged" her in adult life strongly and emotionally because they symbolically echoed the repressed feelings associated with the abuse. She also had an aha that the "multicolored sweater" might be an echo of Joseph's "coat of many colors," and that working with dreams, as she was doing now, and as Joseph did in the biblical narrative, was where she could "watch" the "bug" reveal its true nature and turn itself into the "snake" (in the garden of innocence).

Over the years, I have been particularly struck by the dreams in which the dreamer observes this kind of metamorphosis all the way through from beginning to end "without blinking." It seems to me that this metaphor of actually observing the change from one shape into another is associated with particularly courageous and conscious self-exploration during psychospiritual growth and transformation.

A much more common experience is to "look away for a moment" in the dream, and when one looks back an instant later, the transformation has taken place. In my experience, this more common dream metaphor also shows psychospiritual growth and change, but that which has taken place beyond conscious awareness, and which reveals itself in the dream, and in waking self-awareness, only after most of the transformation has been accomplished "out of sight." This "offstage" dream transformation usually reflects serious introspective work in waking life.

As the group continued to explore Julia's dream, it also became clear that the molestation(s) had in fact taken place in bathroom(s). The dream reproduced her actual childhood flight to the place of supposed privacy and safety, and her newly surfacing memories revealed that the bathroom had turned out to be a *particularly* dangerous place because of its perpetually closed doors, and its "sanitary" isolation and seclusion from the rest of the school. As we worked, Julia became upset, but refused to call a halt.

I was deeply struck by Julia's strength and determination and her readiness to work with and face these repressed memories and the feelings that accompanied them. It was almost as though her dreams had been waiting for the opportunity presented by the workshop to make this leap into this new stage of self-awareness.

The "poetic justice" of having a Catholic institution sponsor the dream workshop that became the venue for Julia to "come out of the closet" with her repressed memories was not lost on her, nor on the rest of us. As we explored the image of the "closet" in her dream a little further, it became clear that it contained not just the amnesic memories of being molested but also the "multicolored" emotions and the creative energies and possibilities for self-expression that had been "locked in the closet" by her amnesia. Julia began to experience some of the physical surges of energy and well-being that often accompany the release of previously repressed material.

The decision to "open the closet" at the very beginning of the dream was clearly a picture of Julia's heroic decision to come to the dream workshop. At another level "opening the closet" also represented the decision to begin to explore her previously dormant creative impulses. At that level, the "multicolored sweater" was a picture of her creative energies and abilities, "hanging in the closet, unused." What had led her to sign up for the workshop was how much it "bugged" her that she didn't feel creatively engaged with her own life.

The act of brushing the "bug" off the "multicolored sweater" began to emerge as a mirroring or an echo of "beating the snake off the little girl," the archetypal wounded child within. This wounded child is always the one who carries the as-yet-unrealized creative energies and possibilities, and the decision to come to the rescue of the child-self invariably results in a release of vibrant emotional and creative energies in other areas of the dreamer's waking life. In Julia's dream, the order of the events appeared reversed. Her decision to deal with what "bugged" her—her pervasive sense of frustrated and unused creative potentials within her, which she desired to unlock—led her to come to the workshop. Participating in the previous evening's introductory discussion and sleeping in the hauntingly familiar setting helped to trigger her dream. The work with the dream then led to her encounter with her amnesic, wounded child within. Her spontaneous decision in the dream to overcome her fear and aid that hurt child part of herself also led to a dramatic release of her creative energies.

The image of the snake "rearing up" to bite the little girl turned out to be a vivid picture of the visual memory of being molested. The heroic decision in the dream to climb down off the bathroom stool and beat the snake off the little girl is also a metaphor of the decision to become conscious about the molestation, and to separate the anger and fear associated with the rape from the possibilities of creative expression held "hostage" by the personal/archetypal image of the wounded child. Old, repressed memories and emotions must be consciously acknowledged and *experienced* in order to clear the way for newer creative energies and feelings to emerge.

The "bathroom" image too emerges with another layer of significance, not only echoing the actual physical setting of the molestation but also pointing to the archetypal association between elimination and defecation and authentic creative/emotional expression. As mentioned elsewhere, there appears to be a deep symbolic association between creative expression and the bodily cleansing functions. With both, we have great freedom to choose when, where, and in whose company to "relieve ourselves" and "bring what is inside to the outside," but we also have no healthy choice whatsoever about whether or not to do it.

To live a healthy and whole life, what is inside us, the "digested" emotional and physical material that nourishes and sustains us, *must* be "brought out" into conscious expression, no matter how "nasty" or "noxious" we may have judged it to be. This must be done regularly, even if it is done completely in private and is shared with no one else. Therefore, Julia's dream might well have made use of the "bathroom" as a setting for the dream actions, even if it hadn't also been a reflection of waking events, because the activities of the bathroom are so deeply associated with "cleaning up our act" and the archetypal desire to live and act in a more freely expressive and creative fashion.

The common feeling in middle life that "something is missing" or that "there must be more than *this*" is often associated with encountering the prematurely closed boundary of creative thought and feeling that has served to protect and prolong some amnesia about childhood trauma. When these feelings of dissatisfaction and "formless" longing and discontent are also accompanied by dreams that point to guilty "secrets," the chances that a repressed, amnesic memory of child abuse is somewhere close to the center of the drama are great. Once again, if and when such feelings begin to surface, and such dreams begin to be remembered, the dreamer can be sure that he or she is actually "ready" and capable of absorbing and dealing with whatever the repressed trauma might be.

The dreamer can also be sure that the ultimate result of releasing the amnesia, and bringing the repressed memories and emotions to fuller conscious awareness will always include a renewed feeling of physical vitality and a reawakened sense of zest and creative possibility in waking life. The energies used to maintain the repression will become available for conscious, creative use in direct proportion to the release of the amnesia and repression.

The dreams of adulthood are always striving to bring repressed material to light, precisely and because each human being is now capable of far more than using his/her energies for continued denial and repression. There are forces inherent in the unconscious, forces that express themselves regularly in dreams, that are always pressing waking consciousness to evolve and express the possibilities of the individual organism and the archetypal creative impulse more fully.

*Chapter Eight*

# LUCID DREAMING AND SHAMANISM

> Last night, as I lay sleeping,
> I dreamt—marvelous error!—
> that a spring was breaking
> out in my heart.
> I said: Along which secret aqueduct,
> O water, are you coming to me,
> water of a new life
> that I have never drunk?
>
> Last night, as I lay sleeping,
> I dreamt—marvelous error!—
> that I had a beehive
> here inside my heart.
> And the golden bees
> were making white combs
> and sweet honey
> from my old failures . . .
>
> Last night, as I lay sleeping,
> I dreamt—marvelous error!—
> that it was God I had
> here inside my heart.

—ANTONIO MACHADO
[Translated by Robert Bly]

ny dream in the midst of which the dreamer has the clear
thought "Oh! I get it! This is a *dream!*" is said to be "lucid."
In a lucid dream, the dreamer recognizes more fully the true
nature of the experience *as it is taking place*, instead of the far more common experience of discovering only upon awakening, "Oh, it was all a
dream."

In the lucid dream state, the "awakened" dreamer can generate
amazing insights and release extraordinary creative energies. Old habits can be transformed energies can be mobilized and directed, problems can be solved and transcended, denials and repressions can be raised
to consciousness and withdrawn, and confusing feelings, emotions, and
intuitions can be clarified and harmonized. These things can also be
accomplished when working with ordinary remembered dreams, but in
lucid dreams, the healing work is often dramatically woven into and carried out within the dream itself, radically and "magically" extending the
range and possibility of dreaming experience.

For example, a man. I will call him Alex, reports:

I am fleeing from a frightening, fiery dragon through a scorched and
charred and still-smoldering landscape. I run and run, until the magical
moment of realization that this is all a dream! I suddenly "get it" that my
terror, and the pursuing monster, and the whole scene are simply things
that are happening in my dream. At that point, I turn and face the dragon
and demand to know what is it doing, chasing me around and terrorizing
me like this in my dream? The fire-breathing dragon stops and replies
telepathically, "I am your smoking addiction!" As the monster "speaks,"
I have an ironic appreciation of how appropriate and even funny it is for
my smoking addiction to appear as "a fire-breathing dragon."

In that moment of lucid realization, the dragon suddenly seems to
change. It doesn't really look any different, but its "expression" seems
to change. It begins to look winsome, almost charming—"Puff, the
magic dragon"—more like a big, old, familiar, friendly family dog than
a menacing, deadly fire-breather.

My lucidity allows me to look even more closely at the "transformed" monster, and I see clearly that there is nasty, sticky brown slime

covering its entire body, and that noxious smoke is oozing and sputtering from every orifice, even from around its eyes, and from under and between its scales. I smell this awful, rancid, repulsive odor coming from it. My revulsion returns, and in the dream I look at it and say with all my heart, "Get away from me! I no longer want you in my life!"

When he awakened, Alex was amazed to discover that he no longer craved the sensation of smoke in his lungs. Perhaps even more important, the desire for the instant and reliable sense of "companionship" that smoking had always given him was also gone. He has not smoked since the dream.

A crucial part of Alex's addiction to cigarettes was a fear of loneliness, and the accompanying desire for at least the illusion of control over this fear through the reliable gratification of "lighting up" anytime he felt lonely. His failure to recognize these dynamics appears to have been the main stumbling block to his "kicking the habit." The dream's compelling image combining both the negative and "positive" elements of the addiction allowed Alex to recognize these previously unacknowledged dynamics with full emotional awareness. The "fire-breathing dragon" suddenly appears like "a big, old, familiar, friendly family dog." Alex's decision that "I no longer want you in my life!" was made in such a way that it "stuck," because it was made in the face of the "old friend," with full emotional awareness of the "comfortable relationship" that was being given up.

In the lucid dream the appearance of the addiction as a "family dog" strongly implies that Alex's smoking habit may have been unconsciously fostered by his family and that he may have been predisposed to smoke addictively by watching and being drawn into parental substance addictions and emotional denials in his childhood. In any case, the illusory emotional security that smoking provided had to be *consciously* acknowledged in the dream before it could be *consciously* relinquished in waking life.

In my experience, spontaneous lucidity is associated with corresponding moments of "lucidity" in waking life. When a person realizes that his or her true circumstances are in fact substantially different from what he or she had always supposed, then a spontaneous lucid dream is likely. In such a dream, the true nature of the sleeper's experience—i.e., that it is really a dream—is recognized consciously, in a metaphoric reflection of the similar realization about what's really going on in waking life. Most often, this happens when a person withdraws a set of habitual projections in waking life.

When I withdraw a projection(s), I have come to realize that, despite what I have always believed, other people's thoughts and feelings don't shape my circumstances and cause me to feel the way I do. On the contrary, my own unacknowledged emotions, my unquestioned assumptions, and my limiting projections on other people create this repetitive situation and the feelings I always have in "response" to it.

For example, if I repress and consciously deny my feelings of anger and hurt, I inevitably project those energies onto others. I will experience those around me as angry, hostile, insensitive to me, and overly sensitive to their own feelings. As a result of this distorted perception, I will live in a constant state of frustration and depression, occasioned by how "unfairly" I believe I am being treated. When I suddenly realize that it is *my own* anger that is causing these feelings, and inflaming my interactions with others, there will be an accompanying lifting of my habitual mood in waking life. In the dream world, I will be able to experience lucidity, particularly regarding symbolic imagery associated with anger and injury.

The emotional aha of recognition with regard to my "true circumstances" in waking life is often accompanied by a corresponding aha of my "true circumstances" in my dreams—that I am, in fact, dreaming.

Spontaneous lucid dreaming occurs most frequently in recurring dreams, particularly recurrent nightmares. As the same dream unrolls in the same way, over and over, at some point the dreamer is increasingly likely to remember, "I've dreamed this before. . . . Wait a minute! I've *dreamed* this before—that must mean that this is a *dream* right now!" The recurrent dreams have come in the service of raising repressed energies to greater consciousness. When denied feelings have been of long duration and the source of recurrent, repetitive dreams and nightmares that focus on the struggle to make them more conscious, the dreamer is increasingly likely to experience spontaneous lucidity since that becomes the most evocative and compelling symbolic expression of the basic healing purpose of the dream.

Alex's "fire-breathing dragon" dream may have been a repetitive dream of this sort, and the "magical moment" of recognition that it was a dream that he reports may have resulted from the preconscious realization "Wait a minute, I've dreamed this before!" Anybody trying to quit smoking is likely to dream about the ongoing struggle, whether those dreams are remembered at the time or not. In my experience, even unremembered dreams can serve as a trigger to lucidity. The surfacing in memory of previously forgotten dreams is a reliable indicator that the main issue(s) the dreams are addressing are becoming increasingly conscious in waking life as well.

In the West, the collective realization that a "lucid" state of enhanced conscious self-awareness while dreaming was even possible is relatively new. Hervey de Saint-Denys wrote in 1865 about his discovery of his ability to "dream on, knowing he was dreaming." He coined the phrase "lucid dream" to describe his experience, but his work has languished in relative obscurity for more than one hundred years.

General interest in lucid dreaming has been growing rapidly in the industrialized West over the last three decades. This interest was initially spurred by the reprinting of Kilton Stewart's seminal essay "Dream Theory in Malaya" (see Appendix I), which inspired a whole generation to begin to explore the possibilities of lucid dreaming for personal growth and communal living. Later, this general interest was further stimulated by Stephen La Berge's pioneering work at the sleep laboratory at Stanford University, which proved that lucid dreaming is a skill that can be taught and that lucid dreams can be observed and confirmed by scientifically trained outside observers.

In the Far East, however, lucid dreaming has been a focus of intense and sustained attention for more than nine hundred years. For centuries, Hindus, Buddhists, and particularly Tibetan Buddhists have seen in lucid dreaming a spiritual discipline of the highest order of importance. This is because many of them believe that the experience of the discarnate soul after death is exactly the same as the experience we call dreaming when we are alive.

The notion that sleep is like "a little death" and that dreaming is like the experience of the soul after death is clearly an archetypal idea. It can be found in the religious and poetic traditions of almost every people. For example, a traditional saying among the Plains Indians of

North America is that "to die is to walk the path of the dream without returning." *From this archetypal perspective, changing one's fundamental relation to the experience of dreaming always holds the intriguing promise of changing one's relation to death itself.*

In the Buddhist tradition, the central story is that after his life of renunciation, austerity, meditation, and intense spiritual search, the former prince Siddhartha Gautama of the warrior-caste Sakya clan decided to focus his consciousness in deep meditation until he penetrated to the heart of the mystery of life. Buddhist sacred scripture relates that he seated himself beneath a bodhi (or bo) tree and entered a meditative trance, vowing not to break his concentration until he understood fully.

The spiritual force of his meditation was so great that the demons of desire and delusion sensed it directly. They realized that their vast empire was about to be conquered and overthrown by Gautama's efforts. In a last-ditch effort to distract the meditating man from his cosmic purpose, the Demon King, Mara ("illusion"—a masculine form of *maya*), assembled an army of fearsome demons—war, hunger, pestilence, plague, thirst, famine, drought, misery, anger, fear, illness, uncertainty, violence, loss (to name only a few)—and assaulted Gautama's mind and body simultaneously, accompanied by howling storms, lightning, thunder, tidal waves, terrible earthquakes, and volcanic fire.

In the midst of his meditative state, Gautama did not flinch, because he realized that all the horrible demons and cataclysmic events were simply apparitions—emanations of his own undisciplined thought forms. He refused to stir or feel any fear or revulsion at the horrific appearance of these "demons," remaining in a state of kindly calm as they attacked him. In some versions of the story, the force of Gautama's meditations transforms the horrible weapons of the attacking demons into flowers as they are hurled at him. The weapon-flowers fall gently in sweet profusion at his feet, becoming offerings of love and gratitude from Nature and the Earth herself for the gift of universal salvation that Buddha offers.

Mara, frustrated and filled with terror himself at the failure of his concerted attack, changed his strategy. Now he called on his incredibly beautiful and seductive daughters—lust, intelligence, passion, desire, falsehood, acquisitiveness, power, attachment, revenge, skill, and dissatisfaction—and sent them to beguile the young man into abandoning his meditation. But once again, Gautama saw that they too were

merely projections of his own mental energies, mere shadows of pleasure, "images in a dream," rather than the true joys of communion with
the Ultimate. Once again he was unmoved as he contemplated them,
remaining expansively calm.

In this fashion, the former prince penetrated consciously to the
center of the true nature of reality and achieved enlightenment. From
that moment on, he became Gautama "the Fully Enlightened One"—
Gautama "Buddha." As a result of this spiritual achievement, he also
became known as Sakyamuni, "Wise One of the Sakya Clan," and
Tathagata, "Master of 'Suchness' (the One True Reality)."

This story of how Buddha achieved enlightenment is at the center
of all the myriad forms of Buddhist teaching and belief, just as the story
of the crucifixion and resurrection of Jesus is at the center of the many
varieties of Christian practice and conviction. The man Jesus becomes
"Christ," "the Anointed One," by virtue of his experience and transcendence of the suffering on the cross and of death, just as the man Gautama
becomes "Buddha," "the Enlightened One," because of his experience
and transcendence of suffering and the fear of death under the bo tree.

The parallels do not end here, but for purposes of exploring the
ancient Asian tradition of lucid dreaming, this brief synopsis should be
sufficient to demonstrate that both Buddhism and Christianity resonate
with many of the same archetypal energies, address many of the same
psychospiritual questions, and employ fundamentally similar metaphors,
albeit with the differing cultural accents of East and West.

For several centuries, Buddhists all over Asia have understood that
one of the most significant aspects of this central teaching story is the clear
parallel between the Buddha's meditative self-discipline and archetypal
self-realization under the bo tree, and the relatively rare experience of
the dreamer who recognizes in the midst of the dream that the seemingly
real and compelling events he/she is experiencing are only "emanations
of his or her own thought forms." Thus, lucid dreaming, the recognition
that the dream *is* a dream while it is taking place, becomes a concrete
psychospiritual discipline for the "imitation of Buddha" that parallels the
"imitation of Christ" in the Western tradition.

This spiritual understanding that "awakening" in the midst of dreaming is the primary means to enlightenment is shared by many Buddhist

sects (such as Ch'an, Shingon, Tendai, Zen, et al.). In many of these traditions this understanding leads to a belief that all living, and life itself, "is but a dream" and has "no true substance." This is the origin of the Buddhist theologica_ assertions that "all is void, and without substance, like a dream." For many Buddhists, this is not simply a poetic analogy but an absolutely accurate, technically sound, diagnostic statement of the human condition. For this reason, the ability to become more conscious and self-aware in the "dream state" (understanding that for many Buddhists, this includes all of waking life as well) is the single most important spiritual discipline that can be undertaken.

In the tantric and Tibetan traditions of Hinduism and Buddhism, this general belief that dream and waking are one and the same at the core (in that they both acquire their feeling of urgency and drama and reality from the unconscious projection of the individual's own thoughts and emotions) is extended to include a detailed analysis of the experience of the "entity" (what Christians tend to call the "immortal soul") after death.

Like the Plains Indians and many others, the Tibetan Buddhists believe that when a person dies, he or she enters a dream and does not awaken. The shape and structure of the after-death dream of the discarnate soul is archetypally determined. He or she "goes down a dark tunnel into the light" and is greeted by the images of people, usually loved ones and family members, who have died and "gone before." Once the dreaming soul makes the transition into the light, he or she experiences whatever specific forms of "heaven" he or she has been prepared by the life just ended to expect. Many Westerners having near-death experiences have described similar images.

A Roman Catholic experiences "welcome into the communion of saints." A Protestant might arrive in a land filled with cloud forms and be issued robes, a halo, and a harp. A devout Moslem man may be transported to a delightful cookout with great food, wonderful music, and satisfying sex. (What "heaven" is like for devout Moslem women is less clear). A Buddhist is transported into an experience of the layer-cake heavens of Mount Meru, or Amitabha's "Pure Land," where he or she basks in the divine presence. These postmortem "dreams" of the discarnate soul, whose specific imagery is determined by the cultural expectations instilled by the life just ended, are called "bardos," or "bardo worlds," by the Tibetans.

However pleasant these after-death bardo experiences of heaven may be, they are not eternal. In fact, say the Tibetans, they last only about forty earthly days. Toward the end of the prescribed forty days (in itself an archetypal intuition, reflected in the religious beliefs and ritual mourning practices of many different peoples around the world), the bardo world begins to become worn and frayed and starts to disintegrate. The food starts to rot; the fountains dry up; the weather turns bad; the musicians go home; the sun begins to go down, red and menacing; evil-smelling winds begin to blow the leaves off the trees; and in the horrible gathering dusk and rancid smoke, *demons appear.*

These "bardo demons" are likened to the demon armies of King Mara, and the devout Buddhist is admonished to "imitate Buddha." The spiritual task of each discarnate soul in the bardo world is to do again what Buddha did—to remain meditatively calm and *inwardly unmoved* by the horrifying attacking demons, just as Buddha did underneath the bo tree.

This is, in fact, the whole point of the *Bardo Thodol,* the so-called *Tibetan Book of the Dead.* It is a long prayer designed to *remind* the discarnate soul that the apparently real and compelling experiences it is undergoing in the bardo world are "just a dream" and that *all* the joys and terrors of the postmortem existence are exactly like dream images. Over and over again, the *Bardo Thodol* reiterates: "Remember, O Nobly Born [in some traditions, the names and nicknames of the deceased are inserted here], all that you see and hear and feel *are only emanations of your own thought forms.*" The discarnate soul is believed to be still vaguely attached to the body and still able to hear little bits of what is said in the presence of the corpse, so the *Bardo Thodol* is recited over the body—for the full forty days, if the deceased or the grieving family can afford to hire the chanters and preserve the physical remains for that long—to improve the chances that the deceased will remember that the bardo experiences are ultimately illusory (just like the experiences of waking, incarnated life, say many Buddhists). In the postmortem bardo realm, as in waking life, the achievement of final oneness with the Divine, or "nirvana," to use the ancient Sanskrit technical term, can only be accomplished by overcoming the attraction and attachment to the illusory dream joys and splendors, as well as the fear of the illusory dream demons.

The problem is, say the Tibetan Buddhists, that the vast majority of people lose their meditative calm and detachment when they are faced with the pleasures of the "bardo heaven," or later when they are assaulted and pursued by the "dream demons" of the bardo world. People flee in terror, in exactly the same way that most people flee in terror from the monsters and demons in their nightmares when they are alive.

Here is where the so-called "laws of karma" become exquisitely refined and precise. The bardo demons are "dream figures" created by the discarnate soul's own fears, regrets, and "sins." Like the figures in a dream, they represent unlived, unfulfilled, or ignored, violated, and suppressed aspects of the dreamer's own psyche. The "demons" embody the "sins" of the departed soul exactly and precisely, just as a person's nightmare images exactly embody the dreamer's own unlived life and unacknowledged memories and feelings.

In this way, the deceased is "judged" for his or her "sins" and condemned to a particular rebirth with exquisite justice and precision. However, the "karmic judgment" is not actually handed down by any external authority (even though in the bardo/dream it may appear that way), but is instead accomplished unconsciously by the "dreamer," in the same way that dream images are created while we are alive.

The worse the "sins," the more horrifying and terror inspiring the bardo demons. As the demons attack, the discarnate soul begins to flee in terror through the disintegrating landscape of the bardo, seeking with increasing desperation for some escape or sanctuary. Somewhere in this horror-stricken flight, so the doctrine goes, the fleeing soul realizes that the only relief from the inexorable demonic pursuit will come through seeking "refuge" by slipping between two creatures while they are mating. The fugitive soul slips between the couple in the midst of their sexual embrace, and *bam!*—the karmic trap has snapped shut and the soul is reincarnated again. The fugitive soul has escaped one set of demons but fallen into the hands of another, back on the wheel for another go-round in another body. (It is worth remembering that the "carn" in "incarnation" is the same as the "carn" in "chili con carne"—to be incarnated is to be made out of meat.)

If the "sins" of the life just passed are *really* bad, then the bardo demons who embody them will be *really* bad—so bad that the fleeing soul may not even hold out for human parents. The soul may slip in terror and desperation between the first mating pair of armadillos or cockroaches or whatever he or she comes across, just to escape the horrible pursuers. This is how, say the Tibetans, a life of particularly heinous sins may result in reincarnation in a "lower," nonhuman form. This is not, as the old Hindus say, because the "lords of karma" render a judgment and command it, but rather because the discarnate soul condemns itself unconsciously and inevitably to its own unique dream.

However, most people's "sins" are not sufficiently horrible to overcome the natural human revulsion toward incarnating in a lower animal form. The discarnate soul flees through the bardo searching with increasing desperation for a human couple in erotic embrace, and thus do the vast majority of all human beings on earth come to be born, say the Tibetans. The shining possibility of nirvana is lost, and the soul blunders and stumbles into incarnated life again, driven by terror and the failure to grasp the true dream nature of the bardo experience.

The newly reincarnated life offers the opportunity to grow and develop spiritually, and it again provides the chance to realize that all the attractions and repulsions of life and afterlife are shadows and dreams. This cycle of life, suffering, death, and rebirth repeats endlessly until the soul achieves enlightenment. It was to relieve this cycle that Buddha entered his heroic meditation under the bo tree.

For orthodox Hindus, nirvana, the complete union of the seemingly separate individual consciousness with "the ultimate ground of all being," including its own, is the highest spiritual aspiration and achievement. Overcoming fear of the bardo dream demons allows the discarnate soul to "reunite with God" (in Western terms) and get off the endless wheel of attraction and fear and successive reincarnation.

The Buddhists reformed this ancient Hindu theology, just as Christians reformed the more ancient theology of Judaism. As part of that "revisionist" reform, the Buddhists, and particularly the Tibetan Buddhists, say that there is an even higher spiritual calling than the achievement of nirvana. Like Christianity, this "higher calling" involves consciously embracing, embodying, and living out the archetype of Willing Sacrifice.

If the discarnate soul can face the bardo demons with unruffled calm, like Buddha, then the threshold of nirvana, "total union with the Divine," opens up, with all its transcendent joy and bliss. At this point the discarnate soul has full, free choice, and the Buddhists say it is an even higher spiritual calling than merging with the Divine to relinquish voluntarily the bliss of nirvana and *choose* consciously to reincarnate for the specific purpose of easing the suffering of other, unenlightened beings, still trapped in "samsara," the illusory world of painful, frightening physical/historical reality (which is actually a dream).

The entities that make this choice are called "bodhisattvas," those on the path to Buddhahood who sacrifice their own salvation for the relief of the suffering of others. The bodhisattva renounces the joys of nirvana and instead of fleeing into reincarnation blindly and in terror, chooses consciously, and with love, the life he or she will live, selecting a life that will be of particular service in spreading enlightenment and "alleviating the suffering of all sentient beings."

To make and keep the so-called bodhisattva's pledge, or vow, is the highest spiritual act in the Tibetan Buddhist tradition. In it, the devotee swears to renounce nirvana each time the opportunity presents itself and instead chooses to reincarnate again and again "until all sentient beings are enlightened." The most important meditative discipline that supports this pledge is the cultivation of what is now being called in the West lucid dreaming, the ability to recognize while a dream is in progress that it is in fact a dream, and to act accordingly.

The leaders of the Tibetan Buddhist tradition—the Dalai Lama, the *karmapa*, and all the various *tulkus* and *rimpoches*, et al.—all claim to have unbroken memories of several of their most recent earthly lives and bardo experiences between reincarnations. Each "order" of Tibetan Buddhists preserves the biographies and bardo stories told by previous leaders and believes that its current leaders are reincarnations of the specific bodhisattvas named in their sacred texts and chants. The current Dalai Lama, for example, is believed to be a reincarnation of the Bodhisattva Avalokiteshvara, "the Bodhisattva of Complete Compassion."

As a practical matter, this "lineage transmission" is accomplished by monks leaving their monasteries and searching among all the baby boys born forty days, plus nine months, after a great reincarnated bodhisattva has died. The monks charged with this search watch their own dreams for indications of where to look, and they seek a child exhibiting the traditional physical signs of the reincarnated bodhisattva. These signs are many and varied. One of them is said to be a particular spiral swirl of hairs just where the eyebrows meet above the nose.

If the monks discover more than one child with the required birthmarks and other confirming signs, terrible schismatic disputes are likely to break out. Many of the competing orders of monks in the Tibetan tradition trace the histories of their separate organizations back to schismatic disputes over whether or not this process of finding the right baby was carried out correctly at some point in the past. Another example of this archetypal idea that great souls reincarnating anew exhibit physical and other more subtle signs by which they can be recognized by initiates, even when the child is very young, is Annie Bessant's public identification of the young child Krishnamurti as "the avatar of this age"—a title he later politely refused when he reached young adulthood.

In the Tibetan tradition, the child that is observed to exhibit the "sacred signs" is then removed from his parents and raised by the monks on a steady diet of lucid dream incubation rituals and other spiritual exercises, along with traditional accounts of the earthly and bardo "biographies" of all the previously recorded lives of the bodhisattva of whom he is supposedly the latest incarnation. Then, when the child's education is complete and he has committed all these traditional stories to memory and demonstrated his spiritual powers in other ways, he is asked to recount the story of the most recent bardo journey. This story is then added to the tradition that will be taught to the next child "exhibiting the signs" at birth nine months and forty days after the bodhisattva's latest death. And so the tradition continues.

This tradition has been operating for almost a thousand years and shows no signs of fading away, although since the invasion of Tibet by the Communist Chinese and the dispersal of the various Tibetan religious refugee communities to places such as Australia, England, Canada, and the United States, there is now a great and growing controversy within the refugee community of believers about whether or not girl children should also be examined for the "sacred signs," and whether or not the traditional bodhisattvas might now be preparing to reincarnate as women in these new social and historical circumstances.

Given this system of belief, and the strength, resilience, and ritual complexity of this tradition, it is understandable why such emphasis

should be placed on the ability to dream lucidly and why so many concrete techniques to promote lucid dreaming have been developed in
Tibetan Buddhism.

One of the simplest and most effective of these techniques may be
rendered as follows:

### Tibetan Lucid-Dreaming Incubation Exercise

I lie down in my sleeping place.

I focus my intention to be aware in my dreams that I am dreaming.

I hold this conscious focus of intention calmly, without either urgency
or inattention.

I lie on my left side, knees slightly bent.

I hold my hands, palms together, under my chin, fingertips touching
my left cheek.

I visualize a glowing, self-luminous blue lotus bud inside my throat,
centered behind and slightly below my larynx. I visualize this bud
slowly opening into full blossom.

As it opens, I visualize the "seed syllable," "aum," written in glowing, self-luminous, white Tibetan calligraphy (ॐ) resting
in the center of the lotus blossom, slowly revealed by the opening bud. As I visualize this, I imagine the corresponding sound:
"ommmmmmm . . ."

[In the Hindu-Buddhist tradition, "aum" is believed to be the first
sound, analogous to the "word" that was "in the beginning" in
Judeo-Christian scripture. It is from the "aum" that all vibra-
tional forms—that is, all seemingly separate physical and spiritual
reality—are born anew and afresh in each passing instant. Visualizing and mentally re-creating the sound in this fashion dupli-
cates the beginning of the cosmos and (re)creates the world of my
dreams consciously.]

I continue to visualize the image, imagine the sound, and maintain the
posture, holding my calm intention to enter the dream world fully
awake and self-aware . . . until I discover that I have fallen asleep
and am now dreaming.

I find that this technique regularly produces lucid dreaming, even if the
dreamer does not believe in the Tibetan Buddhist theology that inspired

it. Some evidence suggests that a committed believer is even more likely to succeed. Using techniques of this sort, it is possible to pass from fully awake consciousness into the experience of the dream with no discernible loss of self-awareness, and of course, to retain the full realization that the dream *is* a dream as it transpires.

Many effective techniques for incubating lucid dreams have originated in many different cultures. Don Juan, the Yaqui Indian shaman, instructed the anthropologist/adventurer Carlos Castaneda to "set up dreaming" by reminding himself, each time he catches sight of his hands in waking life, that the next time he sees his hands in a dream, he will *remember* that it is indeed a dream. The Buddhist and tantric practitioners who use almost exactly the same incubation technique recommend that each time the would-be-lucid dreamer catches sight of his/her hands, he/she should utter the equivalent of a Christian "ejaculatory prayer" and say, "Look! I *am* dreaming!" As this association between catching sight of one's hands and the realization that one is dreaming becomes habitual, lucidity is achieved with increasing frequency in the dream world. Both Don Juan and the tantric Buddhists agree that the hands are not particularly magical in and of themselves but that the dreamer is more likely to have a body in the dream than not and that he or she is therefore more likely to catch sight of his/her hands than any other one "cue" or "trigger image" that might be selected.

The contemporary laboratory dream researcher Stephen La Berge has developed an effective technique that he calls MILD (mnemonic induction of lucid dreaming). His technique, like Don Juan's, also emphasizes memory. He has discovered, and many others have verified, that it is often easier to *remember that one wants to be lucid* as a first step, or "trigger," to becoming lucid. He recommends reminding oneself at both regular and random moments during the day that one does indeed want to remember the desire to be lucid in the coming night's dreams. The steady repetition of this intention does regularly have the desired effect in sleep of the dreamer's remembering the desire to be lucid, which in turn produces lucidity.

Each of these techniques, and many more besides, has been demonstrated to work well in the experience of many different dreamers. Different attitudes and temperaments may be drawn to different incubation techniques at different times. Most people achieve lucidity spontaneously from time to time throughout their lives. As suggested above, the most usual context for unstudied, spontaneous dream lucidity is the recurring nightmare.

At such moments, some of the profound advantages and benefits of lucid dreaming become clear. Like the Buddha under the bo tree, the lucidly "awakened" dreamer can transcend the fear and confusion in the dream. "This is a *dream*; that means that I don't have to be afraid! My physical body is not here in the dream the way I thought it was; it's safe asleep in my bed. I don't have to be afraid of this dream experience the way I always have been." It was just such a spontaneous, lucid, "Buddhist" realization that actually allowed Alex to turn and face the fearsome "dragon" and quit smoking in the dream discussed above.

In a nightmare, the lucid dreamer can overcome fear and continue with the dream instead of simply "escaping" by waking up, which is the most usual response to a nightmare. The lucid dreamer who stays in the dream can turn to the pursuing demons and confront them. One of the best strategies is to ask the seemingly menacing and hostile figures or elements in the dream what they are up to: "What are you doing here in this dream? What do you want?" (just as Alex did). If a dreamer can gather his or her wits together sufficiently in the lucid state to ask a question of this sort, he or she will always be rewarded with an answer. Most often it will be an answer of profound importance to the dreamer's waking life.

Here, the Buddha's one-line summation of his message, "Fear not," takes on new meaning. In the context of meeting and responding to the archetypal symbol dramas of both dreaming and waking life, Buddha's "Fear not," Jesus' "Love your enemies," and Apollo's "Know thyself" all reveal themselves as different ways of saying the same thing.

Awake and asleep, loving my enemies and knowing myself require letting go of fear; to let go of fear requires increasing self-knowledge and the discovery of love in myself for my enemies (both within and without, for they reflect and create one another); to know myself, I must release my fear and meet my enemies with an open heart. Each admonition is a practical prescription for achieving the same essential state of simultaneous internal and external creative, dynamic psychospiritual balance and harmony. This state of dynamic balance and creative harmony is often achievable in the midst of a lucid dream, if the dreamer can only remember that is what he or she desires.

Some contemporary Western dream theorists have become concerned in recent years about the current upsurge of interest in lucid dreaming. They fear that the practice of incubating lucid dreams may "poison the well." They worry that the self-deceptive waking ego may consciously manipulate and attempt to "control" the dream, thus stifling the natural wholeness and health-promoting quality of the dream. Although this may seem like a reasonable and fairly sophisticated concern, in my experience, the concern is mistaken and exaggerated.

The concern that lucid dreaming may be dangerous is a species of hubris and self-deception in itself, resting as it does on an unexamined and unquestioned assumption that the conscious mind is inherently superior to, and stronger than, the dream. This is simply not the case. The presence of ego consciousness in the lucid dream does not alter the fundamental function of the dream state itself. The lucid dream ego (the "me character" in the dream who realizes he/she is dreaming) is secondary to the dream itself. The dream remains autonomous and is *not* under the *control* of, or at the disposal of, the conscious will. The archetypal elements that are the foundation of the dream are so much older, so much wiser, and so much stronger and more subtle than even the most disciplined, habitual lucid consciousness that "control" of the dream state is simply impossible. At best—and it is pretty good!—all that lucidly dreaming ego consciousness can do is increase conscious *influence* in the dream.

Some of the concern expressed by academic theoreticians has been provoked by the exaggerated claims and rhetoric of popular promoters of lucid dreaming who regularly promise that if you buy their books or listen to their training tapes, "you will learn to control your dreams!" In my view, this is simply false advertising since *control* is impossible; *increased influence* is all that can be achieved, and it is a much more interesting and valuable accomplishment than "control" would be, even if it were possible.

The stories that are offered as "proof" of lucid "dream control" almost invariably focus on turning and facing down and overcoming the monsters and other pursuers in nightmares. Alex's dream of the "fire-breathing dragon" is an example of this kind of "control." Reading that account, the reader might assume that Alex's lucid ego "took control" of the dream and determined the positive outcome, both of the dream itself and the subsequent waking-life success in quitting smoking. However, it seems clear to me that the story of Alex's dream, and all the other similar lucid-dream stories of overcoming monsters, are more properly understood as examples of the lucid dreamer's *cooperating* with the dream's energy of ultimate health and wholeness rather than controlling or manipulating it

Even before he became lucid, Alex's dream was trying to get him to turn and face the "hidden" issue(s) of his smoking addiction. When he became lucid and did confront his pursuer, he was not "hijacking" his dream and "controlling" it, he was in fact *cooperating more consciously and fully* with the original healing and consciousness-raising "intent" of his dream.

If a lucid dreamer uses his or her lucidity simply to avoid a monster or a problem in a dream, it is my experience that the dreamer will then inevitably meet the same or a similar situation again, either later in the same dream, or in a subsequent dream. The multitude of lucid-dream stories that come from the Tibetan and other Asian traditions suggest that no matter how dedicated and skilled the lucid dreamer, the dream remains autonomous and defies counterproductive manipulation and control. There are even stories in the Asian and Western mystical traditions of skilled and dedicated groups of lucid dreamers in concerted telepathic rapport who delude themselves that they are controlling the course of their shared dream, only to discover that the dream has used them for its own purposes.

If the lucid influence of the "awakened" dreamer on his or her dream is ultimately in harmony with the deeper nature and purpose of the dream, as Alex's was when he turned and faced the "fire-breathing dragon," then the dream ego may *appear* to "take control," but only because, like an aikido artist, it is in ultimate harmony and cooperation with the deeper energies and meanings that exist below the surface of appearance in the dream.

If the dreamer insists on using his or her lucidity in a trivial or misguided way, then the dream will either simply ignore and override the lucid intervention, something that happens far more often than the promoters of "franchised" lucid-dreaming techniques ordinarily care to admit, or the dreamer will simply awaken, having, in effect, "made an appointment" to meet the central drama or issue of the aborted or mis-used lucid dream again in some subsequent dream.

In this important sense, lucid dreaming is not that different from ordi-nary dreaming; the dream brings information to the dreamer's attention, but how he or she responds is still up to conscious reflection and deci-sion. Deluded and misguided decisions may regularly be made, even by people who have succeeded in becoming lucid in their dreams, but this is a further reflection of self-deception and denial, not a comment on the dreams themselves. (For further exploration of this issue, see Chapter 10.)

In avoiding self-deception and premature closure of creativity in the world of lucid dreaming, the skills and insights of the ancient shaman have proven reliable.

The basic "theology" of shamanism around the world is always the same: *everything is alive.* The spirit entities and energies that animate all things must become known and named in order to interrelate with them more consciously and fully. Academic anthropology has given the derog-atory name *animism* to this spiritual worldview and has categorized it, and the liturgical and ceremonial practices that accompany it, as symp-toms of an "infantile" and "primitive" stage of organized religion and psychospiritual development.

However, as a statement about the true nature of the dream world, "everything is alive" is a highly sophisticated and absolutely correct anal-ysis. In the dream, everything *is* alive, whether it appears to be at first glance or not. This is the essential "animistic" truth at the heart of Fritz Perls's Gestalt approach to dreams: everything and everyone in the dream is a living representation of some aspect of the dreamer's total being and psyche. Even the supposedly "inanimate" machines and chairs and tables and rocks and earth and clouds and ground itself in dreams are alive and articulately conscious, if I only have the wit and wisdom to turn to them and speak to them with courage, openness, and respect.

In Gestalt work with dreams, the dreamer reenters the dream and reimagines and reexperiences the dream from the subjective points of view of other characters or figures in the dream. In these exercises, even the stones and the trees, conscious and self-aware, will speak with the "shamanic" explorer, offering startling insights, reframed interpretations of the action of the dream, and deeper understanding of the waking life dramas that the dream reflects and shapes.

The lucid dreamer needs to remember that everything in his/her dream is alive. The life in all dreams, and in waking experience too, for that matter, is a blending of the individual's own personal vital energies with the larger life of the archetypes and the cosmos itself.

There is an archetypal intuition that one life force animates all. Such a view of the dream world is not only ancient shamanic wisdom, it is also in absolute accord with everything we know about psychology and are learning from the continuing laboratory exploration of the biology and chemistry of dreaming.

The "animistic" worldview if applied to the waking physical world, can have a positive and profound effect on ethical behavior, overcoming fear and anxiety, and informing a satisfying emotional and spiritual rapport with the "synchronicities" and other manifestations of archetypal patterns that appear in our everyday lives. This psychopolitical fact alone should make "animism" worthy of closer and more serious examination. When it is also understood that contemporary scientific research is approaching this same ancient archetypal idea from another quarter, there is even more reason to reconsider it.

There is increasing reason to suppose that this "primitive" worldview may also be the most accurate and sophisticated scientific hypothesis as well. The so-called "Gaia hypothesis" proposes that the earth itself appears to behave like an immense living organism that regulates its planet-wide metabolic activities with large-scale ecological mechanisms that parallel and mimic (and may be the original paradigm for) the homeostatic, self-regulating metabolic activities and systems of individual animals and plants. This hypothesis may be seen as a revival of the ancient matriarchal agrarian theology of the earth as the living body of the Great Mother, which in turn grew out of the hunter-gatherer "animistic" theology of shamanism.

Contemporary physics and cosmology tell us that every atom of the physical universe was apparently first born in the undifferentiated heart of the "Big Bang" that now appears to be the most likely origin of the universe. As Carl Sagan puts it, we are all "star stuff." The fact that some of those undifferentiated and supposedly "inanimate" atoms formed organic molecules and evolved over the millennia into all the living things on the planet (including me sitting writing this, and you reading it) suggests strongly to me that the most useful way to view those atoms may be that they were *alive* (or at the very least carried the potentiality of aliveness) all along.

The distinction between "animate" and "inanimate" upon which modern science has rested for four hundred years appears more and more to be a distinction between obvious and subtle. There are those organized collections of atoms with relative speedy metabolisms that are obviously and observably alive, and then there are those organized collections of atoms that seem to have slower metabolic rates that up till now we have mistaken for "inanimate," when actually their life is simply too slow and subtle to be observed with our short attention span.

For the practicing shaman in a nontechnological culture, such a suggestion is only stating the obvious. No one can get a verbal answer from a stone or a star with our limited waking ears. But in the timeless world of the dream, the healing trance, and the collective myth the "subtle" spirit energies that are the life of rocks and water and wind and stars can be touched and communicated with. Viewed as an expression of basic human consciousness, "animism" begins to echo with Carl Jung's formulation of the "archetypes of the collective unconscious."

One of my own lucid dreams may serve to illustrate a lucid encounter with archetypal energies.

I was traveling, facilitating a weekend workshop in group dream work and staying at a private home, when I dreamed:

> I enter the room where I am supposed to be staying carrying my bags. I am mildly surprised to discover that it is huge, with a high ceiling crisscrossed with steel beams like a big empty warehouse. There is a folding cot/bed, a straight-backed chair, and a standing lamp, all grouped together in the center of the room. These are the only objects in this huge, empty space. The tall, industrial, "wrinkle-glass" windows on all sides of the room let in diffused light that reflects dully off the expanse of polished cement floor.
>
> I trudge over to the center of the room, set my big bag down on the chair, sit down on the bed, and put my smaller bag down on the bed

beside me. I am quite tired, and I want to lie down, but I am wearing my three-piece "preaching suit" and I do not want to get it wrinkled. I am annoyed that there doesn't appear to be any place to hang up the suit when I take it off and change into more casual and comfortable clothes.

Suddenly, a door on the far left corner of the huge room opens and two "janitors" come in, dressed in greeny-brown coveralls, and pushing wheeled buckets ahead of them with their mops. "Oh!" I think to myself. "So much for privacy! This is intolerable!"

I stand up and prepare to meet them. I decide there is no point in hassling with them. I will just have to get back to my "hosts" and tell them that I won't stay in a place where people can walk in on me unannounced at any time.

As the two "janitors" approach, I notice that they are both Asians—not just Asians, Tibetans. They draw nearer and we make eye contact. I suddenly understand that they are not just "janitors," they are refugee Tibetan Buddhist priests, men of tremendous learning and personal authority in the Tibetan religious refugee community who are working as janitors.

Or are they? I suddenly get the clear idea that this janitor business is a disguise—a kind of "test." Will I be able to recognize them for who and what they really are, despite their industrial coveralls and janitor's tools?

Not only am I sure that they are important Tibetan religious leaders, I suddenly understand that I am *dreaming!* I control my mounting excitement and ask myself, What do I most want to do in this dream, now that I am aware that I am dreaming?

I turn to them and greet them telepathically. "Welcome! I understand that I am dreaming and that you are figures in my dream." They both break into broad smiles, and I notice that one of them is slightly younger than the other, but they are of the "same rank," and that the relationship between them is one of complete ease and equality. I gather that they are from different, "competing" lineages, the Red Hats and the Yellow Hats, and that this cooperation and ease and friendship between them is quite extraordinary.

I want very much to ask an important question of these exotic wisdom figures in my dream—what do I most want to know? How can I phrase my best question in this moment, avoiding the pitfalls of unintenional ambiguity that I know from experience will result in losing lucidity and ability to participate consciously and creatively in the dream.

"Please tell me," I ask telepathically, "how may I best enhance and deepen my relationship with the Divine, without diminishing conscious self-awareness?"

They both laugh appreciatively. I feel a sense of accomplishment—this is the best question I can think of to ask with my whole being in this moment.

The older man tells me, telepathically, "Make a perfect altar according to our tradition."

I feel a wave of disappointment. I have read a treatise recently in waking life—a gift from my Tibetan Buddhist–devotee half-sister—about the elaborate ritual preparation of an altar in the particular "Vajra-yogini" practice she follows. I remember the basic points, and I know that I could do it with the book in front of me, but I am disappointed at what seems to me to be a mechanical and ritualistic response to my query, which I had hoped would elicit much more from my dreaming self. Why is my dream giving me such an unsatisfying response to my best question in this moment?

My attention is suddenly drawn over to my right, and I see that there is now a fully and beautifully prepared Tibetan ritual ceremonial altar standing in the middle distance in the huge room.

I am amazed—it wasn't there a moment ago, and now it is there, with every detail of offering and ritual utensil correct and perfect. I laugh. I understand that these two figures have helped me reach into my memory for the specific, detailed information gathered and stored from reading my sister's gift book, and they have helped me to project and manifest this "perfect altar" in the dream. I realize that I also have a detailed memory and understanding of the subtle and multiple symbolism of each implement and element, and also of the overall design and significance of the altar as a whole. I am very pleased.

With this rush of pleasure and understanding comes an even more deeply felt sense of the nature of this dream. I realize with deepening surprise and excitement that I have made a mistake. I look back at the two men and think/say, "Thank you! Thank you for helping me. I'm sorry. I didn't realize . . . I now understand that you aren't just figures in my dream; you are archetypal figures. You have a reality independent of me and my dream. Thank you for visiting me and manifesting in this dream in this way."

As I address these thoughts to them, they both smile back even more broadly. I now realize that they are no longer dressed in their janitor's coveralls, and I am no longer in my three-piece suit. All three of us are now dressed in full ceremonial Tibetan robes "for the impersonation of celestial beings." Each of us is also wearing a traditional helmet/hat with metal "rays" or "petals" radiating upward and outward around a sort of segmented central spire like a pagoda. I understand that these ritual headpieces focus the energy of the cosmos in our minds and bodies through the subtle harmonics of their shape and structure.

We are now standing, each facing the altar, one on each side, with the fourth side framed in a beautiful diaphanous cloth backdrop. We somehow "enter" the altar together, each moving toward the center from his respective side. The dream continues, but in such a way that I have no words or images to convey it.

This was and is a very satisfying dream for me. The lucid awareness that the two dream figures were "archetypal" and have a reality independent of me and my dream, and yet were right there, full and relational figures in my dream, was and is quite moving. The most frustrating part of the dream is also the most exciting—the point of "entering the altar," which in some sense I know to be the world of the archetypes themselves. The feeling is of concrete physical forms as well as even more real, nonphysical forms that have their most authentic existence beyond the surface of appearance and that are indeed in some sense the source of all appearances. Being able to interact personally with these figures, knowing that it was a dream, is something I cherish and continue to find fascinating.

At another fundamentally related level, the dream is also a playful confrontation with evolving shadow issues in my personal psychospiritual growth. To this day, I remain deeply and fundamentally suspicious of all religious and secular authority, particularly authority that is founded on esoteric dogma or on any kind of specialized knowledge or information not easily or immediately available to everyone. At the same time, however, in order to pursue my life as a dream worker and community organizer, and to write books for other people to read and learn from, I have to admit to myself that there is legitimate authority that stems from knowledge and experience. In order to embrace my own calling, I can no longer reject all external authority as potentially illegitimate or ignore the maturing of my own authoritative experience, as I once did.

The admonition from the dream priest to "build a perfect altar according to our tradition" symbolically sums up the ambiguity of this shadow drama of authority for me. The solution, as always, requires me to know myself, let go of fear, and embrace my "enemy" (the "illegitimate authority") with love and respect and wholehearted enthusiasm. The dream offers me an opportunity actually to do this—to trust my own character and unconscious processes, including the multitude of things in my memory that I cannot call up immediately by an act of conscious will. In this sense, the dream offers me another opportunity to deepen and extend my knowledge of my own creative possibilities and in so doing to move past the shadow "door guards" of my suspicions and mistrust of myself and other "authorities" and to move closer to the wellsprings of the archetypal creative impulse in my life.

When I first recorded this dream in my journal, I consistently "misspelled" the word *altar* as *alter*, emphasizing unconsciously the pun level of the dream referring to the necessity of "altering" my attitudes and behavior. For me, the "Tibetan monks" are a particularly charged and ambiguous image of "illegitimate spiritual authority." Recently, the head of one of the Tibetan refugee monastic communities in the U.S. knowingly infected several of his devotees with AIDS, and I am very much aware of the shadowy role certain Tibetan priests had in advising Hitler and others high up in the Third Reich. At the same time, I am also very drawn to the ways in which certain archetypal religious intuitions and philosophical ideas are given elegant and compelling and psychological sophisticated form in the Tibetan tradition. For these reasons, the image of "wise Tibetan monks" who make "rigid, ritualistic demands" is a particularly apt image for my own ongoing struggles with the issue of authority in my life.

The unfolding of my creative possibilities requires me to embrace this shadow of "esoteric authority" and consciously honor and make use of the understanding that grows out of my years of study and experience. My fear is that I will misuse my authority, as I have seen so many others do. The irony is that unless I admit and consciously embrace my own authority, I will *inevitably* misuse it in some unconscious, projected fashion. Embracing one's skills and abilities is often even harder than acknowledging one's foibles and failings.

The testimony of male and female shamans from around the planet, from all periods of history, suggests that the encounter with the "spirit world" has always felt and seemed much like my experience of this dream. The "spirits" always give gifts and offer playful but ultimately serious challenges to grow in wisdom and courage simultaneously. They always appear in multiple disguises and engender a sense of being in the presence of entities and energies that are beyond the limited sense of individual self, even when those disguises are penetrated. In this way, the "eternal" archetypal encounter in lucid dreams with the energies of the collective unconscious often rediscovers the basic insights and metaphors and "reinvents" the specific techniques and strategies of ancient shamanic spiritual practice.

The experience of a shaman is always revitalized by contact with nature in an unspoiled and undeveloped state. However, unless the energies awakened in this encounter are applied to the realities of the contemporary technological/linguistic world, the "shamanic revival" is only another means of self-deception and denial and withdrawal from the arena of responsible creative encounter, possibility, and change.

The true shamanic tradition is open and adventurous. It is *more* conscious, complex, and multidimensional than ordinary "rational" dealing with life, not *less*. It is a practical worldview that acknowledges the archetypal patterns of the collective unconscious as pragmatic realities. It embraces the vision and the dream as practical means of communion with real energies greater than the ego. The true shaman, in nontechnological societies as well as in modern industrial settings, is always more open to new technologies and ways of doing things, new social relationships, and new ways of framing and conceptualizing experience than his or her more conventional neighbors. True shamanic exploration is the exact opposite of "superstition" because it always remains open and nondogmatic, regularly searching beyond the known and the socially agreed and accepted, not acknowledging conventional wisdom as the limit of the possible.

To substitute the conventional wisdom of nontechnological societies for the conventional wisdom of our own culture is the ironic antithesis of the authentic global shamanic tradition. Too much of the contemporary shamanic revival involves embracing the theatrical trappings of traditional shamanic praxis without grasping the fundamental pragmatic point: everything is alive, and the more I know about and commune with that life, the greater the range of creative possibility I will be able to imagine and manifest. This is as true of dealing with the subtle symbolic energies of automobiles and computers as it is of dealing with animals and "illness spirits."

While I was working as a senior therapist at St. George Homes, Inc., a Berkeley, California, residential treatment program for schizophrenic and autistic adolescents and young adults based on Jungian therapeutic principles, I had the following dream:

I find myself floating in a dim, gray, undefined space. "Eric," one of the most violently disturbed boys in the program, appears before me, laughing and rolling his eyes in his most withdrawn and "crazy" mode. I watch him for a long time, and as I watch, I begin to see his aura. It is a strange pinkish color and extends out around him on all sides for about fourteen to twenty inches. It undulates slowly and changes shape, like a cloud of gas. As I watch, I also notice that there are strange black "spindles" or "spikes" sticking out all over him. These ugly black shapes are about a foot long, about half an inch wide at the base, where they attach to his body, and taper evenly to nasty, sharp-looking points.

I feel terribly tired and have a great desire to go to sleep. As I struggle with my fatigue, I have the thought that there is no point in falling asleep because I am already asleep . . . I'm already asleep and this is a dream.

Now that I am aware that I am dreaming, I look at Eric even more carefully. Is he "just" a projection of my own injured, "crazy kid" side? Yes, I am dreaming, so he must be that, but even while I formulate this thought clearly, I keep having the feeling that he is more than that. . . .

My exhaustion is increasing, and even though I am lucid, my mind seems to be fuzzy and slow. Why is my dream offering me this image of Eric with these ugly black spikes imbedded in his aura? What health and wholeness is this dream promoting?

I realize that whatever layers of meaning this dream may carry, the spikes are ugly and look as though they don't really belong there. I have the ironic thought "What's wrong with this picture?" and I decide that no matter what these "spikes" are, I had better remove them. I will myself to move forward toward Eric and tell him telepathically that I am going to "uproot" the spikes from his aura. I am surprised at my spontaneous choice of the word *uproot* in the dream.

As I begin to pull the spikes out of the aura with my dream hands, I realize that the word *uproot* is appropriate. I have to pull them out, rather than simply breaking them off, because they seem to extend below his skin for an inch or so, and I have the clear idea that if the "roots" are not totally removed, the "spikes"—whatever they are—will simply grow back again.

I finally succeed in pulling out all the spikes I can see, front and back. I am tremendously relieved to have completed the task. I give in to my feeling of exhaustion and let go of the dream and allow myself to fall away from Eric into the blackness.

In itself, the dream is not terribly unusual. All of us who worked at St. George Homes dreamed about the kids in our charge quite often. The relatively deep therapeutic work we did with the schizophrenic and autistic adolescents on a daily basis inevitably brought us face-to-face with our own unresolved emotional dramas, transporting some of us to the edges of our own psychospiritual boundaries, as well as bringing us closer to our most creative and transformative energies and possibilities. One of the inevitable results of this deeply stirring therapy was that we staff members regularly dreamed about healing "the kids" as a metaphor of our own internal growth and healing.

However, one of the things that makes this dream more compelling than many of the other "healing the kids" dreams, particularly with regard to lucidity and shamanic praxis, is an event that took place the following day.

The next morning, I was walking down a tree-shaded street in North Berkeley, going from one of the residential treatment houses to another, in the course of my regular work, when I caught sight of Eric walking down the street toward me in the company of a residential treatment staff trainee. As soon as he caught sight of me, Eric broke away from his staff attendant and came rushing full tilt down the sidewalk toward me.

I felt an immediate flush of fear. From my experience with Eric, I expected an unprovoked and violent onslaught. I stepped back off the cement sidewalk onto a lawn and prepared to receive and neutralize Eric's imminent attack as best as I could. To my surprise and relief, however, Eric careened to a stop just inches from my face and only shouted at me.

"You stole something from me last night!" he said angrily. "Give it back!"

I had not yet had a chance to tell anyone, even my wife, about my dream that morning, and I experienced a rush of surprise and disbelief when Eric accused me of "taking something from him last night." The trainee ran up and hung around nervously just behind Eric.

"I was asleep at home in my own bed last night," I said.

"No! You took something from me last night!" Eric continued, refusing to be put off. "Give it back!"

Although "participating in the patient's delusions" is discouraged as therapeutic practice, it has always seemed to me that emotional honesty and authenticity is an even more important element of therapy than theoretical purity, and since I did have a feeling that I had "taken something" from him the night before, I decided to pursue the conversation carefully.

"Okay. Tell me, what did I take from you last night?"

"I can't remember . . ." Eric replied, "but I know you took something! Give it back!"

"How do you feel?"

Eric seemed taken aback by the question. Eric was not ordinarily either willing or able to say anything at all about his feelings, but that morning he looked surprised, then replied, "Okay—I feel okay."

"Well, that's pretty unusual, isn't it?" I said, taking advantage of the sudden change in the tone of our conversation. "So, maybe what you lost last night isn't something that you really want back."

We looked at each other for a long moment. This was also unusual and surprising, since Eric ordinarily refused sustained eye contact with anyone. Then he nodded slowly, eyes still meeting mine, apparently convinced by my reply to just stay focused on the surprising new awareness of "feeling okay" and not pursue the issue of his "loss" any further.

"Yeah," he said with uncharacteristic calmness and clarity. "Yeah, maybe you're right." And with that he turned to his staff companion and they walked off together down the street.

This may seem like a story implying "magic" and "superstition." It is certainly the kind of experience that shamans from around the world have reported as evidence that their craft is effective and worth pursuing. It is also the kind of subjective dream experience that can be expected when one explores the dream world in a consistent and increasingly conscious fashion over time, particularly if that exploration includes regular sharing of dream memories with other people with whom there is some depth of emotional involvement. Depth of feeling and authentic emotional connection are the opposite of "superstition."

The reader may dismiss my apparent cross-dreaming with Eric as mere chance, or luck, but that is not how I see it. I suspect that that event, and the many others in my years of dream work, are a result of cultivating and consciously inviting intuition in the search for the aha of recognition of "hidden" symbolic significance beneath appearances.

Assuming that Eric was responding to a dream that depicted me taking something from him, it seems reasonable to me that Eric's dreams might well have used my image as an identifying mask of the part of his own psyche that was actually capable of healing some of his intrapsychic wounds. The program at St. George Homes was carefully designed to evoke such healing projections and "transferences" from the clients onto the staff, and in this instance, our efforts may have met with some success.

It also seems reasonable that I may have been sufficiently attuned to Eric's progress in therapy to be preconsciously aware that this transference was taking effect, and that he was on the threshold of some integration of his dissociated personality. This assumption seems more than casually born out by his uncharacteristic control of his habitually volatile and physically violent behavior, and his willingness to make and sustain eye contact throughout our conversation.

Under these circumstances, I might well have had a dream of "healing Eric" in part to bring this unconscious observation of his increased readiness to engage in new, more appropriate behaviors closer to the surface of my therapeutic awareness. It also seems reasonable to imagine that at precisely the same moment, he might well have been dreaming of my image performing a symbolic act of healing that felt to him like "theft" of his old habitual "crazy" responses.

In any case, I can say with certainty that my dream helped prepare me to be open to interact with Eric on the street in a positive way and with a positive outcome that was unusual for him and that seemed to have some lasting positive effect on his behavior.

I also know that something that might as well be called telepathy happens in dreams on a regular basis (see Chapter 3) and that this phenomenon links individuals across "bridges" built of emotional relationship and the strength of their respective emotional responses to similar symbols. In this instance, the emotional connection between Eric and myself, and our shared emotional focus on therapy and "healing" (symbolized in my dream by "removing ugly black spikes from his aura" and in his dream by my "stealing something from him"), makes me suspect that there was indeed a genuine element of "shamanic" telepathic cross-dreaming woven into this connected set of dream and waking experiences as well.

Dr. D. T. Suzuki, early in his efforts to bring the religious philosophy and meditative practice of Zen Buddhism to America, gave many lectures in Los Angeles. One evening, so the story goes, he spoke for about an hour and a half and afterward took questions from the audience. A young man spoke up and said, "I've been listening carefully to you, and I haven't heard you offer any definition of this 'enlightenment' you keep talking about. Could you please tell me what you mean when you use that word?"

Dr. Suzuki reportedly shook his head in frustration and said, "If you can ask me such a question, you have not understood a word that I have been saying. 'Enlightenment' is beyond verbal definition. It is an experience. It can only be apprehended directly through sustained meditative practice."

The young man would not be put off so easily, however, and pressed his question. "Yes, I understand, but some sort of definition would help me think about where even to begin looking in my own experience. I honestly don't understand what you're talking about, and I really would like to."

Once again Dr. Suzuki demurred and said words to the effect of "Read my lips: no verbal definitions of 'enlightenment'!"

The young man was particularly persistent, however, and pressed his question a third time. "Dr. Suzuki, I'm an American, and we Americans like to have definitions of things so that we can think about them clearly. If you really want to spread your ideas on this continent so that they will take root and grow, you're going to have to give some sort of answer to questions like mine sooner or later. So, granted that there is no such thing as an adequate verbal definition of 'enlightenment,' could you please tell me what sort of an answer you might give if you were going to answer the question?"

Dr. Suzuki became very grave and replied, "Young man, I'm not sure if you realize what you have just done, but in the lineage I come from, it is the tradition that if the student has the courage and tenacity to ask a question three times in the face of the teacher's refusal to answer, the teacher is then obliged to respond. So, even though I am afraid that my answer may mislead you more than it will help you, I will give you a definition of 'enlightenment.' I would say that 'enlightenment' may also be understood as *habitual intuition*."

Alan Watts related this story when similarly pressed to answer the same question. He added a comment to the effect of "Misleading though it may be, 'habitual intuition' remains the best definition I can think of. And you know, one of the things that means at a practical level is that to most uninitiated observers, 'enlightenment,' and what happens in the enlightened person's life, *looks like luck*."

One of the reasons I believe so deeply in exploring and sharing dreams is that in seeking the aha of recognition, the intuitive faculties are exercised and attuned. Sooner or later, the inveterate dream worker discovers that the intuitive aha of recognition of significance becomes more conscious and reliably available, i.e., "habitual," in waking life as well. Working with dreams can claim to be an authentic "spiritual discipline" because it regularly increases "habitual intuition" (which, in turn, also has this curious tendency to "look like luck").

On grounds of preconscious observation and therapeutic intuition alone, Eric's and my cross-dreaming can be seen as quite meaningful, far beyond mere "luck." However, I must admit that the high incidence of this kind of "cross-dreaming," and the other "shamanic" dreams and experiences of this sort I have had over the last forty-plus years, also leads me to keep a very open mind with regard to the reality of what has traditionally been called telepathy, and its role in "shamanic healing."

Even if my dream did not prepare me for the unplanned therapeutic encounter with Eric on the street, it is still a picture of the ongoing effort to heal and transform the "crazy kid" elements of my own psyche. I know that Eric's image appeared in my dreams in part because I identified with him and his emotional symbol dramas, since they were a grotesquely exaggerated parody of my own. I also know that if I am actually engaged in some of my own healing in relation to those dramas, I am going to be a better therapist to other people trying to accomplish the same or similar things.

It is ancient archetypal wisdom that "only the wounded can heal." All over the planet, the "gods of healing" are themselves sick and wounded. The therapist or counselor who is actively and creatively engaged with his or her own psychospiritual growth and reconciliation will also be of great use to others. In my experience, those who are not, are not. As Carl Jung was fond of saying, "People learn from who we *are*, rather than what we *say*, and to believe otherwise is a disease of the mind."

My experience over the years convinces me that whenever the dreams of a therapist/counselor and his/her clients "overlap" in this way, or indeed, whenever people dream about each other, it is meaningful and ought never to be dismissed as "mere coincidence." Such "coincidences" are clearly at the heart of the archetypal phenomenon Jung called synchronicity (an acausal but deeply significant relationship between seemingly chance events). The native shaman or shamanna also perceives such synchronous events and believes that they result from closer communion with the "spirit energies" that animate all things. I am increasingly convinced that these are simply different ways of talking about the same thing.

The concepts, vocabulary, and insights of the ancient shaman are of particular value because they raise intuitive awareness, personal courage, and the awareness of beauty to the same importance as abstract theory and rational thought. I know from experience that personal energies of this kind are of the greatest significance in growing and releasing the creative energies in my own life. I also know that these "personal" traits and energies are profoundly effective in nurturing healing and transformation in others as well.

*Chapter Nine*

# DREAMING AND THE EVOLUTION
# OF THE ARCHETYPES

*The archetype is a kind of readiness to produce over and over again the*
*same or similar mythical ideas . . . when an archetype appears in a dream,*
*in a fantasy, or in life, it always brings with it a certain influence or power*
*by virtue of which it either exercises a numinous or a fascinating effect, or*
*impels to action.*

—C. G. JUNG

The "archetypes" reveal themselves in repeating patterns of energy, form, and symbolic significance, visible in our contemporary experience and throughout history. As the Greek therapist Evangelos Christou says, "It is not so much that the archetypes are in us; the more important truth is that it is we who are surrounded by and immersed in the archtypes." We apprehend their influence in both our interior and exterior experiences on a daily basis. Not only do archetypal patterns and symbol dramas regularly manifest themselves in our dreams, we also live and act them out, both consciously and unconsciously, in our waking activities, repeating the same recognizable mythic themes with seemingly endless variations in our individual and collective lives.

If we look back over the entire history of the planet, and the more recent history of the human species, these archetypal energies can be seen manifested in multiple, interconnected patterns of physical form and structure, symbolic meaning, and psychospiritual significance. These archetypal patterns appear to evolve and change as we develop ourselves, both individually and collectively, and our dreams offer evidence of this.

However, as Carl Jung has pointed out, whether the archetypes of the collective realm actually evolve or not is a question we cannot answer with certitude. Everything we know of them comes from our limited perceptions of their specific appearances in our own lives and from the accounts that have come down to us from our ancestors. We infer the existence of "archetypes of the collective unconscious" in much the same fashion that Plato deduced the existences of his "ideal forms" from the play of their shadows on the wall of his cave.

Given this inevitable existential limitation to our ability to perceive archetypes directly, we cannot say whether the "developments" we view in the archetypes are true changes in the energies themselves, or merely developments in our ability to perceive and conceptualize aspects of their nature and energy that were always present. Like Plato, we are limited to talking about the "shadows" rather than the objects that cast them. However, from the inescapable point of view of human awareness, this is a distinction without a difference, because to us they do *appear* to evolve, albeit with majestic slowness.

The realm that Carl Jung called the "collective unconscious" or the "objective psyche" is made up of these "archetypes." The reality of this realm is demonstrated by the spontaneous appearance of archetypal forms, even and particularly in situations where there is no "imitation" or "borrowing." For example, there are the fundamentally similar forms of dreams and spontaneous art productions of small children all over the world and the fundamentally similar cultural expressions of totally separate and isolated societies in different periods of history.

We human beings have a deep predisposition to express certain universal aspects of our social and personal experience in repeating archetypal images and symbols. These archetypal figures exhibit the same essential form, regardless of the specific variations we put on them.

Jung proposes that the archetypes are "instincts," inborn in us with the same persistence and individual variation as our instincts for self-preservation and reproduction. (For suggestions about readable works that discuss the different archetypes, see Appendix I.) In this chapter, I will focus primarily on the appearance in dreams of a single archetype and its role in the evolution of individual consciousness on the one hand and the development of the objective psyche on the other.

The "Willing Sacrifice" is an archetypal form of crucial importance in the continuing evolution and development of both individual and collective human consciousness. The Willing Sacrifice appears in the endlessly varied and yet essentially similar and repeating story of "the one who gives up individual life by choice so that others may live."

Historically, the story of the Willing Sacrifice almost always appears first with the central archetypal character in animal form, which then "evolves" into a more and more fully human shape. In the "evolution" of this archetypal symbol drama, it becomes clear that the Willing Sacrifice is and always was the Divine, even in its earliest animal shape. As discussed in the previous chapter, both Christianity and Buddhism embody the Willing Sacrifice at the center of their sacred narratives, linking it simultaneously to both the development of individual psychospiritual awareness and the "salvation" of humankind and the world as a whole.

Conscious self-awareness, intelligence, curiosity, courage, creativity, and compassion appear to be important to the manifestation and development of the archetype of Willing Sacrifice, in ways that parallel the evolution of humanity itself. The more we embody these extraordinary qualities in our individual lives, the better off we are as a species. Expressing these human energies appears not only to assist in the development of human consciousness, but also in the apparent unfolding of the archetypes themselves.

Acts of courage and consciousness and compassion are not abstract or generalized. They exist only in specific, individual cases. The cumulative effects of individual achievements of awareness, relationship, and creative expression shape and direct whole societies and cultures. In this sense, it can be said that the archetypes require individual human lives—individual acts and experiences that develop individual conscious awareness—in order to manifest, grow, and develop. As Bodhidharma says (in the "Wake-Up Sermon," translated by Red Pine), "When you're deluded, buddhas liberate mortals. When you're aware, mortals liberate buddhas. Buddhas don't become buddhas on their own. They're liberated by mortals."

Carl Jung, in his essay "Answer to Job," offers a specific example of this process. His analysis of the Book of Job shows the archetype of the

Divine itself evolving in direct response to Job's suffering and question-
ing, and the consequent increase in human ethical and relational understanding that Job's suffering creates. As Jung points out, even if the Divine
itself does not actually change, but only shows a more complete face to
the human observer as a result of Job's lamentations and cries for justice,
and our reaction to them, it is still a tremendously important step in our
human ability to see the archetype of the Divine, and in that sense alone
it can be viewed as an "archetypal development."

Sometimes, archetypal forms will appear in dreams in obvious and
dramatic ways, in images that are clearly "mythical" and "numinous"
and charged with special energy. Such dreams invite the dreamer and
dream group members to enter the realms of the religious and the spiritual. Jung called these "big dreams"; they have layers of meaning beyond
the personal. They reach into the transpersonal.

However, my experience is that an element of the "big dream"
exists in every dream, no matter how seemingly "small," fragmentary,
or personal it may appear to be. In waking life and dreams, the basic
background of all experience is always archetypal, whether the figures in
the foreground appear to be "larger than life" or not. For example, I have
often found that archetypal elements are hidden in ordinary-seeming
dreams and suddenly emerge into the foreground in response to a dreamer's particularly courageous or creative action. The "ordinary dream" is
transformed into a "big dream," right in the midst of the ongoing action.
Sometimes this transformation takes place later in group work with a
seemingly "mundane dream," when the group's projections highlight
the aspect(s) of the dream that echo with the feelings and struggles of all
humankind.

In these transformations, it seems to me that the archetypes themselves are helped to grow. Archetypal energies are influenced by individual experience, in much the same fashion that the individual dreamer's
experience is influenced and guided by collective archetypal energies.
This "individual influence on the archetypes" may not be overwhelming or decisive in any single instance, but I believe that in encounters of
this kind the whole species, and by implication the entire cosmos (since
everything is alive and profoundly interconnected), is brought to fuller
development and self-awareness.

The archetypes are capable of evolution, just like the human species.

Personal work influences the development of archetypal forms, just as the
archetypes influence personal growth. This may sound very theoretical,
but I believe that "ordinary people" do this psychospiritual work of evolution on themselves and the archetypes every day.

Let me offer a concrete example. "Carmen," a woman in her late fifties, bitterly divorced for some time from her successful doctor husband
of many years, reported the following dream:

It is registration day for the new semester at the local community college. I have arrived early because I do not want to miss getting into the
classes I want and need. I know the best and most important classes will
fill up quickly as soon as registration begins.

However, when I go into the gym where registration is being held,
a male administrator tells me that the hours have been changed from
what was originally printed in the bulletin, and now registration will
not begin until after lunch. I am annoyed, but I don't say anything. I
leave, and when I go outside again, I run into a friend of mine. She is
also trying to register and has been told the same thing.

We go off together and buy bag lunches at the cafeteria. Then we
go sit outside on the lawn by the gym to eat and wait for registration to
begin. As soon as we sit down, though, a fat campus policeman comes
along and tells us that we can't sit on the grass. We are annoyed. "Since
when!" I want to know, but we get up and move. We decide to leave
the campus. We walk across the street and sit on a bench in the park
to eat.

However, just when we get comfortable, a regular city cop comes
along and tells us that there is a new regulation that says that people
can't eat sitting on the park benches anymore—something to do with
controlling the homeless population. We are both getting more and
more angry and frustrated, but we get up again and go back across the
street to the campus because now it's almost time for registration to
begin.

However, when we get there, the building is already open, and
when we go inside, the same administrator tells us that they changed
the hours for registration *again*, after we left. It was moved up, and now
it's all over, and all the classes are filled and closed and my friend and I

can't register! I'm so angry and frustrated I start to cry in the dream, but there isn't anything I can do—the administrator is cold and uncaring.

I get back in my car and drive home again, fuming and raging because I've wasted my whole day, and because now I can't get on with my life because of this bureaucratic screwup.

When I get home and go inside, I notice a funny disturbance in the air down in front of the fireplace in the sunken living room. As I pause and look at it, it turns into a "special effect," like the "transporter" on *Star Trek*, and I see this *demon* appear in front of me.

He smiles and says to me in a real matter-of-fact way, "Okay, now it's time for you to go upstairs and get your daughter and bring her down here to me and sacrifice her to me." I know this has to be done by cutting her throat with a knife.

I am stunned. I don't know what to do. As I stand there, terrified and dumbfounded, the demon starts to get annoyed and says something like "Hurry up now! Get on with it! I haven't got all day!"

I start to say "No!" but he just holds up his hand and says, a little more gently, "Come along, now. Don't be difficult. You know you have no choice!"

It feels as though he's right—as though I don't have any real choice. I can feel my body starting to move and turn to go upstairs and get my daughter. It's like I'm in some sort of a daze or a trance, like he's forcing me to do this with hypnosis or something.

I turn away from him, and once I can't see him anymore, the idea comes into my mind that maybe I don't have any real choice, but I'd rather die trying to fight him than just go off and do his awful bidding like this. I don't care if he does kill me—I'd rather die than sacrifice my daughter to him like this!

I don't know where I get the courage, but I turn around all of a sudden and hurl myself at him and start hitting and scratching at him and shouting, "No! No! No! No!"

He and I fight, and I'm amazed that he doesn't just annihilate me in the first second! I realize that *I am fighting him*, and he hasn't beaten me yet! I fight harder, and we start to roll around on the floor on the carpet in front of the fireplace.

Then I see that he's starting to change shape and turn into my

father, right before my eyes! I'm even more terrified. I realize that if he
succeeds in turning himself all the way into my father, he will be able
to force me to do what he wants. I know that I have to stop him, so I
scratch and claw at his face even harder and keep on shouting, "NO!
NO! NO!"

We fight and fight and fight. It seems to go on for a long time, but
he doesn't succeed in turning into my father. Then he breaks off, pulls
back from me, and shimmers and bubbles and disappears. I'm on all
fours on the floor, panting and crying.

Just then, my daughter wakes up in her room upstairs. She's crying
too. She comes out of her bedroom up to the railing on the second-floor
balcony that overlooks the living room and calls down to me, "Oh,
Mom, it was awful! I just had the most horrible dream! I dreamed you
were going to sacrifice me to some sort of terrible demon!"

On the face of it, this is clearly a dream about one woman's personal
struggle with sexism and abandonment. The drama of "betrayal" and
"having the rules change" without prior warning or consultation reflects
her experience of divorce and her subsequent struggle, both to earn a living and to retain her sense of self-worth, in a sexist society that does not
honor women in general and older divorced women in particular. Her
fears about having to earn her own living, particularly when all she was
"trained" for was to be a socially correct wife and mother, are given clear
and poignant shape in the dream, particularly in her anxiety about having to take "the right classes."

At another level, this is also a dream about Carmen's heroic struggle
with her own internalized oppression. All the frustrations and injustices
and hypocrisies of the first part of the dream are dramatic metaphors for
Carmen's experience of "unfair" sexist discrimination and oppression in
waking life. The oppressive rules and schedule changes are also a picture of internalized injuries to her self-esteem and imaginative possibility
wrought by living her whole life in male-dominated, upper-middle-class
American society.

The return to her "home" in the middle of the dream, and the
appearance of the terrible "demon" on the hearth at the very center of
the house, are indications of the dramatic extent to which the injuries to

Carmen's self-esteem have been introjected. They are in the very heart (hearth) of her psyche (home).

However, it is important to remember that the "demon," the arrogant "administrator," and the two insensitive "policemen" are also a portrait of a shadowy aspect of the dreamer's own psyche. They are all reflections of the dreamer's animus, the archetype of the deepest intuitions about what it feels like and means to "be a man." In general, the ability of women to make creative use of their internal decisive and assertive masculine (animus) energies is greatly impaired by growing up with the oppressions of sexist society, just as the ability of men to be in expressive touch with their feminine (anima) feeling and relational energies is regularly stunted by the same collective oppression. Like all animus dramas, Carmen's dream is clearly connected with unresolved dramas with her father—the man who first defined the category "man" and who first instilled the internalized oppression of sexism most successfully.

I am convinced, however, that this dream goes far beyond Carmen's personal struggle and is deeply connected with archetypes of spiritual authority and submission that are even older than the four-thousand-year history of patriarchy. In this dream an ancient archetypal symbol drama is acted out again, only this time it turns out a little differently from what we have come to expect. Although this is clearly a dream about Carmen's very personal rage and frustration in reaction to the "stacked deck" of patriarchal society, Carmen's heroic actions in the dream go beyond a simply personal response to this collective reality.

The "administrator" and the "policemen" may be seen primarily as "personal animus figures," but the shape-changing "demon" in this dream is an even larger and more significant archetypal figure. In him we can see an animus figure with more complex dimensions, an ancient, archetypal figure who has been demanding for millennia the sacrifice of the next generation of children on his altar. The archetypal echoes of the practice of child sacrifice by the Carthaginians, of the biblical narrative of Abraham and Isaac, and of Jacob's wrestling with the Angel, are unmistakable.

In Carmen's dream, I believe we are privileged to witness a moment of important transformation in the archetypal symbol drama itself, not only in the individual life of the courageous, imaginative, loving woman that Carmen is, but also in the inherent structure of the collective energy pattern itself, or at least in the face of the "myth" that we are able see, given our current individual and collective state of development.

When Jacob wrestles with the Angel and holds his own until the dawn (of increased conscious awareness), the Divine rewards him with the promise of the Promised Land, and the entire Jewish people (to say nothing of the Christians and Moslems who come after) are profoundly affected. When the sacrifice of Isaac is "canceled" and the sheep is substituted, the ritual practice of child sacrifice is abandoned, and the collective circumstance of human civilization evolves in a most important way. I believe that in overcoming the demon in her dream, Carmen is participating in an event of equal archetypal collective significance.

The demon's mythic appearance, his extraordinary arrival and departure, and his "magical hypnotic power" all suggest clearly that he is an archetypal figure and that there are archetypal issues and possibilities at stake in the dream. The collective drama is given shape by, and is deeply interwoven with, the issues of creative autonomy and selfhood that are at the center of Carmen's personal struggles with the collective reality and internalized oppressions of sexism. From the moment of the appearance of the demon onward, her struggle, while it remains deeply "personal," echoes far beyond the confines of Carmen's own life and unique biography. It resonates with and inevitably calls up the struggle of all people against internalized oppression of all sorts. Because of the archetypal collective nature of the dream struggle, in a profound sense the outcome echoes into our own lives and affects us all.

The figure of the demon is an archetypal form of Carmen's own personal internalized demon. Only when the demon threatens to become purely "personal"—by turning into the image of Carmen's own father—does she know she will have "no hope." This can be recognized as a symbolic statement of the extent to which Carmen is still, in middle age, "a good girl" who continues to live out the values and ideas absorbed from her father in childhood. But at another, more important level, if the "demon" becomes "merely psychological," merely her own father, then even if she succeeds in defeating him, the nasty oppressive world as a whole remains unchanged. This image grows directly out of a great psycho-spiritual truth. Unless I feel connected to a pattern of meaning and a worldview larger than my own personal successes and failures, no matter how good I feel, I will still sense an emptiness in my life. If I live in a world that has no meaning beyond my own biography, my own personal pains and joys, I will experience an emptiness that always threatens to render even my most joyous moments "meaningless." Only through participation in a universe whose ultimate meaning is larger than my own life and life span can this psychospiritual problem be resolved.

The central drama of the second half of the dream pivots on the demon's "order" to sacrifice the daughter, and the dreamer's resistance and refusal to submit to this command. The symbol drama suggests strongly that Carmen has realized that she must overcome her own internalized oppression. Here again, the growth and transformation of the archetypal struggle in the dream involves embracing and embodying the Willing Sacrifice. Carmen decides in the midst of her dream, with her whole heart, that it is better to *die* herself in the effort to resist and defeat the demon than it is to live on at the cost of her daughter's sacrificial death.

The "trance" that the demon creates is an evocative metaphor of the life that is only partially lived, limited by the unquestioned assumptions of conventional wisdom and opinion. The "trance" is also a picture of the effect of the internalized oppression that leaves the victim with the sense that he or she "has no real choice" but to be a victim and to "stew" in the rage and frustration that inevitably accompanies the conscious awareness of being a victim.

If she remains unwilling to sacrifice herself in the struggle with the demon (i.e., if unwilling to let go of her lifetime self-image) Carmen is telling her "daughter" that self-reliance and success are impossible for a woman alone. The stronger the helpless, self-pitying rage and resentment "at men" and "at the system" the stronger the ironic, self-defeating message is. The "daughter" who must be protected is both the actual daughter in waking life and the "daughter" of new creative possibility within Carmen's developing psyche. The dream suggests that if rage and frustration are all she feels and all that determine her actions, this is the symbolic and emotional equivalent of "sacrificing her daughter to the demon."

Each time any individual overcomes the "trance" that Carmen experiences in her dream, the collective, archetypal "trance" of common wisdom and consensual reality is lifted a little. This "trance" of conventional thinking is a daily reality for us all that habitually limits our awareness of our true character, strength, imagination, and creative possibilities. This collective "trance" can only be broken through individual acts of courage and awareness, such as the struggle and willing sacrifice of Carmen in her dream.

Every person who succeeds in breaking the "trance" of conventional attitudes, whether toward gender stereotypes or other limitations on creative possibility, manages to break the chain so that these attitudes and self-limitations are *not* passed on to the next generation. In this way, the individual dreamer contributes in a most profound and real way to the liberation of all people, and of the planet as a whole.

Each time an individual overcomes fear and creatively embodies the Willing Sacrifice in his or her dreams and waking life, the archetypal energies themselves are influenced and helped to change and evolve. The archetypal shape-changing "father/demon" that Carmen confronts in her dream has plagued humanity for millennia, and as we move to rid ourselves of his lethal "trance," we succeed or fail as individuals. Our individual triumphs and defeats, aided and supported by the people closest to us who share our lives, feed back into the realm of the archetypes, in the same way that the archetypal energies embodied in our dreams and myths influence our waking lives.

Any meeting with archetypal energies in the dream world, or in waking life, that is characterized by courage, imagination, love, and willingness to sacrifice one's immediate interests and sense of self for the longer-term benefit of others has its effect on the archetypal energies themselves, as well as on the individual consciousness that enters the engagement. Whether or not we can measure either aspect of this influence doesn't matter; at worst, this is a useful way to imagine the "unknowable," and at best it is true.

The Hindus and Buddhists say that the gods themselves are envious of human beings because we alone are capable of the growth, change, and transformation that leads to enlightenment and escape from the endless cycle of rebirth in samsara. This is a mythological metaphor of the intuition that increasingly conscious and self-aware human participation in the symbolic dance and drama of the archetypes is as meaningful and necessary to the "gods" (for which read "archetypes") as it is for us human beings who engage in it.

This notion is fundamentally related to the archetypal idea (discussed more fully in Chapter 8) that death is a continuation of the dream. In this view, after human beings die, they experience dying as an "awakening" and recognize that what they took for the physical reality of waking life was in fact the fleeting and transitory *dream*, and what we took to be "dreaming" is actually the eternal (archetypal) reality that persists after the separation of conscious awareness from the body.

Just as the archetypal energies of the collective unconscious form the foundation of both the dreaming and waking world, so the waking and dreaming experiences of human beings (and other vital organisms) become the arena where those archetypal energies are given vitality, made concrete, acted out, and allowed to evolve and change. As they "are made flesh,' the archetypal energies are, in turn, woven back into the myth and the dream, echoing back into the transpersonal realm that Carl Jung called the "collective unconscious" or the "objective psyche."

I believe that in Carmen's dream, we see a concrete example of this process, a moment where such personal/archetypal evolution takes another step.

Let me offer another dream that for me has this same profound quality of mutual interaction between evolving human consciousness and the archetypes themselves.

This dream was shared with me by a woman, I will call her Grace, who has spent all her adult life as a Roman Catholic nun, working to relieve the suffering of the poor and the dispossessed. When she first had this dream, it frightened and depressed her deeply. Only later, when she worked with it, did she begin to feel the hope and deep transformation it embodies, not only for her personally but for the archetypes as well.

I both observe and participate in the dark scene before me. Only five people are present, with absolutely no sound whatsoever.

A man is lying facedown on the ground, dead, a victim of the earthquake. Near the victim is an ambulance, and the ambulance driver, a paramedic, is dressed in a white suit. Only yards away, I sit on the ground in a circle with a man and a black woman.

The paramedic brings me a goblet of wine and says, "Some of his blood is in the wine."

I take the wine and drink of it and pass it to the woman, who drinks
and passes it to the man, who also drinks . . . all in *profound* silence.

Then I say calmly and spontaneously, "I wonder if he has AIDS."

The black woman replies, "I never thought of that."

Grace had this dream not long after the terrible San Francisco earthquake of October 17, 1989. The "feel" of the dream—the darkness, the
silence, the earthquake victim, the specter of AIDS, the black woman's
comment, the ambulance, and the paramedic—all point to the horrors
and confusions of contemporary events.

Drinking the wine mixed with "his blood" is an inescapable reference to the Eucharist, and the structure of the dream requires us to
imagine, however briefly and preconsciously, a Christ with AIDS and,
by implication, a sexually active Christ. This dream fuses deeply felt contemporary social and political concerns with religious intuitions, meld-
ing them into a single, deceptively simple, poignant "morality play."

When I imagine this dream for myself, one thread of personal
meaning is church-sponsored guilt and shame for being a sexual being,
perhaps even a sexual being drawn to love other women, since the
association of AIDS and same-sex love is inevitable, even if it is also
oppressive and incomplete. But far more important than this, from my
point of view, is the drinking of the wine mixed with blood without
hesitation, without "thinking." It reveals a profound saying of "yes" to
life in all its messiness and injustice, without holding anything back,
without trying to second-guess any of the ultimate consequences.
The "paramedic," in his official uniform, is a "technician"—of rescue and "salvation"—as well as a figure embodying the institutional,
male-dominated church. His (male) authority at the scene of the
"disaster"—the earthquake, the AIDS epidemic, modern life in general—is accepted by the dreamer without question, but she also sees that
he does not participate in full authentic communion with the suffering
victims. The "paramedic" hands the dreamer the wine mixed with "his
blood" and does not appear to drink it himself, unlike the practice of
the officiating priest in waking life. In my version of the dream, this is
both a reflection of the dreamer's continued dependence on the institutional church and, simultaneously, a clear criticism of its hypocrisies and
failings. But even with these feelings, the dreamer participates in full

communion with the victims, without hesitation, even though it may result in her death.

The appearance of the group of three beside the ambulance, two of whom are known (the dreamer and the black woman), and one of whom is unknown (the shadowy man who drinks from the communion cup last), suggests the great archetypal trinity of past/present/future (the past and the present being relatively known, and the future being relatively unknown). In the moment of sharing the cup, "the fullness of time," where past, present, and future meld into one affirmation of life and spiritual vision, is experienced. This sharing of the possibly tainted cup also confirms Grace's conscious effort to embrace the Shadow and the Animus in her ongoing work of personal exploration and psychospiritual development.

Death in dreams is always a metaphor of emotional growth and change. The dead earthquake victim, and the implication that the three communion drinkers will die as well, all point to how profound, albeit difficult and painful, such growth and development are.

As a collective, archetypal metaphor, the dream is a paraphrase of the mystical, prophetic words of martyred Central American bishop Oscar Romero: "Our persecution is nothing more nor less than sharing in the destiny of the poor." Despite the pains, uncertainties, and disillusionments of her personal and institutional religious life, in this dream Grace affirms both her personal life and the life that she shares with all people. In the dream, as in her waking life, she offers up her energy and experience in an act of willing sacrifice for others. In this way, she grows, and in growing she shares the indivisible bond of common humanity with all, even and particularly with those whom the church ignores and rejects, and even with those who seem to be condemned by God, since the "earthquake" is the archetypical "act of God."

When I imagine this dream for myself, I also experience regret over "not having thought" fully about the consequences of sexual celibacy on relations. When I chose my vocation as a religious, I didn't understand, as I now do, how vitally important full, honest physical expression of feeling is to the service of the Divine, but even this profound regret is consciously acknowledged and released in the experience of "communion" in the dream.

The experience of "being both a participant and an observer" simultaneously is the "frame" of the whole dream. As is often the case, this suggests the achievement of something approaching "objectivity" in the assessment of the dreamer's own waking-life struggles. The dream demonstrates a profound and loving acceptance of Grace's own personal emotional upheavals, intellectual doubts, and the ethical complexity of contemporary life, without resorting to either cynicism or repression. The dream offers a compelling image of exquisite balance between contemplation and action in the world.

All of this marks this dream as another of those in which the archetypes themselves are touched and helped to evolve through the medium of deeply felt and wholeheartedly lived individual human life. Both Carmen's dream and Grace's dream have a quality of full participation, of deeply felt experience with nothing withheld. In my experience, this is the hallmark of the dreams and the dreamers in which the archetypes themselves are invited into full transformative relationships with one another through the medium of individual human experience.

In conclusion, let me share another dream of my own, which I had while writing the last draft of this chapter. Many things might be said about the dream, but at the very least, it gives the ideas presented here a "mythological" dramatic-narrative form. Out of a strong sense of having dreamed much more, all I can recall is:

I am both a direct participant and a disembodied observer in this dream. I am attending a gathering of "humans and gods." We are meeting together in a huge stone house that from time to time becomes a medieval castle, an ancient palace, a temple, and other kinds of carved stone architectural spaces as well. All these different spaces are somehow the same place.

Our interactions are intense and multileveled, and I cannot recall or frame them all clearly. However, one "strand" of experience does coalesce more clearly than any of the others: there is a vigorous "old male god"—Caucasian, with a long white beard and a muscular body. Despite his strength, he is in his dotage. In the dream I think of the cartoon character the King of the Sea from Disney's *The Little Mermaid*.

This "old god" is ranting and raving and carrying on in an indignant, arrogant, vengeful, uncaring "Old Testament" fashion. We humans, supported by some of the other gods, deliberate and declare that the time has come when he must see his dark, weak, frightened side consciously. The effect of our firm, concerted declaration is that he suddenly has a negative "vision" of himself that is almost overwhelming. The previously denied aspects of his being seize him and take on physical form, and the "old god" ages and falls to his knees and becomes senile and weak and fearful, à la King Lear, right before our eyes. His body seethes and boils and changes shape continually. All the shapes are old and frightened and deformed.

"I" am shocked, both as one who is participating and one who is a disembodied conscious observer. Even though I participated in the decision to make this happen, I am unwilling to let it go forward without some compassion. I step forward and lift his writhing, shape-changing form up in my arms, like a pietà. I make a strong, ringing "speech" to the assembly that is simultaneously spoken and telepathic about how "not even a dog" should be subjected to this kind of treatment/torture and how he should be allowed to pass and transform with dignity and honor. I call up a vision of how this very god once cremated his old faithful dog with a bolt of lightning, standing and holding the dog as the lightning struck.

I step forward with the seething, shape-changing god in my arms and call upon the lightning to cremate him and release his energies from the prison of the old, shape-changing body they have become trapped in.

I know that if the lightning strikes, I may be immolated and obliterated myself, but I am willing to risk it. I think I may be strong and centered enough to have the lightning pass right through me if I do not offer any resistance to it, and thus there is a chance that I may come out unharmed.

The setting transforms again, this time into a rocky mountaintop in a storm. Out of the dark, billowing storm clouds, a huge blinding waterfall/bolt of lightning cascades down and incinerates the decaying, shape-changing old god, and in fact, I am not harmed. I am so excited and transported by the process and the feeling of his being cleansed and transformed and liberated in my arms as the lightning consumes the outward shapes that I pop awake.

Is this a metaphoric picture, a "little myth," about the ways in which the archetypes themselves are changed through individual human consciousness and action? I believe it is. Do we all participate in this process each time we dream, whether we remember it or not? I believe we do. As we human beings struggle wholeheartedly with our seemingly personal and separate dramas, the archetypal energies of the collective are given shape and made manifest.

We have reached a point in the development of the species where we have taken into our hands the power to destroy the life of the planet. We are using that power, for good and ill, every day. If we are to survive, we must learn as much about our own unconscious depths and creative possibilities as we know about the structure of the atom and the makeup of the stars. Our dreams are an indispensable key to that learning. We must consciously explore this realm further. We can afford to wait no longer.

*Chapter Ten*

# DREAMS AND THE EVOLUTION OF HUMAN CONSCIOUSNESS

*Be wasteful of your life give the whole of yourself without restriction . . . a*
*complete surrender to life and fate. . . . If we live completely, we surrender*
*to the lives [of the ancestors] and redeem them. Also we prepare for a*
*future generation, because we have lived out our own lives; we have*
*fulfilled them and we leave no curse for the following generations—the*
*curse of economized life.*

— CARL JUNG, *Nietzsche's Zarathustra*

In the last sixteen years since *Where People Fly and Water Runs Uphill* first appeared, I have become even more convinced not only that every dream comes in the service of the individual dreamer's health and wholeness while speaking in a universal language of archetypal symbol and metaphor, but also that dreams and dreaming expand the very domain of health and wholeness itself by fostering and reflecting the evolution of human consciousness collectively. My experience also convinces me that Carl Jung is correct when he suggests that the evolution of human consciousness as a whole takes place only in specific individuals at specific times and places. It is only as individuals grow and "individuate" that the species as a whole has any chance of evolving and growing collectively.

Forty-plus years of work with my own dreams and the dreams of others has demonstrated to my satisfaction that through the promotion of growth of consciousness and individual self-awareness, dreams and dreaming also advance collective potential for more evolved consciousness in the whole human species. Sándor Ferenczi is not only poetically inspired but also technically correct when he says, "Dreams are the workshop of evolution."

## PROJECTION AND THE EVOLUTION OF CONSCIOUSNESS

At the outset of this discussion it is important to remember the central and pivotal place occupied by *unconscious projection* in the initial evolution and development of new consciousness and awareness in human beings.

Projection itself is the ubiquitous process in which we catch our first conscious (but not yet self-aware) glimpses of aspects of our own beings that are developing in us more or less unconsciously. As a result of the increasing developmental energy and cathexis of these previously completely unconscious contents, they begin to seep and bubble up from our individual and collective unconscious depths into our dreams and at the edges of our waking awareness. We begin to become vaguely aware of them at the periphery of our conscious awareness and through the hairline cracks in our experience of the waking world. In this completely natural and endlessly repeating drama of evolving conscious awareness, we unconsciously project these newly energized elements outward onto the world and onto particular people and situations that echo the symbolic content of the preconscious material that is rising and thrusting itself into our field of perception.

This is the first step in the unfolding drama of evolving consciousness. The more our conscious self-awareness develops and grows in the general direction of increasing intensity and scope, the more necessary it is for us to *recognize consciously, acknowledge, and withdraw these previously unconscious projections* of our own inner lives from the people and situations in the external world where we first "saw" them.

## PROJECTION IN A NUTSHELL

The basics of projection may be summarized as follows: projection is a ubiquitous *unconscious* process, much like digesting food or having a wound heal; it is *not* something that we do on purpose. This process of projection causes us to perceive aspects and energies of our own being as though they existed exclusively outside ourselves and were the exclusive "property" and responsibility of others.

It is through projection that we usually gain the first conscious, relatively clear (though mistakenly attributed) glimpses of currently unconscious *aspects of our own being* that are pressing and clamoring for more conscious acknowledgment, recognition, and expression in our waking lives.

Even though my projections are always symbolic reflections of more or less unconscious aspects of my own being, at the same time they may also be generally accurate apprehensions of what's actually going on in the outer world. My projections may be either largely true or in the main false, *but either way, the fact that they are my unconscious projections will drastically interfere with my ability to make that most important judgment with any accuracy.*

Additionally, any actual person or situation out in the world will "automatically" draw out of me whatever my own corresponding projections are that echo with that situation or person, because projecting is not a product of, or even initially subject to, will and conscious choice. If I feel *"But it really is true, dammit!"* then the very strength of this feeling itself is an even *more* reliable indication that my perception of that external truth is shaped, flavored, and ultimately driven by my own unconscious projections.

Projections come essentially in two "flavors"—positive and negative. These are known as "bright" (or "golden") shadow projections and simply "shadow projections."[1] Regardless of the "flavor" of my projections, or whether they are essentially true or false, projection is *always* a

---

1. Sometimes, if a person is using the phrase "bright shadow projection," he/she will make the distinction clearer by using the corresponding phrase "dark shadow projection" (as I will be doing myself later in this chapter). When the phrase "shadow projection," or simply "projection," appears alone in the literature, it usually refers to the "dark," apparently negative, shadow qualities that I see quite clearly in others while still remaining blind to their presence within me.

consequence of it being *so* much easier for me to see all these aspects of my own character and personality—good, bad, or indifferent—in *others* than to recognize them, and take responsibility for them, *in myself*. The current entertainment industry slang puts it very succinctly and clearly: "If you spot it, you've got it!"

## PSYCHIC PERCEPTIONS AS A SPECIAL CASE OF PROJECTION

In my experience, the process of projection shapes our perceptions of reality across the board and applies equally to intuitive processes, eliding all the way through to full-blown psychic awareness. When a person has a totally nonrational, "psychic" perception of a truth in the external world, that perception is still "filtered through" and profoundly shaped by that person's personal life, past experiences, and unconscious patterns of anxiety, belief, fear, and attention. The mere fact that the awareness of a particular piece of information is genuinely psychic, and is later demonstrated to be correct, does not mean that it is not *also* a tissue of projection at the same time.

Some psychics are particularly skilled in "picking up" information relating to physical health, while others excel in areas of interpersonal relationship and so forth. In my experience, the particularity of these various unique, individual psychic gifts and talents is always directly related to the practitioner's own history, background, and unresolved psychospiritual issues. The insightful, nonrational "hits" that these psychic folk articulate are projections—*particularly* when they also prove to be uncannily true and accurate.

A constantly deepening awareness of one's own patterns of projection is an absolute necessity for living an increasingly conscious, creative, and psychospiritually satisfactory life in the waking world, whether or not one is interested in, or pays any particular conscious attention to, dreams as a part of that process of inner development. Obviously, paying close attention to dreams is very valuable in this process, because *dreams always give us a clear, symbolic, emotionally resonant account of what the specific shapes and patterns of our unconscious projections are in waking life.*

## THE EVOLUTION OF CONSCIOUSNESS
## IN OTHER SPECIES

It would be an act of foolish human chauvinism to assume that it is only the individual and collective consciousness of human beings that is capable of evolving, or that is actually evolving, particularly at this particular geological moment of immense planetary transformation. There are undeniable indications that the whole ecological balance and dynamism of the planetary biosphere are developing and changing with increasing rapidity. Recently, the accumulating evidence of these ecological upheavals has become inescapably clear in the rhythmic and escalating dance of global warming, coupled with the dramatically increasing proportion of unbonded and loosely bonded carbon atoms in the air, soil, and water of the world. In the midst of this vast and increasingly swift ecological transformation, other species are also developing new, previously unobserved adaptive behaviors, behaviors that we can only assume reflect the consequent extensions and expansions of cognition and self-awareness that these innovative behaviors clearly imply.[2]

To offer only one of many recent dramatic examples, an Associated Press story by Michael Casey (appearing in the "Science and Health" section of the *San Francisco Chronicle* on June 11, 2008) proclaimed, "Monkeys have learned to fish, researchers find." The subhead reads: "Newly reported behavior shows an ability to adapt to environment, food sources." The story goes on to report that researchers from both the Nature Conservancy and the Great Ape Trust have independently observed and reported a startling new, previously unobserved behavior pattern among groups of long-tailed macaques along riverbanks in East Kalimantan and North Sumatra provinces in Indonesia. They have been seen "scooping up small fish with their hands and eating them. . . . The species had been known to eat fruit and forage for crabs and insects, but never before fish from rivers."

Erik Meijaard, one of the coauthors of the scientific report published

2. I strongly suspect that since projection is such a basic and all-pervasive phenomenon in the development of new consciousness and awareness in humans, it may also play a similarly important role in the corresponding development in other species, particularly other primate species.

in the May 2008 issue of the *International Journal of Primatology* describing this new behavior in a species that has been carefully and systematically observed for several decades, is quoted as saying, "It's exciting that after such a long time, you see new behavior."

An increasing number of credible reports like this one, describing new behaviors "suddenly" appearing in several diverse species, are finding their way into the public data stream. It seems there is reason to suppose that the forces of the collective unconscious that manifest in new, seemingly innovative adaptive behaviors and the acquisition of corresponding new modes of interior experience and self-awareness are not, and apparently never have been, limited just to human beings.

## THE ISSUE OF "BRIGHT SHADOW" PROJECTION

The projection of the archetypal "Bright Shadow"[3] also plays a particularly important and dramatically underappreciated role in this process of developing individual consciousness, character, and personality. When the creative energies of the Bright Shadow are "expressed" only in projected form, at the very least it has a direct, negative influence on cultural innovation, which in turn exercises a negative influence on the development of further conscious awareness in countless individuals. When bright shadow energies are withdrawn and given concrete expression, the lives of individuals and whole societies are transformed.

As discussed earlier, the projection of the classic "dark" shadow is demonstrably responsible for all the most oppressive and collectively dangerous patterns of human behavior, from racism, sexism, "ethnic cleansing," and genocide on the one hand, to the increasing degradation and destruction of the ecosystem and the forced extinction of countless species on the other.

The unconscious "engine" that drives this ceaseless human activity that increasingly degrades and destroys the interconnected web of the planetary ecosystem is fueled by *our inherent, archetypal predisposition to identify and equate "wild nature" with unconsciousness itself.* As individuals and

---

3. In case it is not already clear, when I capitalize the names of archetypal terms, I am emphasizing the transpersonal, collective side of the archetypal images named, and making reference to the same names in lower-case letters in order to emphasize the corresponding, necessarily personal side of these same archetypal patterns.

whole societies brush up against and begin to encounter their own deep, ambiguous, disturbing, unconscious potentials and fears, this encounter stirs up creative energy that is *mistakenly literalized and turned toward the seemingly heroic effort to "tame nature" and "exploit natural resources" for human profit, power, and "progress."*

The global industrial "war on nature" is actually at this deeper level an unconsciously projected and thoroughly misguided war on the unconscious itself. As such, it is "ecocide," a form of *unconscious collective suicide.* It is a "war" that simply cannot be won. It makes no more rational sense to talk about "winning" *any* war in this postmodern era than it does to talk about "winning an earthquake" or a "winning a wildfire." "Winning a war on nature" is a particularly obvious contradiction in terms. (See Chapter 5 for a discussion of some of the individual and collective consequences of the unconscious projection of the personal and archetypal Dark Shadow.)

Destructive and suicidally counterproductive though the unconscious projection of the archetypal and personal Dark Shadow demonstrably is, the unconscious projection of the Bright Shadow, both personally and collectively, is regularly responsible for even more harm. I realize that is saying a mouthful, particularly since Dark Shadow projection is deeply implicated as the hidden unconscious source and motive force behind everything from the Holocaust to global warming, from imperialism to child abuse, but in its own way, Bright Shadow projection regularly does even more harm, in large measure *because its terrible effects remain virtually invisible.*

## SHADOW WORK

When a person undertakes the incredibly difficult task of recognizing and consciously withdrawing his or her own previously unconscious Dark Shadow projections, that person accomplishes a psychospiritual task of immense collective as well as personal importance. The short-term collective problem with "Dark Shadow work" is that "evil is ultimately banal." Hannah Arendt is correct; all evil is essentially the same. It is born of shortsighted arrogance, selfishness, and stupidity, and upon closer examination it ends up looking pretty much like all other smug, self-obsessed, and dim-witted evil. Even the archetypal "evil geniuses" of sacred narrative, folklore, literature, world history, and current events succeed only in creating elaborate, baroque variations on the basics of evil: overweening pride, greed, and stupidity.[4]

At the collective level, one of the things this means is that each time an individual person does the incredibly difficult and courageous interior work necessary to recognize and withdraw his/her previously unconscious Dark Shadow projection(s), there is always someone else quite close by who will step up and act out his/her own versions of the same pernicious, ugly, unconscious projections, and so the collective positive effect of the individually heroic act of withdrawing dark shadow projections is often difficult to see.

The Bright Shadow, on the other hand, always carries unique elements that are not reproduced in exactly the same form(s) in the unconscious psyches of others. *The Bright Shadow is composed of the inimitable gifts and unique creative potentialities of each particular person.* When someone does the difficult and courageous work of withdrawing his/her bright shadow projections on others, and starts to take personal responsibility for the unique gifts he/she possesses, there is usually no one else anywhere (let alone in the immediate vicinity) to step up and replace those same projected bright shadow energies, so the collective positive effect of the "bright shadow work" when it is successfully accomplished is easier to see. The world is made into an observably better place for everyone when any one person's unique gifts and talents are made manifest. *And it is also much easier to miss entirely when the withdrawal of bright shadow energies is **not** accomplished.*

## MICHELANGELO REBORN

Let me offer a purely imaginary, paradigmatic example of the archetypal drama of bright shadow projection. Let us suppose, for the purposes

---

4. I thought about using the word "ignorance" here, but I am constantly reminded that there are plenty of uneducated and undereducated people who are really very intelligent and self-aware, and that there are also plenty of highly educated folks who really are moral, emotional, and spiritual morons. Ultimately the issue is not one of "educated versus ignorant," but rather one of "intelligent and generous versus selfish and stupid." Education is *crucial*, but by itself, without corresponding cultivation of emotional, moral, and imaginative capability, it is at worst utterly useless and at best simply not *enough*.

of this discussion, that the great Renaissance artist Michelangelo is reincarnated in a wealthy suburban community somewhere near where you live. He is born as a healthy, energetic boy. He is loved deeply by his upper-middle-class parents, who put his incredibly talented childhood drawings and paintings up on their refrigerator with magnets, and praise him generously for his many other interests and talents, and particularly for his obvious intelligence. They are liberals who believe in the value of public education, so they send him to public school, but in their hearts, they don't believe that public education is really good enough for him, so they also send him off to enrichment camp every summer and pay for various extra lessons and educational experiences during the school year.

Throughout this loving, supportive parenting, they also send him the continuous and unrelenting message that a career in "art" is not an acceptable life choice for an upper-middle-class male child in an advanced industrial society at the beginning of the twenty-first century. And because this incessant and subtle message is delivered to him with *love*, he *buys* it.

There is a very important and difficult point here, especially for intelligent, good-hearted, spiritually aware people. Alas, the Beatles are not entirely correct; love is not *all* you need, particularly if it assumes unconsciously oppressive and limiting forms. *The oppressions that are delivered with love are far more difficult to throw off than the oppressions that are delivered with malice.*

If psychologically and emotionally oppressive ideas and behaviors are visited on an individual, or on a group, with malice (even hidden and disguised malice), then ultimately all that is required to escape and find freedom from those oppressions is to develop enough courage and "upper-torso strength" (both physical and metaphoric) to throw them off and get on with one's authentic life. But when those oppressions are delivered with genuine, if misguided, love, then no amount of "upper-torso strength" and courage by themselves will be sufficient to rectify the situation. Other means must be discovered to accomplish the necessary liberation.

This is yet another reason why paying reasonably close attention to dreams is such a potentially important practice. Dreams always come and take memorable form in the course of serving the dreamer's truest and deepest health and wholeness. For that reason, they always point

symbolically (and sometimes even with blunt literalness) toward potential paths of personal and collective liberation, particularly liberation
from the oppressions that are anchored in place securely in the dreamer's
psyche because they were delivered sincerely with real love, but without the corresponding respect, curiosity, and acceptance that would have
softened and tempered the ultimately oppressive message(s).

## INTROJECTIONS AND "VOMITING" IN THE DREAM WORLD

The technical name for accepting the projections others make on us
and mistaking those projections for genuine aspects of our own being
is "introjection." *All* parents and parental surrogates project on their
children. As I have said before, we *all* do it *automatically*, because it is
a natural, unconscious process, not initially subject to conscious will,
self-awareness, or choice. Our children, of course, return the favor and
project back on their parents and parental surrogates with equal sincerity
and unconscious energy.

One of the things this means is that virtually *everyone* has a network
of erroneous introjects in the unconscious psyche that interfere with living fully and authentically. These introjects obstruct a person's health and
wholeness, and as a result, getting rid of unconscious introjects is always
high on the list of concerns that the dreams are always addressing.

When a person is deeply engaged in ridding himself or herself of
introjects, particularly parental introjects, the process very often appears
in the dream world as vomiting. Once again, this is so frequently the
case in my experience that it is always worth asking when "vomiting"
appears in a dream whether or not it is an archetypal symbolic reflection of the dreamer engaging in the effort to bring introjected material
to consciousness and getting rid of it, regardless of what other levels of
meaning the image may also be carrying.

## "MICHELANGELO" GROWS UP

In the case of our imagined reincarnated Michelangelo, he grows up
in the lap of this kind of unintentionally oppressive love. He accepts the
projections that his parents, and his whole society, place on him—that a

life as an artist is "unthinkable"—and as a result, he is forced to cultivate unusual self-discipline and control from a very early age. He has to discipline himself fiercely to overcome his immediate, natural, instinctive desire to doodle on restaurant napkins and to paint on every blank wall in town.

Because of this constant cultivation of self-discipline, he does very well in school (because, alas, discipline and perseverance are really all that is required for "academic success" in most schools these days). He graduates with honors from high school and goes on to a prestigious university, where his greatest problem is choosing a major. He has difficulty with this task because he can't really afford to "follow his bliss." At this point, he has disciplined himself (as an unconscious "love gift" to his parents) to not even *sense internally* what his true bliss might be (except, of course, in his dreams).

Eventually, he picks a liberal arts major and once again graduates with honors. Now he is faced with the problem of choosing a life path. This time, it takes the shape of choosing specialized postgraduate training. Once more, he vacillates, and eventually he picks law school, because it is one of the paths of least resistance for a liberal arts major and also because he knows he has all the necessary skills of self-discipline and determination for a very successful career as a lawyer.

Not surprisingly, he does well once again in law school and graduates with honors a third time. He returns to his hometown and marries his high school sweetheart. They "live happily ever after." He has a very successful law practice. He and his wife have the appropriate number of children and a dog. He does all sorts of pro bono work and helps build houses for Habitat for Humanity on the weekends.

From the outside, his life looks *perfect*, but one thing that can be said with absolute certainty about this straw man I have constructed is that in his sleep, he will be *tormented* by nightmares because he's *Michelangelo*, and it doesn't matter how well he lives *someone else's* life. It doesn't even matter how "good" and "attractive" or "honorable" that life appears to be when viewed from the outside; it's still not *his* unique, authentic, healthy, and whole life. To use traditional language, he is not living "according to God's will," and his dreams come in increasingly dramatic and emotionally urgent forms, in the service of his health and wholeness, to let his waking mind know that he has lost track of something of absolute importance in the course of his apparent success.

He quietly tries therapy from time to time (not wanting to make too much of a public fuss about it, lest he jeopardize his reputation as a legal ace or compromise his increasing standing in the community as a mentor and role model). The therapists he chooses (alas, like most therapists) have had little or no training regarding the psychology of dreams and don't have much to say to him about his recurrent nightmares. In fact, the therapists he sees are all actually secretly jealous of him and his visibly very successful life (a life that any of them would cheerfully give a couple of fingers off their left hands to have themselves), and so, even though they provide him with impeccable Rogerian nonjudgmental support and active listening, he doesn't end up getting much benefit or relief from any of it.

Because his personal bright shadow is directly concerned with art, he projects it "automatically" onto every artist he encounters. As a result, he develops an uncanny eye for young talent and helps and supports many young artists at the very beginning of their careers by buying their work at good prices. All that pays off spectacularly in the long run, as the artists he picked (long before anyone else noticed them) become increasingly famous and sought-after and his growing collection of their early works increases in value geometrically. And yet he is still tortured by his dreams.

Assuming that he avoids alcoholism and other addictions, and also assuming that he does not have some kind of a blinding epiphany that reveals the true calling of his life, bringing with it the courage to let all his worldly success go and to start over (disappointing and confusing his aging parents, his wife, his associates and friends, and even his children), he will go to his grave still haunted by nightmares, because dreams never give up when there is even the slightest possibility remaining for the dreamer to make a conscious turn toward psychological health and spiritual wholeness. He will die with a gnawing sense that he "missed something" somehow, that he "failed to connect with life" in some important way, despite all the good he did, all the love he gave and received, and the kind, gentle, intelligent, generous way he lived.

This may seem like merely an ironic and vaguely tragic postmodern fairy tale I have woven here out of the whole cloth of pop archetypal psychology, but let me remind you—this imagined man was *Michelangelo reborn.* This seemingly exemplary (at worst, totally harmless, and at best, very useful and productive) life could have—*should have*—included the creation of the twenty-first-century equivalent of the Sistine Chapel ceiling.

Our "successful lawyer" could/should have created the work of art that would be the twenty-first-century *David*, reinvesting the archetypal image and energy of the masculine with the beauty and dignity that the failures and depredations of patriarchy have so deeply injured, damaged, and stripped away. The rehabilitation of the archetypal masculine is something we are all in desperate need of *collectively*. This imagined man could have contributed an immensely important piece to that necessary effort as a *direct result of his own individual efforts*. In my sad invented tale, he fails to find his true calling, and the worst part is—*the rest of us wouldn't even realize what has been stolen from us by his gentle, lifelong, unconscious bright shadow projections.*

Had he been able to recognize his true, healthy, and whole self, and had he been able to act from that foundation of self-knowledge, this man could have energized a collective revitalization of spiritual possibility and religious awareness, to say nothing of the repair and rehabilitation of vilified masculine archetypal patterns. The loss to the life of the whole human community resulting from this one person's failure to live out his authentic life and give concrete shape to his full creative gift is almost incalculable, and the rest of us don't even have any conscious clue about the value of what we have lost. *The misfortune of each individual who fails to live into his/her full being is not only an individual tragedy but also an incalculable loss to the whole world.* It is also an entirely predictable consequence of the collectively recurring patterns of bright shadow projection. Over the millennia, this collective pattern of unconscious projection outward onto others has stolen countless immensely important things from all of us, and continues to rob us today of even more than we can possibly calculate, or even guess.

Our decent family man, patron of the arts, benefactor of the poor, and all-around good guy was also capable of creating a new vision of compassion for our enemies, a work that would have been the worthy successor of *The Dying Gaul*. For centuries, Michelangelo's original sculpture of the dying Gaulish prisoner has awakened a sense of pathos and compassion for the enemy in all those who have viewed it with an open heart.

Our collective need for another emotionally compelling reminder of the necessity to "love our enemies" and "love our neighbors as we love ourselves" has never been greater.

The disastrous consequences of our failure to recognize and love our true selves, and to recognize that *"our enemies" are figments of our unconscious projections*, have also never been greater. The stakes have been raised to global proportions as a result of our collective sorcerer's apprenticeship in science and technology. The need for a more conscious appreciation of the collective consequences of our bright shadow projections, as well as our more familiar dark shadow projections, has become an increasingly urgent priority for our collective survival.

The propensity to "disown" and project the Bright Shadow has always been an archetypal drama of great importance. It is worth remembering that Michelangelo himself had to withdraw his own bright shadow projections on Leonardo da Vinci. Michelangelo grew up at a time when Leonardo was still alive and had won understandable public adulation as the unsurpassable benchmark of artistic and inventive genius and greatness in Renaissance Italy. Imagine how the history of civilization would be diminished if Michelangelo had not been able to recognize and withdraw his own bright shadow projections on Leonardo (of which he wrote in his notebooks). Suppose he had simply devoted himself to slavishly copying Leonardo's work, or had chosen to make his living as an art docent, sharing his deep, sincere, and intimate appreciation of the great man's work with an endless stream of Renaissance tourists, and never expressed his own vision.

Or imagine that Albert Einstein decided to stay married to his first wife and to devote his best energies to becoming the best patent investigator he was capable of being. He would certainly have been an unusually able patent clerk—he was that already—and none of us would have any idea that he could have changed the whole course of modern history with the work of his unique and restlessly inquiring mind.

This universal, archetypal problem of the projection of the Bright Shadow is what the Zen Buddhists are talking about when they say bluntly and metaphorically, "If you meet the Buddha on the road, kill him." It is a shocking little parable that points in laconic Zen fashion toward the central importance of avoiding the terrible consequences of Bright Shadow projection at the psychospiritual level. If you don't metaphorically "kill" the Buddha when you meet him—that is, if you don't withdraw all life energies, both conscious and unconscious, from the inevitable projection invoked by an encounter with the "Enlightened Master"—you, the spiritual traveler on the road of life, will never be able to achieve your own unique experience of enlightenment.

It *looked* as though our imagined lawyer was participating fully and generously in the life of the community, but alas, in this story we know he was not—all because he was unable to throw off the oppressions that were delivered to him with love.

I weave this little story here because I am a dream worker, and for forty-plus years, I have been listening to and working with the dreams of people who might as well be reincarnated Michelangelos. They are people who have been weighed down by the oppressions delivered to them with love and who as a result have failed to become conscious of, or take personal responsibility for, their own unique and wonderful gifts, always finding it so much easier in the short run to "see" them only in their appreciation of others. So many of the dreamers I work with have spent their lives projecting and seeing their own gifts only in others, and being variously exhorted, inspired, and tormented by their dreams as a consequence.

I believe that at some deep level, every human being is a reincarnated Einstein or Michelangelo. We all have unique and extraordinary gifts— gifts that are always ever so much easier to "see" in others than to "own," taking full responsibility for ourselves. As the Australian artist Rowan Williams says, "An artist is not a special kind of person—every person is a special kind of artist." In this sense, all life's challenges and activities are "art." Every good parent, every honest soldier, every ethical businessperson, teacher, farmer, and doctor is "a special kind of artist."

In order to evolve and develop our individual consciousnesses and become truly healthy and whole, we must be more than merely "nice" and "decent." We must each discover, develop, and evolve in the direction of our own deepest authentic character and personality. We must consciously acknowledge and give shape to our idiosyncratic gifts and talents, both individually and collectively. In that crucially important endeavor, bright shadow projection, and the consequent failure to live out and express our own unique gifts and talents, causes more harm, even in the short run, than the endless, ubiquitous, iniquitous, and self-indulgent projection of the dark shadow, which causes unspeakable havoc and misery every day.

*It is always the unique and idiosyncratic gifts, talents, and energies that are reflected and held hostage in the bright shadow. It is also precisely these same energies that are the only ones capable of healing the wounds and restoring the collective health and wholeness crippled by the rampant projection of the dark shadow.* Evolution, both individual and collective, draws us inevitably in the direction of all the archetypal creative energies we first catch sight of in our bright shadow projections.

## SEVEN VARIATIONS IN OUR ABILITY TO REMEMBER DREAMS THAT ARE DIRECTLY RELATED TO AND BOTH STIMULATE AND REFLECT THIS EVOLUTION OF CONSCIOUSNESS

There are a number of recurring patterns in the ways we are able to remember and later recount our dreams that reflect this subtle, nuanced, multilayered process of developing new consciousness and awareness at the individual level. These same images and symbolic dramas also regularly reveal their direct connection to the archetypal patterns of new consciousness and awareness in the collective psyche of the species as a whole. These "styles" of dreaming and, even more important, patterns of *remembering* our dreams can be seen regularly among people all over the planet.

My experience leads me to believe that this individual process of progressive development of character and personality (which Carl Jung aptly called "individuation"—the process of fully becoming the unique, whole, fully alive individual human being that my genetic heritage and personal experience call me to make manifest in the world) also reflects and stimulates collective developments in human awareness. This increased awareness in particular individuals promotes and strengthens the greater integration of intellectual and emotional capacity, and opens the way to extending and deepening intuitive and sensory capability in us all.

These seven particularly recognizable variations in the "style" and quality of dream recall seem to me to reflect this transpersonal enterprise of evolving increasing conscious self-awareness with particular clarity.

The seven types of dream recall I wish to highlight in this connection are:

1. The experience and memory of lucid dreams, in which the sleeping dreamer is aware in the midst of the dream (without necessarily waking up) that "We're not in Kansas anymore."[5]

2. The ability to see, sense, and remember extraordinary beauty in a dream,

3. The dreams in which the awakened sleeper is able to remember "being in more than one place at once," and . . .

4. . . . particularly those dreams in which the awakened sleeper is able to recall that "more than one dream was taking place simultaneously,"

5. Vague and barely conscious dream recollections,

6. Relatively clear and vivid dream memories that also contain "murky," "confusing," and "blank" places in the narrative, and . . .

7. Dreams in which sequentially related *archetypal images* transform and evolve and reveal successively more nuanced, conscious, and developed forms—usually over a series of dreams, and occasionally over the course of a single dream.

In many instances, these categories dissolve into one another, and many dreams will exhibit more than one of these patterns at once. These seven general types of dream recall certainly do not exhaust the list of basic patterns of dream memory that reflect the evolution of consciousness, and of course, *all* remembered dreams reflect the current state of evolution of the dreamer's consciousness and self-awareness, and invite the awakened sleeper to expand his or her awareness even further.

5. I realize that this reference to the 1939 film *The Wizard of Oz* will probably resonate more strongly and clearly with North American readers and filmgoers than with others. The film version of Frank L. Baum's children's classic, *The Wizard of Oz*, has become a part of the cultural heritage of the modern world as a whole, and this playful reference to the movie is the opening suggestion that we would do well to expand and deepen our working definition of "lucid dreaming" to one that gives consideration to *behavior* in a dream as much as, or even more than, the current definition, which is completely focused on purely linguistic cues.

These particular seven "varieties of (remembering) dream experience" are, in my experience, among the most commonly encountered
and most immediately recognizable indicators that this archetypal process of personal individuation is taking place. They are indicators that
also reflect and stimulate the collective development of human awareness
and acuity at the same time. Dreams that match these patterns, and most
particularly *the dreamer's expanding ability to recall and recount these types of
dreams,* also imply, evoke, and energize the processes of the evolution of
collective consciousness as a whole.

## (1) LUCID DREAMING AND
## THE EVOLUTION OF CONSCIOUSNESS

Spontaneous dream lucidity (as opposed to lucidity achieved through
intentional incubation exercises and meditative techniques) is most often
a symbolic reflection of an increasing clarity and depth in the dreamer's
waking perceptions, attitudes, and conscious understanding. Most often,
spontaneous lucidity in dreams reflects the recognition and withdrawal
of previously unconscious projections in waking life.

Let me offer an example. Let us imagine that I am a person who is
aware of growing tension in my workplace. I have noticed that my colleagues and coworkers are increasingly frustrated and angry, and consequently less willing to cooperate cheerfully with one another than they
have been in the past. This perception irritates and depresses me, and
makes me nervous and apprehensive.

Then, after a while, I come to a deeper, more honest insight that it is
actually *I* who am getting angrier and less cooperative. I realize that I am
actually *much* angrier and more disappointed than I have allowed myself to
admit, because I was passed over for promotion in favor of a younger, less
qualified, and less skilled colleague with less tenure on the job than I have.

I slowly realize that I have been repressing and denying the true
strength of my feelings evoked by this situation. As a result of this insight,
I come to understand that one consequence of ignoring and repressing
my own feelings of anger, resentment, and distress has been to make
it much easier for me to "see" these strong feelings in my fellow workers than to recognize them more fully and take more conscious responsibility for them in myself.

In reality, many of my colleagues *do* share many of these same feelings about the inappropriateness and unfairness of the most recent round of promotions, *but not to the degree that I have been "perceiving"/projecting.* Now that I consciously admit to myself the depths of my own rage and disappointment, I see that my fellow employees are not nearly as upset about all this as I thought. I now realize *I* am the one who's *really* angry.

In this example, it is important to remember that it was not mere whim or perversity on my part that I repressed these negative feelings. I don't like feeling impotently angry and frustrated, and since there is nothing I can do about the situation—short of resigning from my job, which I am simply not prepared to do—I now also comprehend more clearly *why* it was so much easier to "see" my own anger and frustration in the others around me, rather than to admit to the full strength of these feelings and "own" them, consciously and uncomfortably, in myself.

A situation like this is an archetypal drama. The individual characters, sets, and costumes are always unique to the particular person, moment, and situation, but the basic shape of projection dramas is universal and remains essentially the same. In such a situation, the conscious admission of previously ignored or denied feelings, attitudes, and ideas will very often serve as a trigger for a corresponding moment of lucidity in dreams.

In other words, since I have come to a clearer understanding of my true circumstances in the waking world, this new waking clarity is then symbolically reflected in the dream world by coming to a clearer and more accurate understanding of my true circumstances in the sleeping world—namely, that *I am asleep and dreaming.*

More and more people are cultivating lucid dreaming as a means of expanding and refining new states of consciousness. My experience is that dream lucidity is indeed "a knife that (potentially) cuts both ways." The cultivation of lucidity in the dream state can and sometimes does lead to corresponding expansion of self-awareness and the ability to see into the previously unconscious and hidden patterns of waking life. In my experience, however, while spontaneous dream lucidity is almost always associated with increased conscious awareness and clarity, most often as a result of the withdrawal of previously unconscious projections in waking life, lucidity cultivated by itself for its own sake often fails to awaken new understandings and clearer perception of the waking world.

In fact, I have seen a number of situations in which it seemed to me (i.e., I projected) that "cultivated lucidity" was being used unconsciously as yet another form of denial and further separation from uncomfortable and challenging realities of waking life. (The fact that I *know* I am capable of this order of self-deception in my exploration of my own dreams makes it all the easier to "see" it in others. And just because it's projection doesn't mean that it isn't also quite possibly true. I acknowledge this archetypal drama of self-deception facilitated by lucid dreaming consciously in myself, and it still looks true to me as I see it in others.)

At another level, many dreamers who are successful in cultivating more or less regular dream lucidity are led to believe that their lucid dreams no longer have multiple layers of meaning and no longer even address the waking world symbolically (e.g., Karle, et al.). In my experience, this is simply not the case. All dreams, whether they contain an obvious element of increased conscious self-awareness of being asleep and dreaming or not, have multiple layers of meaning and continue to address waking consciousness through manifold strata of unconscious metaphor and symbol. Many of these layers of "hidden," unconscious implication and significance continue to be essentially unseen and unknown to the lucid dreamer in the midst of the lucid dreaming experience itself, no matter how dramatic, consciously appreciated, and emotionally satisfying the other lucid elements of the dream may be. (See, for example, the lucid dream of "Alex" confronting the "fire-breathing dragon" of his smoking addiction, in Chapter 8).

Whenever dream lucidity is elevated ideologically to a position of importance and significance above "ordinary dreaming," the likelihood that it may also be unconsciously and ironically recruited as a tool of repression and denial in waking life is significantly increased.

As I see it, one of the best ways to tell if and when the cultivation of lucid dreaming may be unconsciously co-opted to serve repression and denial is to take regular and careful note of whether the feelings and insights gained in the pursuit of lucid dreaming are having the effect of bringing me into closer, more intimate, and more satisfying contact with others in the waking world. At the same time, it is also important to monitor whether or not my lucid dream adventures and insights are contributing to an increase in the vibrancy of my waking creative/

expressive life. If the answer to either or both of these basic questions is "no," then it may be wise for me to put less of my energy and attention into dreaming lucidly and more into deeper, more consciously "lucid" appreciation of my waking-life relationships and creative/expressive possibilities.

Dream lucidity is a marvelous and potentially very important state of mind, offering many exciting possibilities for psychospiritual growth and development (as well as problem solving, creative inspiration, and just plain rambunctious, guilt-free fun). Dream lucidity is not a "magic formula" that somehow relieves the lucid dreamer of the task of deepening conscious self-examination. In fact, in my experience, lucid dreaming makes increasing demands on the dreamer's awareness in the waking world and on the dreamer's responsibility to search even more energetically and honestly for the most self-aware, generous, loving, and creative possibilities and paths of action in his or her life.

### A Weakness in the Current Definition of "Lucid Dreaming"

Currently, the generally accepted definition of "a lucid dream" is one in which the dream character with whom the dreamer identifies in the dream, the "dream ego," has the verbal understanding, either clearly thought or spoken out loud in the dream: "This is dream" or "I am dreaming," etc. Alas, forty-plus years of research using this definition does not seem to me to have turned up much in the way of new information about the lucid dream state itself, or even about the various ways to cultivate it.

Some people argue that Steven LaBerge's NovaDreamer electronic sleep mask represents a genuine advancement in the cultivation of lucid dreaming, since it mechanizes the process of recognizing cues that the experience in the present moment is a dream and not a waking-life event. When the motion sensors built into the NovaDreamer mask detect rapid eye movement under the dreamer's closed eyelids, they activate light-emitting diodes set into the mask in such a way as to appear in the dreamer's area of peripheral vision. With practice, the dreamer learns to associate these winking lights intruding gently into the experience of the dream with the realization "I am dreaming" or "Oh, there are the winking lights—that means this must be a dream," and thus to become lucid without waking up.

The machine works well to promote lucidity in REM sleep, but it does not work to alert dreamers to non-REM dream states, and thus tends to reinforce the idea that REM dreams are really the most interesting and important ones. For this reason, anyone who wishes to become lucid in order to gain better control over any of the various parasomnias (sleepwalking, bed-wetting, night terrors, sleep talking, etc.) will almost certainly find that this instrument is not particularly helpful in that potentially important effort, since all the evidence points to these parasomnias occurring during non-REM dreaming states.

Whether one is a fan of the NovaDreamer machine and its imitators or not, this very important field of inquiry into the nature and importance of lucid dreaming seems to have fallen short of offering any significant new insights into, or even casting any new light on, the many ancient lucid dreaming traditions, such as Temiar Senoi dream practices, Western ritual magic and Gnostic traditions of lucid dreaming, or the lucid dream practices of the various sects of Bon and Tibetan Buddhism.

I believe this apparent failure is due in large measure to the inadequacy of the founding definition itself. This definition rests firmly (and for the most part unconsciously) on the naïve assumption that current language forms are fully capable of defining and cultivating new states of consciousness and awareness without the language forms themselves having to evolve or change. Everything I know says that this unquestioned assumption is incorrect, and that continuing to rely on it is hobbling the field of lucid dream inquiry and is ultimately counterproductive.

### Defining Lucid Dreaming by Behavior Rather Than Language

All images and situations that are remembered from sleeping dreams, whether they are lucid or not, arrive in their place in the dreamer's remembered narrative because of *the totality of their associations and resonances, both conscious and unconscious, both personal and collective.* Archetypal images and symbols, for instance, take memorable shape in the dreamer's memory in large measure because of their inherent transpersonal/collective symbolic associations and significance, *whether or not the dreamer is consciously aware of these broader associations and implications.*

In my experience, the word "dream," like any other element of the remembered dream, appears in a dreamer's narrative because of the totality of associations that it carries.

In English (as well as most of the other languages with which I am familiar), the term "dream" itself carries a range of connotations, many of which are undeniably negative. To call someone "a dreamer" in casual conversation in almost any language is *not* a compliment. In ordinary social conversation, the word "dreamer" inevitably carries a certain stigma, an implication of "idle fantasy" and "pointless flight of ungrounded imagination," often for the apparent purpose of avoiding and ignoring the hard realities of life. *All* of these connotations resonate with the word in the dream world, whether or not the individual dreamer consciously embraces or subscribes to these implications. For this reason alone, it seems to me that relying on a functional definition of dream lucidity that depends on the appearance of forms of the particular ambiguous word "dream" (complete with all these inevitable, negative associations and implications) in the dreamer's memory of the experience constitutes a major stumbling block to exploring the dynamics and the evolutionary implications of lucid dream awareness itself.

For many frequently lucid dreamers, the more often they become aware that they are dreaming without waking up, the more interesting, engaging, and exciting their dreaming becomes, and *the less likely it is that the word "dream" or "dreaming" will figure in their otherwise lucid awareness*. I believe this is primarily because for them this inevitable level of implication of "trivial," "self-deluded," and "unimportant" that the word "dream" carries in common usage *simply does not reflect most lucid dreamers' evolving experience of lucid dreaming itself.*

For this reason, I believe the definition of "lucid dreaming" might well be expanded to focus on the behavior and self-awareness of the dreamer, or "dream ego" in the dream, rather than rely completely on the inherently limiting and inevitably ambiguous language form, "dream." I believe that any dream in which the dreamer "knows" in some fashion that "in this situation" (without necessarily naming it as a "dream state"), the social rules, ethical parameters, and laws of physics are "different" from those that "usually apply," *and in which the dreamer thus behaves accordingly in the dream*, deserves to be categorized as lucid.

### *"Diving off the Ferry"*

Let me offer a clarifying example from my own dreaming. The other night, I dreamed:

I am riding on the ferry from Seattle out across the sound to the Channel Islands and the northern tip of the Olympic Peninsula. The sun is setting, and the air is fresh, sweet, warm, and caressing. I walk out onto the deck, feeling the thrumming of the ship's engines through the steel deck plates and on up through the soles of my shoes: I am surprised to see that no one else is taking advantage of this marvelous moment to smell the air and bask in the last rays of the setting sun.

I lean on the rail and revel in the gorgeous "rightness" of the moment, appreciating the beauty of the small, tree-covered islets as they slip by and enjoying the beautiful aerial dance of the wheeling seabirds, who do seem to be taking advantage of these last warm rays before the sun disappears below the horizon.

Then, out of the corner of my eye, I notice an unexpected flicker of movement off down the deck to my left. I turn and see that a woman in a tan, possibly camel's-hair, coat has come out onto the deck. Like me, she is now leaning comfortably on the rail. She is beautifully illuminated by the golden sunset light. Then I see her suddenly leap up onto the rail with great grace and agility and jump overboard!

I am stunned. For a fraction of a second I see her fall, feet first, her coat flaring out around her like a strange parachute or an upside-down flower opening face downward. . . .

"Hey!" I shout stupidly. For a tiny instant, I am caught in an internal dilemma about whether to shout the standard, immediately understandable and urgent warning, "Man overboard," or whether I should shout, "Woman overboard!" because I know she is female. The instant I become aware of having this thought, I decide that clarity and urgency are far more important than the niceties of gender address.

I tear off my jacket and shout, "Man overboard!" referring to myself as much as to her. I clamber much less gracefully than she did up and over the rail, and dive headfirst into the water in an effort to rescue her.

I hit the water, and it is cold! The sudden chill shocks me, sharpens my senses, and energizes me.

I see that she has disappeared beneath the surface of the water, so I dive and start to swim downward. I am surprised at how clear the water is and how far I can see. . . . I would have thought that the low angle of the setting sun would have made things appear much darker and harder to see under the water, but for some reason it hasn't. . . .

Then I see her! She is below me, still off to my left, and she is sinking like the proverbial stone. I start to swim down toward her, increasingly aware that I am holding my breath and that at some point I am going to have to make a judgment call about how deep I can dive and still have enough air to make it back up to the surface. . . .

Now I see to my amazement that the woman is not passively sinking—she is actively swimming downward into the cold, increasingly dark depths! It comes to me in that moment that although I thought I was diving into the water to save her, she is actually "leading and guiding" me! I am stunned—I had no idea. . . . I redouble my efforts to catch up with her. As I swim downward, I also become aware that I am no longer straining to hold my breath; I am breathing easily—breathing underwater! With this realization comes the clear thought: "All that work that I have been doing remembering and facing my childhood fears—particularly the terrible fear that the authorities would somehow discover how crazy my manic-depressive single mother actually was, and that they would institutionalize her and put me into foster care—must be paying off, because here I am, deep in the waters of cold, dark emotion that I used to experience as utterly overwhelming, and this time, I am not being overwhelmed!"

With that thought, I redouble my efforts to swim down and catch up with my underwater guide, but I see that she is somehow aware of my every move without even appearing to look at me. As I swim faster, she speeds up and maintains the same teasing, enticing distance between us, as we plunge ever deeper into the surrounding darkness.

We are now swimming down through very cold, almost pitch-black water. I can barely make out her shape, arrowing through the water ahead of me. Then I see what appear to be colored lights in the depths. I peer at them as we swim even deeper and realize that they look like the lights of a city—a great, circular underwater city! It's huge, and very beautiful! (I become aware that I am waking up. I try my best to stay asleep and in the dream. I want to go on dreaming and experience whatever is going to happen next! But it is over. I am waking up.)

From my point of view, using the definition of "lucid dream" that I am proposing, this becomes "a fully lucid dream" at the moment when dream-ego "me" recognizes that "I" am "breathing under water," and "I" have a clear thought about one important level of what this ability to breathe underwater *means* symbolically. This all happens without any conscious reference to the idea that "I am dreaming" or even that there are two separate states involved, dreaming and waking. In fact, the "lucid insight" about one important layer of the symbolic meaning of my experience at that moment in the dream blends waking-life thoughts, feelings, and interior work with spontaneous dream imagery and self-awareness into a single, seamless reality.

By the currently accepted definition, this is, at best, a "pre-lucid dream," since it has many seemingly lucid elements, but the crucial verbal realization "this is a dream" is still absent. Not too surprisingly, I do not find this to be the best terminology either, since the term "pre-lucid" also carries and promotes the distinct implication of a "self-evident" hierarchy of value, with "lucid dreams" being of greater import and value than "ordinary dreams." Once again, in my experience, "self-evident" and immediately appealing though this notion may be, it is simply not true.

I believe this hierarchical attitude that "naturally" places lucid dreaming above other forms of dream experience is itself *symbolic*. Not only does it reflect the archetypal association of evolving consciousness with lucid dreaming, it also implies a belief that the current state of human intellectual capacity and verbal self-awareness is the epitome of evolved consciousness and that "the evolution of consciousness" means simply extending the current state of waking awareness and understanding further into the dream world without any growth or fundamental change.

Even though the general association of lucid dreaming with evolving consciousness is solid and demonstrable, the adoption of this attitude without further thought or feeling is, in my view, a special case of *mistaken literalism;* it is a literalistic interpretation of what is an essentially symbolic event.

It is an error to assume that because of this *symbolic* association, lucid dreams are somehow automatically "better" or "more evolved" than nonlucid dreams. *All* dreams are important (witness the "maybe pastel colors" dream), and setting up such hierarchies of value for dream experiences almost always ends up reflecting, reinforcing, and reifying the unconscious limits of the *current* states of self-awareness, thought, feeling, sensory acuity, and intuitive ability, rather than extending and developing them further. For this reason, such an attitude is very likely to postpone and frustrate any developmental steps beyond these unconsciously assumed limitations into genuinely new states of awareness and consciousness.

From my point of view, dreams like the one recounted above, in which it is clearly understood that the dream reality and the waking reality are so intimately connected as to be *one*, and that they coexist as related elements of a single, greater, all-embracing reality (a contemporary reflection of the archetypal *unus mundus* of medieval philosophical and spiritual reflection), represent a fairly high order of self-awareness. It seems to me that such dreams are at least as "lucid" as the dreams in which the unconsciously ambiguous defining word "dream" appears.

It is also important to remember in this connection that lucid dreams are *only one way among many* in which the evolution of consciousness reflects itself in the ways that dreams are experienced and remembered. To focus exclusively on lucid dreaming as the primary dreaming mode in which the evolution of consciousness is depicted and fostered is a limited perspective, and is itself a species of mistaken literalism.

### Multiple Layers of Meanings in Lucid Dreams

*Lucid dreams are not stripped of their multiple layers of unconscious meaning and implication.* For example, the question in this dream, "How long can I hold my breath?" is *not* a literal question. At one level, it does reflect the "literal" physical reality of the chronic sleep apnea from which I suffer with increasing severity as I age. This level of implication is clearly present in the dream, but I recognize it with the "aha!" of insight only after I have awakened and am thinking about the dream in retrospect.

At another level, this thought about "holding my breath" in the dream is also simultaneously a metaphor of my waking mind's initial refusal to open itself to the healing and transformative influence of the unconscious. It requires "ego-me" to relinquish the illusion of "heroic" conscious control of my life in that moment in the dream and to accept and embrace my oneness with the thing that I initially experience as definitely "not me"—the cold waters of the unconscious that surround and threaten to "drown" me.

The figure of the "suicidal" woman who turns out to be my "guide" is also overdetermined, polysemic, and multivocal. In this dream, the woman who jumps off the boat is at one level a transpersonal, archetypal trickster figure, "tricking" me into "risking my life" by leaping overboard "myself." At another level, she is also an image of my personal feminine consort (anima) figure, carrying and energizing my ambivalent but ultimately emotionally persuasive longings for greater conscious awareness of the hidden depths of my own being. Because dreaming-me is tricked into following her into the symbolic cold, dark depths, I am able to catch a glimpse of the amazing, surprising place where my personal psychology touches and joins with the archetypal energies and patterns of the collective unconscious, the glowing, mandala-shaped "city" beneath the waves.

In order to truly grow and evolve, I (like so many others) must follow my feminine soul into the frightening and disorienting depths of my unconscious emotional being, no matter how fearful and symbolically "life-threatening" that journey may appear to be. Such a willing descent into the depths of personal unconsciousness (albeit the result of being "tricked" into it) always leads eventually to the levels of archetypal unconscious symbolism that we all share collectively.

Pursuing and attempting to rescue this part of my personal, emotional, feminine consort self in the dream involve "me" being tricked into losing my previous, habitual strategies for acquiring a sense of self-worth and self-importance. It is worth noting that at one point in adolescence (during the era of the dating wars and the "parade dress uniform" of camel's-hair coats), I struggled with suicidal feelings, which I now associate with my underdeveloped relationship with my personal and collective Consort. My "heroic" act of "attempted rescue" in the dream lead inevitably to an even deeper participation in the archetypal drama of "Willing Sacrifice" enacted in the dream in a more lucid and self-aware fashion in the symbolic "depths."

These dream activities in turn symbolically reflect and lend support and motivation to similar acts and situations in waking life where the demands of emotional, psychological, and ultimately spiritual growth require me to relinquish old patterns of behavior I engage in habitually in order to acquire and foster feelings of self-worth and self-esteem. Giving up these increasingly outmoded strategies and behaviors requires that I become more aware of them first and then alter my actions on the basis of these new understandings.

### The Necessity of "Willing Sacrifice"

This lucid dream offers multiple examples of transpersonal, archetypal images and symbolic experiences embodying organizing principles in the unconscious that are deeply collective while remaining absolutely and uniquely personal.

The archetypal drama of Willing Sacrifice unfolds in the dream, as the woman purposefully jumps off the boat, and is continued as "I" willingly jump into the water in the seemingly conscious "heroic" effort to "rescue" her. She turns out to be much less in need of "rescuing" than "I" am myself. "I" willingly and consciously push the envelope of how long I can hold my breath without "drowning." This is also a "willing sacrifice" of my own comfort and apparent safety in the dream. This action seems to be a necessary precursor to the realization that "I was deluded—I am not so much attempting to rescue her as she is leading and guiding me!" Each successive "willingly accepted risk" in the dream strips away another layer of habitual self-image. Ultimately, the evolving drama of "willing sacrifice" leads to the discovery of the "glowing city at the bottom of the sea."

The "underwater city" reveals a segmented, circular, mandala shape as "we" swim down toward it. The perceived beauty of the mysterious, previously hidden city beneath the sea makes it emotionally and intellectually clear in the dream that diving to these depths is *worth the risk*. The dream creates a situation in which the dream ego is "tricked" into hazarding its habitual sense of self in order to connect more consciously with the energetic essence of this "breathtakingly" beautiful, "divinely orderly" energy and symbolically collective structure "in the depths."

## (2) "BEAUTY" IN THE DREAM WORLD AS AN ARCHETYPAL SYMBOL OF PSYCHOSPIRITUAL WHOLENESS

*Anytime a dreamer reports an "aesthetic response" to beauty in a dream, it is a very reliable indicator that whatever the image or situation is in the dream that evokes that response is itself a symbolic representation of reliable psychospiritual truth in the dreamer's waking life.* In this dream, the beauty of the sunset scene at the beginning and the startling beauty of the "underwater city" at the end are both clear examples.

The discovery of what I am calling "reliable spiritual perspective," particularly when it appears in a dream along with an element of willing sacrifice, is also a key element in the evolution of consciousness and self-awareness. A reliable spiritual perspective is one that allows me to remain calm and clear, flexible and creative, communicative and attentive, loving and able to be loved, *even in the midst of my own deepest sorrow, regret, and confusion.* In this important sense, the awareness of "beauty" in a dream is another archetypal narrative metaphor of the "alchemy" of psychospiritual evolution, or "individuation." When a person achieves a firm grasp, or even a brief glimpse of such a state if mind and heart, it is very often an occasion for dreaming of something "very beautiful and awe-inspiring." This archetypal association is so reliable that it is always worth asking when such a moment is encountered in a dream whether the dreamer is approaching, or perhaps is already in the midst of achieving, such a realization.

### The Alchemy of Individuation

Carl Jung demonstrated exhaustively through his historical research that "alchemy" was (and in the dream world still is) an archetypal metaphor of the process of deconstruction and reconstruction of consciousness and memory that leads to individuation—that is to say, the achievement of emotional, psychological, and ultimately spiritual maturity.

The interior work that a person must do in order to remain fully aware of the deep meaning and value of life in general, and his or her life in particular—especially in the face of the "worst things," the greatest miseries and sufferings of his or her life—is symbolized on the one hand by the awareness of beauty in a dream, and on the other by the "lapis," the "philosopher's stone," and "alchemical gold" in the medieval and Renaissance alchemical texts and drawings. To be able *to live consciously, fully, lovingly, wisely, and creatively while also being equally aware of all the worst things in human life **is** alchemy.*

### Excrement and Alchemy

Very often, this archetypal drama of "alchemical transformation" involves images of excrement and "shit" in the dream world. We human beings appear to be inherently predisposed to symbolize the worst things in our lives as "shit." In a dream, the appearance of excrement (from the tiniest desiccated cat turds all the way to the "hell world" made entirely of revolting bodily waste stretching to the horizon) is a very reliable indicator that the dreams are touching on "the worst things" in the dreamer's life.

As a child, the "worst things" include all the terrible things that other people have done to me, along with the worst things that ever happened to me through misadventure. As the child grows into adolescence and young adulthood, the category of "the worst things" expands to include all the worst things that I have ever done or participated in doing to others. Ultimately, as I mature into authentic emotional adulthood, the basket of "worst things" tends to expand again to include the worst things that human beings have ever done, whether I was there to witness and participate in any of them directly or not.

Because dreams with images of excrement tend to focus on the "worst things," at the emotional/psychological level, whenever "shit" appears in a dream, there is always reason to inquire about the dreamer's state of mind and whether or not he or she is struggling with depression in waking life. The sudden immersion in conscious contemplation of the worst things in one's life (most often precipitated by cascading events in the outer world beyond his/her ability to avoid or control) is a predictable occasion for a descent into depression and melancholy.

At a deeper psychospiritual level, the dreams of excrement that accompany and reflect the growing conscious awareness of the "worst things" is also *a shining promise*. As Carl Jung's researches have demonstrated, because "shit" is an archetypal metaphor of "the worst things," it means that in the dream world, *"shit" is the* only *"base matter" that can actually be turned into true gold in the end.*

The bowdlerized "lead" of the early alchemical texts is itself a metaphor of "shit" (as Jung's studies revealed). Translated into more immediately recognizable contemporary psychospiritual terms, this means that the consciously felt sense of transcendent meaning and communion with the Divine and the deepest sense of meaning and value in my life must be able to remain consciously robust and to withstand the direct experience of, and full immersion in, the "worst things." Unless it passes the test of full encounter with the *absolutely* "worst things," the resultant psychospiritual awareness will not prove adequate to the demands of the dreamer's life experience.

If the "base matter" with which the archetypal alchemical process begins is anything less than the undiluted "shit" of the authentic worst things in a person's life, then the seeming "gold" of the emotional/spiritual perspective that is born from the encounter will almost certainly turn out to be "fool's gold" and will not be able to withstand the "real worst thing" when it finally forces its grotesquely ugly head into the field of conscious awareness.

If a person's spiritual perspective is based solely on pious practices and on carefully avoiding the worst pains and miseries of life, then (short of the completely unpredictable intrusions of grace, or baraka, or Avalokiteshvara, or the Paraclete, or whatever name your particular culture and tradition chooses to call it) the only possible outcome of such a carefully "edited" spirituality is deathbed despair. I will find myself on my deathbed with the worst things in one hand (because they actually happened, and it is simply impossible to go on pretending that they didn't) and a spiritual perspective in my other hand that has been carefully crafted my whole life long to avoid them.

One of the strongest implications of the dreams in which "shit" appears is the promise that despite the likelihood of accompanying depression and misery, the absolutely necessary first step in the archetypal drama of alchemical transformation of the "worst things" into the "gold" of adequate spiritual knowledge and perspective is being taken.

The "worst things" have been encountered and are still a focus of consciousness in waking life, and a dream reflecting that situation in images of "shit" also silently promises that if the dreamer continues to remain courageously conscious of the whole difficult process, and goes on about the business of living and loving and creating with a whole heart (no matter how anguished and filled with pain that heart may be), then eventually this sustained encounter with the "worst things" *will* enable and bring about the transformation of that same, seemingly irredeemable "shit" into the "alchemical gold" of spiritual vision and experience that is strong enough to thrive and nurture the dreamer even in the terrible, scaly grip of the "worst things."

### "Willing Sacrifice" and the Evolution of Consciousness

Staying conscious and fully alive even in the face of the worst things *is* an archetypal act of Willing Sacrifice. In the "Diving into the Depths of Puget Sound" dream, there is a distinct implication that the courage to "risk all" is *necessary* in order to reach the place where the "beautiful mandala city" can be glimpsed. Certainly, in my childhood, the looming specter of my mother's mental illness and the possible destruction of our beleaguered little family was the simultaneously archetypal and personal "worst thing" in my life at that time. Doing the waking-life work to face it both literally and symbolically in the "cold depths" is a specific example of the archetypal drama of Willing Sacrifice in the service of "willing sacrifice" and the evolution of consciousness in my own life.

I could not even face those fears consciously most of the time as a kid. As an adult, I see that honestly naming, facing, and owning those fears was, and still is, an essential, archetypal element in the continuing drama of my own evolving consciousness today. In this particular dream, the apparently "suicidal" gesture of the woman who jumps off the boat, followed moments later by my own willingness to "jump overboard to rescue her," and later by the sacrifice of limited understanding and the willingness to go past the supposed "fail-safe" point in my "dive," are all concrete examples of the archetypal drama of Willing Sacrifice. The clear archetypal shape of the events in the dream suggests a two-way link to the collective drama, and the likelihood of similar evolution of courage and consciousness on a collective level as well.

Willing Sacrifice of this kind, in my experience, is necessary in order to open up to the gifts of new psychospiritual awareness that await us all "in the depths," and of whose amazing "impossible" existence in the dream I was previously unaware. The more lucid I am in the dream world the more easily I will be able to "recognize my true circumstances" and *to overcome the fear that prevents me from growing and becoming more self-aware in the dream, as well as in waking life.*

## (3) "BEING IN TWO PLACES AT ONCE"— MULTIPLE SELF-AWARENESS AND THE "DISEMBODIED OBSERVER PERSPECTIVE" AS MARKERS OF EVOLVING CONSCIOUSNESS

Many dreamers have already had the experience of being in more than one place at once in a dream. Often people remember dreams where they watch themselves acting in a dream from an elevated, "disembodied" perspective, while simultaneously experiencing the dream through the apparently physically embodied dream ego. Usually, the disembodied observing presence is less emotionally involved in the action than the seemingly embodied self, and often is a focus for a broader perspective, both visually and emotionally, than that carried by the seemingly embodied dream-ego figure.

One of the very likely implications of any dream that assumes this generic form is that it is addressing, in symbolic terms, an issue in the dreamer's waking life that the person cares about deeply. The "disembodied perspective" in the dream is most often an archetypal metaphor of having achieved a hard-won, relatively objective view of this situation, in spite of the deep desire for particular results and outcomes.

At the same time, the disembodied observing perspective in dreams is also a symbolic form evoking the "successful" repression of strong feelings and emotions—a preconscious act that may have been necessary in order to achieve the relatively "objective" view in the first place. Symbolically, the "body"—the locus of feeling and emotion—has been "removed" from the experience of the dream, making the more "objective" intellectual understanding of the situation less fraught with complication, pain, and difficulty.

### Looking at Things Through Glass, Breaking Glass, and Breathing Underwater in Dreams

This "disembodied observer" mode of dream experience and memory is fundamentally related to another, somewhat less common, but still quite frequent dream experience—namely, looking at things through glass or some other transparent substance. When a dreamer looks through glass at something in the dream world, it is a very reliable symbolic indicator that in waking life the dreamer is attempting to understand his or her life in purely conscious and intellectual terms, and is repressing unwanted feeling and emotion in the process. The emotional distance symbolically implied by "looking through glass" is similar to the emotional distance symbolized by the disembodied observing perspective.

Just as I can easily tell in waking life whether the scene I am viewing through glass is being distorted by the glass itself, the clarity of the images seen through glass in the dream is also a very reliable indicator of whether or not the waking intellectual analysis and understanding of the situation in question is accurate or distorted. Like the museum display case in waking life, the message of the glass surface in dreams is "Look but Don't Touch."

Breaking glass, or even coming upon glass that has already been broken in a dream is almost always a metaphor of the emotional impact of a waking-life situation "breaking through" the barrier of detached intellectual comprehension and beginning to make itself felt. In this sense (as mentioned above), the experience of "breathing underwater" in dreams is also regularly associated with the issue of accurate intellectual analysis versus feeling the full emotional impact of a waking-life problem or the memory of waking life trauma.

When a dreamer finds himself or herself "breathing underwater," it is always worth asking if some aspect of this dream may be celebrating the achievement of a level of emotional maturity that he or she had not achieved the last time this "overwhelming" set of feelings was encountered.

The metaphor is particularly touching and evocative for me, because it makes the situation very clear symbolically. The "waters" (of strong emotion and feeling) are just as deep and potentially "overwhelming" as they were last time. (This is not a metaphor of "rising above it" by "walking on the water," or of minimizing the feelings—"I am only in water up to my knees," etc.) The dream points out that "I" am still "in way over my head," but "I" have other aspects of my being that I can call on besides my intellectual capacities residing in my "head." Now (often without my having realized it consciously) "I" have this miraculous new emotional strength that allows me to be totally in the midst of these feelings and *not* be overwhelmed the way "I" was in the past. All my experience led me to expect "drowning," only my new (usually hard-won), emotional maturity allows me to experience the tremendously intense feelings with their full force and *not* "drown" in them as I did in the past.

In this symbolic sense, the particular dream experiences of "breathing underwater" and "breaking the glass" are both dream metaphors that celebrate the evolution and development of consciousness at a very personal level. People who are able to grow and mature in this way, so that their dreams offer up these archetypal metaphors of dramatically evolving emotional strength and self-awareness in their personal lives, are also "volunteering," whether they realize it or not, to have their lives become a venue where these developmental/evolutionary energies assume a collective role and quality as well.

Every person who does the personal work of individuation is also fueling and facilitating the collective evolution of human consciousness at the same time. Collective evolution of consciousness takes place only in individual lives. My experience suggests very strongly that the particular dream metaphors discussed here (particularly because of their archetypal quality and universal appearance in the dreams of individuals who are from diverse and widely separated cultures and who speak very different languages) are most often markers of the interface between the personal evolution of individual consciousness and the potential of symbolically similar development of greater consciousness in the whole human species.

## (4) REMEMBERING MULTIPLE SIMULTANEOUS DREAM REALITIES

This implication of dual impact in both the personal and collective realms is also carried by those dreams in which the dreamer is able to recall more than one dream "happening" at once. In some sense, this is an apparent "extension" or "development" of the dream of multiple perspectives and loci of consciousness within a "single dream." Over the years, in my experience, dreamers tend to remember and report the "disembodied observer" dreams before they start remembering and reporting dreams where "multiple realities are all taking place at once." It may not be necessary for this development of consciousness to take place in this sequential fashion, and at the same time I have yet to meet anyone who reports the "multiple simultaneous realities" dreams who does not also report remembering "disembodied observing presence" dreams that preceded them.

The experience of multiple simultaneous realities is first cousin to the "disembodied observing presence" dreams, but instead of experiencing the same dream setting and events as the seemingly embodied dream ego/"I," the multiple "dream egos" are experiencing what appear to be quite different dreams with different settings and characters and situations, all taking place at the same time.

Another example may be helpful here. The dreamer who shared this dream with me is an old friend of mine. She shared this dream with me in the early spring of 2008, while I was on the road, facilitating a weekend dream work seminar on the East Coast.

It is also worth noting that all of the rest of the dreams discussed in this chapter are "lucid" by the definition proposed above. Even though the verbal knowledge of the experience being a "dream" does not appear in any of the narratives that follow, the dreamers' decisions and actions all indicate a courageous, conscious acceptance of the "radical differentness" of the situations in which they find themselves, together with a willingness to act in ways that they would not undertake in waking life. It is this expanded state of mind and heart that is the more accurate and productive definition of dream lucidity.

### July 4, 2007: What price will I pay/Protecting the mainframe

This dream was *not linear in that it felt like there were two dreams happening at the same time rather than one dream after another* [emphasis mine], though I will tell them in a linear way.

Poetry, elaborate multi-windowed comic-strip panels, and split-screen film and TV are other ways that might be utilized to convey this kind of multiple, simultaneous dream experience, but for the purposes of an ordinary written dream record, there are few practical alternatives to express this other than to say bluntly, "There were two dreams happening at the same time, though I will tell them in a linear way."

#### THEME 1

I've heard about a healing modality from someone at work, and I want to check it out. I'm interested and considering doing it, but I can't seem to find out what it is going to cost me. There is a kind of secrecy about it. I call to set up an appointment, but it is not clear. I'm somewhere else now in an office in a house and I try again. *(This movement to a new place seems to reflect getting to the house/office in the other part of the dream* [emphasis mine].*)* I find out that I have to make a commitment for an initial set of sessions and it will cost a fee plus some other charge, but you don't find out the price until you are through with the initial plan. That leaves me wondering about doing it. I ask someone else who has done it, but she can't tell me. It's to be kept a secret. I ask again are we talking hundreds of dollars, or thousands of dollars, but she won't say, though she hints that it will be fine.

## THEME 2

This feels like a science-fiction kind of theme. There is some kind of war going on in a futuristic world, and there is a band of military police after me. I'm on a mission to save my people, and I'm trying to get to a certain destination. I'm being pursued by the band of MPs, who are trying to bring me back somewhere to a prison of sorts or to somewhere where my freedom would be taken away from me. I have certain powers and abilities but I am also aware that I have a limited amount of energy left to use them. I have the ability to shape-shift into the elements, but I also have to plan well and conserve my energy if I am going to complete my mission. I'm crossing a big bridge that looks something like the Golden Gate Bridge. There is lots of backed-up traffic on it, but I am flying above it. The MPs are also chasing me and are getting close. Below me on the bridge there is also a car of sorts that is filled with them. On the driver's side of the car there are no doors, and they are hanging out and holding on to the car as it goes along. I seem to have someone with me, someone younger, I can't get a clear picture, but I am talking with this person and explaining what is going on, much like I am narrating this dream. To protect us from this band of MPs in the sideless car, I turn into the wind. I become a ferocious wind and blow with hurricane force at them and knock them out of the car, but I am careful not to overdo it, so I won't use up all my energy, like wearing out my batteries to do these specific shape-shift things.

I continue to try to get where I'm going, and the MPs who are in the air are closing in on me. I turn myself into fire and hurl balls of flame at them. It buys me some time, and I get to my destination. It is a kind of house with an office in it. There is someone there, and I'm telling her that the MPs are coming. She doesn't seem to be aware of what is really going on or the urgency of the situation. She seems young and naïve. She thinks everything is okay, and I try to explain that she is being used by the people who have hired her. She is supposed to be protecting something, and they want to get to it. They have put her in charge because they think she will let them in. I ask her where it is, and she brings me to it to show that it is quite safe.

We are standing in the entry room of the house. The door to enter seems to be on the right rather than the front of the house. We go into the next room and then into a locked room that is behind that. It seems to be a little reception office with nothing but a desk and chair. Then we go into the room to the right of that; it is kind of like we made a big U-turn and are in a room behind the room we first started in. It is also locked, but she has the key. We walk through the door, and the room, which is a little bigger than the outer office, is filled with some kind of mainframe computer system. It is very large, with lights blinking on and off. It is like the control room for something. I tell her that this is what they are looking for. I suddenly have a moment of panic as I realize that I didn't lock the outer office door behind me. We are standing in the doorway between the two rooms. And just as that thought crosses my mind, I look up and an older woman is walking through the door, and I know we have been caught.

I strongly suspect that all us humans (and who knows—perhaps all vital organisms?) are dreaming multiple (perhaps uncountable), simultaneous dreams all the time. I suspect the big deal is not so much to *dream* in this fashion; the big deal is to have evolved waking consciousness and self-awareness sufficiently to begin to *remember* dreaming in this fashion upon awakening.

### Living with Paradox and the Evolution of Consciousness— The Image of Bridges in the Dream World

Jung suggests—and my experience is that he is absolutely correct— that any religion or spiritual practice can be understood as "mature" and "immature" on the basis of its relationship to paradox. Immature religion and spiritual practice attempts to eliminate paradox, while mature religion and spiritual practice acknowledge irreconcilable paradox and attempts to prepare and support the participant in living fully and well in the full awareness and experience of inevitable paradox. My experience leads me to believe that the evolution of consciousness at both the individual/personal and collective/species-wide level is also deeply bound up with the encounter with archetypal paradox.

In the dream world, "bridges" often appear as archetypal images of the ability to "live with full awareness in the midst of paradox." Bridges are architectural creations of human consciousness and skilled physical effort that allow people to travel back and forth across chasms and other spaces that would otherwise be very difficult, if not impossible, to cross. This waking-life truth about bridges is also symbolic of the ability to hold "both sides of a paradox" consciously in mind rather than "taking up permanent residence on only one side or the other." For this reason, it is always worth asking whenever a bridge appears in a dream, even if it is "in the background" and seemingly "unimportant," whether this dream might have as one of its foci a maturing relationship with intellectually, emotionally, psychologically, and ultimately spiritually irreconcilable paradox.

### The Notion of an All-Powerful, All-Good God Creates the Problem of Evil

For those who have been brought up to believe in, or have chosen to believe in, "an all-powerful and all-good God," the question of "why then do the innocent suffer?" is an example of such an irreconcilable paradox. The generation of the concept of "all-powerful and all-good divinity" itself *creates* the paradoxical "problem of evil." Immature religion and spiritual practice attempts to eliminate the paradox by asserting things like "If they suffer, then they can't be innocent!" or "Even if they are 'innocent' in this life, they must be paying for sins in a past life!" Mature religion and spiritual practice says, "This is a paradox I cannot resolve, so I must content myself with doing my loving and creative best to relieve suffering in myself and others in whatever ways I can in the full face of this paradox."

The appearance of the "bridge" implies that this is a dream about learning to live fully and openly in the midst of intellectually and emotionally irreconcilable paradox. I know the dreamer and her life circumstances. She works for a spiritually oriented organization, which, like all organizations, spiritual or otherwise, operates in practice like a dysfunctional family. If it were my dream, one of the inevitable paradoxes informing this dream is the tension between the wonderful shared vision that inspires us all and the petty, irritating, unjust realities of day-to-day administration in a community of occasionally less-than-enlightened personalities.

In "Theme 1," the ambiguous "cost" of the "new healing modality" calls up for me the archetypal pattern of the "Pearl of Great Price." The Pearl of Great Price is a symbol of the effort necessary to accomplish the task(s) of psychospiritual growth and evolution of conscious self-awareness, and also the goal of the process—the "transformed evolved state" itself. Questions of monetary value in the dream world are very often symbols of the true medium of exchange that we use within our psyches and with one another—namely, our energies, both physical and nonmaterial.

The "price" of the Pearl of Great Price is always the same: it is *everything I have.* If I am down to my last dollar and change, it costs a dollar and all my change; if I have just cashed in all my Microsoft stock, it costs all the millions I have acquired down to the last penny, plus whatever walking-around money I also happen to have. This is an archetypal symbol of the simple fact that in order to truly grow and evolve as a psycho-spiritual being, I must commit myself to that process wholeheartedly and sincerely. No one gets to invent a fake person who does not embody and express the wholeness that each of us is and is capable of becoming, and then have that fake "puppet" achieve the great transformation of aware-ness, learn the great secret, experience the great truth—the truth of who I *really* am.

For this reason, the "price" of growth and evolution of awareness in terms of energy and honesty is always the same—it's all I've got—and just as the dream says, it only *looks* as though "I may not be able to afford it." After the price has been paid (and it doesn't have to be paid until I'm well into the process, until I understand just what the price is), it is always "worth it." In fact, it turns out to be the only thing that's worth it.

In my imagined version of this dream, the "mainframe computer" in Theme 2 is also an archetypal image of the goal of the process, the rea-son for the journey from the beginning. It is an image with many of the same symbolic resonances as the "shining underwater city" of my earlier dream (right down to the multiple shining lights). The "mainframe" is a repository of the world's knowledge and creative energy. It connects one with all. It is Pearl itself, viewed from a different angle.

Because it is a "mainframe," it also implies a *collective* level of thought, feeling, sensation, and intuition. In my imagined version of this dream, the presence of an image like "mainframe," with its inevitably collective implications of "connectivity" with countless other computers, includ-ing "personal computers," suggests that the dreamer's personal struggles and personal individuation dramas have reached a point of depth and intensity where they resonate with issues of collective evolution of con-sciousness as well.

The timing of this dream, occurring as it does on "the fourth of July," also suggests the increasingly terrible personal and collective paradox that more and more Americans are struggling with—namely, that our nation, supposedly dedicated to the equality of all human beings, and to the ideals of peace and participatory democracy, is waging a bloody, ill-conceived international and domestic war that threatens to efface or even destroy those very ideals. The "MPs" in my imagined version of the dream call up the specter of a military police state and the sense of constant injustice and fear that it evokes. No one wishes to put themselves and their loved ones in harm's way by speaking the truth to power, particularly in a police state like the one we are evolving into, but we also all know somewhere in our depths that all that is required for evil to prevail is for good to remain silent.

My imagined version of this dream gives shape to deep and not fully acknowledged fears and disappointments about America herself, and about being an American on the Fourth of July.

At this level, particularly when I imagine being a woman having this dream, I believe that the "flying MPs" are not just images of the literal "Military Police," enforcing martial law on the civilian populace in a time of unpopular war, they are also "Maternal Principles." It is an archetypal problem for us parents—and for mothers in particular in this masculinist, sexist society—to feel called upon to sacrifice not only our time and energy for our children but even to give up our authentic being and life energy. To give up the truth of my own authentic, evolving being is a perversion of the archetype of willing sacrifice, and yet it is asked of me and other parents over and over again by the society that both nurtures and supports me on the one hand, and asks me to pretend to be someone other than who I am on the other. I am asked to give up my right to the Pearl of Great Price and pretend to be satisfied with the half-life that is thrust upon me by conventional wisdom, by church, state, education, and popular culture.

This uneasiness reflects my uneasiness about the oppressions of the workplace, and the oppressions of the family, as well as the increasingly inescapable oppressions of my own government. In my imagined version of this dream, the question of discovering my own truth and following my own authentic path to a place of newly evolved consciousness requires me to see all these other pressures in my life with greater clarity, including my responsibility to "be there to help others, even at the cost of my own life."

In my dream, one of the reasons why I feel as though "we have been caught" at the end of Theme 2 is that "I" feel caught in the gap between the possibility of my own evolution and the fulfillment of the nurturing roles and responsibilities that have always been close to the core of sense of my own worth and well-being as a parent and as a worker in an enterprise devoted to the nurture and betterment of the lives of our particular "clients" in a conscious effort to contribute to the betterment of the whole world community. Imagining myself as the dreamer of this dream, I am filled with all the intense feelings that fuel the collective Prophetic Voice, and at the same time, I am always thinking about the best outcomes for the particular people around me and for the ones I specifically love, even though they are farther away, and for everyone everywhere.

The competing demands of these ways of being and feeling in the world are in conflict in me, and I have yet to find an adequate path through the paradoxes these conflicting feelings and loyalties create.

I also *fly* and wield the powers of Nature herself in this dream, and the very fact that the dreamer has *remembered* this dream, with its multiple simultaneous realities, suggests to me that she is well on the way to embracing these paradoxes with a full heart and to finding a creative, energetic, loving path over the "Golden" bridge that connects them all.

Whether or not these projections are actually true for the dreamer's original experience, only she can say. They are certainly true for me in my imagined version of this dream, and if you, the reader, find any of these suggestions provocative and moving, then you have discovered something true and valuable about *your* imaginatively acquired version of this dream as well.

*Remembering Multiple, Simultaneous Realities as an Archetypal Symbol of Compassion*

Perhaps the most important implication of this multiple, "double" dream related to the evolution of consciousness is the dreamer's ability to *remember* the two seemingly separate, simultaneous dream experiences (which become "narratives" when expressed and shared with others). *The ability to recall and hold in mind seemingly different, simultaneous realities is, in itself, both an archetypal symbol of compassion and the single most necessary concrete strategy to manifest compassion in the world.*

Compassion, at the most immediate and practical level, rests upon and requires the ability to hold more than one worldview, or set of psychospiritual organizing principles, consciously in mind at once. In my experience, any activity that actually grows from this multiple, simultaneous perspective is compassionate, and any attitude or activity that does not rest on this foundation of multiple, simultaneous awarenesses does not deserve to be called "compassionate," regardless of the other words used to describe it.

There is a certain kind of sentimentality that equates "compassion" with "pity." In this way of thinking and feeling, there's ordinary pity, which makes a person feel bad contemplating another's pain and distress, and there is "big," twelve-cylinder, turbocharged pity, which may actually be powerful enough to move a person to take some sort of helping, ameliorating action, and this "amped-up" version of pity is understood as compassion. In my experience, pity and compassion are opposites ("true contraries," in the language of William Blake).

Pity emphasizes and grows from a vivid sense of how different the one experiencing the pity is from the object of his or her contemplation, while compassion always grows out of a vivid sense of connection and similarity to the object of attention, despite the often huge and obvious differences in their respective appearances, circumstances, and points of view.

In this way of understanding compassion, being able to remember two or more seemingly different and apparently unconnected simultaneous dreaming realities, to say nothing of being able to sense places where these two realities touch and influence one another (as in the above dream when the dreamer reports, "This movement to a new place seems to reflect getting to the house/office in the other part of the dream"), turns out in practice to be an archetypal metaphor for *the basic practice of compassion: holding other people's worldviews vividly and consciously in mind while dealing with them from one's own differing but consciously compassionate point of view.* Note that this does not mean being overwhelmed or "convinced" by the worldview or opinions of the other(s), but holding them and their attitudes consciously and fully in mind, even if/when these attitudes also awaken my antipathy and are fundamentally repulsive to me. It is also important to note that at the Gestalt level, this kind of compassion "begins at home." It is born out of the difficult interior work of recognizing and remaining conscious of the "other" within. This interior work is absolutely necessary, in my experience. Recognizing the potentially conflictual and disharmonious parts of the previously unconscious self reflects and paves the way for the corresponding compassionate work in the world.

Pity is reserved in practice for people we basically feel superior to, while compassion embraces all people as emotionally worthy and valid and of equal and profound importance. True compassion even extends to people who are truly our enemies, people who will do us serious harm and injury if we are foolish enough to allow them to. Feeling compassion for such people is difficult, and also *absolutely necessary* if we are ever to end, or even ameliorate, the cycles of gender, ethnic, and class hatred and violence that threaten in every era to destroy us and the societies and cultures we cherish.

In my experience, over the years with many dreamers, and in particular with this dreamer, the ability to remember and recount dreams with different simultaneous "narratives" is a hallmark of deepening and widening compassion evolving hand in hand with the development of the dreamer's new consciousness and self-awareness in waking life. The collective, archetypal images and situations in these simultaneous dream realities (the "new healing modality," the "ambiguous price that must be kept secret," the "big bridge," the "mainframe," the direct "magical" identity with the classic archetypal "four elements"—particularly "wind and fire," etc.), all point very clearly to the *collective, transpersonal* resonances of these dream images and metaphors. The appearance of archetypal images of this kind and the roles they play in the dream(s) imply a connection to the parallel evolution and development of collective awareness, creative response, and consciousness going hand in hand with the dreamer's personal development.

## (5) DREAMS THAT ARE DIFFICULT TO RECALL AND THEIR IMPLICATIONS FOR THE EVOLUTION OF CONSCIOUSNESS

The dream that stubbornly defies all efforts to recall it clearly is not so often greeted with the same excitement and enthusiasm as the lucid dream, or the dream of multiple simultaneous remembered realities, but in my experience, it is often just as intimately connected to the evolution of consciousness as these more immediately gratifying and intriguing dreams.

When new consciousness is "brewing" in the opaque depths of the unconscious, it will almost always cast its incomprehensible shadow ahead into dreams before it arrives in a more consciously evolved, understandable, and memorable form.

Once again, let me offer an example, because I am convinced that examples often make the necessary general points more clearly than abstract discursive prose is able to. A dream work client of mine, a divorced woman entering middle age who is engaged in an ongoing search for a spiritually oriented community that can meet her needs for human connection and creative spiritual stimulation dreams:

Someone has told me about a new church in town that in the dream I think might be worth checking out. I have gotten all dressed up in my best churchgoing clothes and driven over to where it's supposed to be, and there it is! They even have a parking lot so I don't have to park on the street. I arrive in plenty of time before the service. I park and go inside.

The dream gets frustrating here. I know I am there for the whole service. I know it's a great service. I like the people; I like the theology; I like the music—I like everything about it. While it's going on, it's all perfectly clear and wonderful, but when I wake up, I can't recall any of the details!

My memory picks up again more clearly as I'm coming out of the church. It's a beautiful sunny day, and I notice with surprise that while we were inside, someone came through and repaved the parking lot with fresh blacktop. I am a little annoyed, because I am afraid that I will get nasty tar on my lovely new shoes, but I manage to walk very carefully back to my car without ruining my shoes, and I am quite relieved.

Then I notice something very odd—the people who did the repaving have blacktopped right over some of the cars in the parking lot, leaving these great big black car-sized humps! I'm very relieved that they didn't pave over my car, and I wonder briefly how they were able to pave right underneath some cars without disturbing them, and paved right over on top of others, burying them completely! Then I get even more distressed, because as I try to leave, I discover that these paved-over cars are arranged in such a way that I can't get out of the parking lot! Every exit is blocked! I drive around the parking lot getting more and more upset. Finally, my upset wakes me up.

In the short run, the most immediately important level of this dream turned out to be the physical health implications. This dream, and the work the dreamer did with it, alerted her to the fact that she had cancer. The dream drove her to her doctors sooner than she would have gone had she not remembered the dream. The relatively early diagnosis enabled her to undergo surgery that successfully removed the tumor(s) and to receive post-operative care that allowed her to return to her "regular life" fairly quickly.

The physical-health warning embodied in the "car-sized lumps that blocked egress from the parking lot" occupied her whole attention for quite a while. As her recovery become more solid, the "forgotten but viv-idly experienced church service" began to take on increasing importance in her memory. At one level she experienced an "aha" of insight that it was a metaphor for "heaven" and that the reason she couldn't remember it was that she was not destined to die from the cancer. The "glimpse of heaven" that the dream provided was not clearly remembered because she believes "it is not meant for people to know in detail about heaven before they die."

At another level, the "forgotten church service" slowly began to reveal itself as a metaphor for the internal development of her longings for spiritual clarity and a spiritual community. The brush with her own mortality suddenly seemed to make the mundane world around her "come alive." Her desires began to evolve, and she began to encounter more and more moments in waking life where she noticed that she was feeling much the same way as she had felt in the dream during the service. It became increasingly clear that the inability to remember the specifics of the service that were so clear in the dream was also a symbolic reflec-tion of the state of the progress of the development of her own spiritual awareness at the time she first dreamed the dream.

An increased conscious understanding of the spiritual implications of her "brush with mortality" followed her recovery. Her spiritual longings and awareness were even more intense as she reclaimed her "new life" from the threat of the cancer. Her spiritual energies became more focused, and she realized that the memory of her excitement and clarity in the church service in the dream was a foreshadowing of her subsequent evolution toward more spiritual awareness of meaning and purpose in her life and the collective life of humankind. The dream "announced" how wonderful it would feel when she achieved it. It also "announced" that it had not yet reached that level in the waking world but was sufficiently developed to offer an intimation of its immanent arrival, even before her consciousness could grasp the concrete details. The current state of this evolutionary, psychospiritual "work in progress" was reflected symbolically in the inability to recall all the delicious details that had seemed so clear in the dream. It also continues to promise that if the dreamer continues to do her inner and outer work, "more will be revealed."

Over and over again, this pattern of remembering a vivid sense of detail and clarity in the dream, and being unable to call up those same details when awake, turns out over the longer run to be a *promise* of things to come, even though at the time it is experienced primarily as a cause of frustration. In my experience, such dream memories affirm that consciousness *is in the process of evolving.* Despite the inevitable frustration in the moment, the promise is that it will evolve to a point where the "lost" feelings and thoughts will become clear, not only in future dreams but in waking life as well.

Mircea Eliade, the eminent comparatist historian of religion at the University of Chicago, has reported a very similar dream (quoted in *The Sun* magazine, March 2006, p. 48).

And suddenly, I understood; everything became extraordinarily clear and simple. Everything: life, death, the meaning of existence. And even stronger than this revelation was my surprise: how had no one on earth yet understood this thing, so extraordinarily simple? . . . I had the feeling that a message had been transmitted to me, that I should remember [it] so as to be able to communicate it to men. I woke up . . . with this idea in mind: not to forget what I had seen. A second later, I had forgotten.

Many of the things that have been said about the previous dream of the woman "attending the new church service" could be said about this dream as well. The sense of "perfect" understanding, with no fuzziness or feeling of confusion or being "overwhelmed"—even though the size and scope of the insight is immense—coupled with the utter loss of detail an instant later, is essentially the same in each dream. This pattern is a hallmark of this kind of dream where immense spiritual insight is evolving in the personal and collective depths, and casting its developing "shadow" in front of it before it arrives in more fully developed individual consciousness.

## (6) CONFUSION OVER WHAT'S GOING ON IN THE DREAM AS AN INDICATOR OF EVOLVING CONSCIOUSNESS

Another pattern of dream recall that reflects evolving consciousness is even more counterintuitive. The dream in which the dreamer is not even sure what is actually taking place is also, in my experience, significantly linked to the evolution of consciousness. Such dreams are usually characterized by the dreamer reporting a fairly coherent narrative and then saying things like "And then I can't remember what happens exactly. Maybe I see my old friend George, and maybe I don't—I'm not sure."

It actually makes a certain amount of logical (if not emotional) sense that something genuinely *new* would appear somewhat "confusing" on first encounter. It isn't necessarily how we want to feel, but it is a species of hubris to imagine that I will be able to see and understand the genuinely and radically new and different in my life with the same words, ideas, images, and feelings that I habitually make use of to describe, understand, and relate to what I already know and believe about my life. Anything that can be framed adequately in the old, familiar language and concepts of my life is probably actually not that new and different.

When a dreamer reports "confusion" and uncertainty about what is actually happening in a dream, it is often because that dreamer's consciousness is evolving in ways and directions that he or she had not previously anticipated. This is particularly true when the confusion involves apparently contradictory, or seemingly mutually exclusive, events in a dream.

For example: *I dream that I go driving in the country with my sister. I don't remember whether I drive or she drives. We arrive at a little country store and decide to stop and see what they have for sale.*

Such a narrative implies that the dreamer may have two conflicting memories: one in which he or she is driving the car, with the sister sitting in the passenger seat, and another in which the roles are reversed, while they still pass through the same countryside at the same moment. In waking life, such a situation would be impossible, but this is, after all, a dream. Often when questioned about these moments of "uncertainty," what transpires is that the dreamer actually has two fairly clear memories, but they are, or rather would be, mutually exclusive in the waking world, and so they get reported as "confusion." As noted earlier, *the ability to remember more than one reality at once in the dream world is directly associated with the development of a compassionate perspective in waking life, as well as the evolution toward higher levels of consciousness and self-awareness, even though they are often reported as "confusion" in the early stages of development.*

Sometimes this "confusing dual perspective" is also associated with the focus of the dream shifting from the past and the present to the relatively near future. This is particularly true, in my experience, when the multiple simultaneous "versions" appear toward the end of the dreamer's narrative. The best analogy I can think of for the "future orientation" of such moments is that of a person playing chess. The player imagines several different combinations of moves ahead in order to anticipate which particular move is likely to produce the best outcome(s), before actually touching and moving the piece on the board. These "considerations of future moves" often appear in dreams as this sort of "confusion," where the same scene is experienced simultaneously with multiple variations.

From an interpretive perspective, it is often valuable to concentrate on the "unchanging background" that marks and reveals such confusing moments as simultaneous versions of the same scene. The single unchanging background often reflects, in symbolic form, the basic structure of the situation that was previously hidden from conscious "view" and consideration. If the dream worker directs his or her attention to this unassuming but consistent background, rather than focus on the different but essentially similar "moves," then a deeper and more accurate view of the whole situation will often reveal itself.

Whether or not these "multiple simultaneous realities" reflect the dream's focus on future events, the ability to remember more than one reality, or simultaneous "version" of a dream, is still a very reliable indication that the dreamer is beginning to be able to hold more than one thought/feeling/worldview consciously in mind at once. This ability to maintain "multiple awareness" in a dream, *and to remember it upon awakening*, is a symbolic event that most often reflects a deepening self-awareness and increasingly sensitive and compassionate connection to the world.

## (7) DREAMS IN WHICH OBVIOUSLY TRANSPERSONAL AND ARCHETYPAL IMAGES METAMORPHOSE AND CHANGE

A friend and colleague of mine dreamed this in April 2008:

### Dangerous Snake Turned Friend/Something Feels Resolved

Have lost much of this dream . . . a professor, like a researcher, is living out in a tropical forested area . . . somehow he becomes trapped. I do not know how he is trapped. I do know that he is trapped. Maybe a landslide? He is unable to leave. There is a large poisonous snake— maybe that's why the researcher is trapped—the snake is blocking his way? The snake is in a tree and has use of the whole area, watches the professor/researcher . . . the researcher is trying to protect himself by being as far from the snake as possible . . . like, back in a small clearing . . . all the professor has to eat is oatmeal and he continues to fix it in order to survive . . . I think the scene changes . . . the ordeal is over . . . the professor/researcher has got out . . . he is explaining how he was not harmed by the snake . . . that the snake grew to trust him and he the snake . . . I realize how good this is . . . I imagine myself in this predicament and know that I, if I could have, would have killed the snake, would have felt bad, but would know that that is what I would have done without even thinking about it prior, even though I respect snakes and want them to live, but, if it is threatening me, I would have killed it . . . I think I am at a door to a large building—the snake and the professor(?) are there, the snake seems almost human . . . its head seems human, like a distinguished bald black man . . . someone says

wait, tell a really surprising part of the story, that the snake learned to
eat oatmeal, even likes it . . . the snake nods in agreement . . . I imagine
the researcher leaving the oatmeal by the tree, that the snake is curious
and begins to eat it, that the snake and the researcher begin to trust
each other . . . I realize again how bad I feel that I would have killed
the snake w/o a second thought . . . I feel grateful for the snake and the
professor . . . a kind of warm feeling . . . a feeling of making friends . . .
something in me feels like I resolved some kind of conflict within me,
something has healed in my life (??) end.

One of the most intriguing images in this dream is the snake itself.
First it's in a tree and "has the use of the whole area." This is its first, primary form in the dream and in the archetypal world of ancient religious
symbolism. It evokes all the classic images of the "Snake in the Tree"
from Sumeria and Mesopotamia, all the way up to the biblical Snake
twining around the trunk and up into the branches of the tree that bears
the Forbidden Fruit of the Knowledge of Good and Evil in the Garden of
Eden. It also calls up for me the Kundalini "snake" of physical/spiritual
energy that lives in the bottom of the torso and climbs up the "tree" of
the central nevous system into the "spreading leaves and branches" of the
brain and the cerebral cortex.

Once the "snake" appears in this "primeval" archetypal form, in the
equally primeval setting of the "tropical forest," it starts to evolve, mirroring and stimulating the dreamer's own internal evolution. It appears
to be on its best behavior, and even starts eating "oatmeal." It grows and
changes into a strange, hybrid creature with a human head, "like a distinguished bald, black man."

The evolution in a dream of a clearly archetypal figure like "Snake"
into increasingly more complex, "human," ambiguous, thoughtful,
stimulating, unexpected, and surprising forms filled with even greater
mystery, etc., almost always marks that dream as a turning point in the
individuation process of the dreamer. In this instance, as the dreamer
remembers and accepts his "trapped" status with the "snake," he is also
brought closer to accepting more of his (highly tabooed and suspect)
deeper masculinity. This amounts to a relaxation of his lifelong habits of
defense, and denial allows the dreamer to grow and to see more clearly
and consciously some of the ways in which he has kept himself "trapped"

by his ideals and ethics, his religion and his fears, and his general desire to be a stereotypically "good man," rather than to discover the particular and unique "good and bad man" that he actually is.

This is a tremendously important piece of "research" in my view, and points to the dreamer's personal developments being sufficiently close to, and resonant with, the dramas of collective human consciousness itself to attract collective, transpersonal, archetypal energies of growth and change to constellate in and around his personal efforts. In so doing, he also "willingly" (if not fully consciously) offers up the experience and the details of his own life as a venue, or a vehicle, for those same collective, archetypal energies to "incarnate" and make use of as an "incarnated" setting for their own dramas of growth and change.

Some of these energies appear as the primal "tropical forest" itself, which transforms first in the dream into "a small clearing," and then into "a door to a large building," indicating both the evolution of the dreamer's awareness of and comfort with the collective/archetypal "background" of his very personal struggles, as well as his own "willingness" to change and evolve. Most important, these collective patterns of energy and consciousness also appear as the *evolving, shape-changing* "snake."

The dreamer's willingness to overcome his natural fears and let the "researcher" in him remain conscious of the dream events as they occur allows the archetypal "snake" itself to take on a more consciously clear form and shape. Those same archetypal energies and collective, transpersonal patterns that are given specific shape initially in the "snake" are focused in the consciousness and memory of the dream, and as the dream evolves, they are given an opportunity to grow and develop themselves. The snake shows his potential for more conscious and communicative behavior by transforming its head from reptilian to human form, "like a distinguished bald black man." The transformed, evolved head still shows the symbolic "blackness" that is one of the most frequent symbolic markers for its relatively recent emergence from the archetypal "blackness" of unconsciousness. It now also transforms and grows to reveal the image of the "Wise Old Man," its wisdom and maturity symbolically reflected in the "distinguished" and "bald" masculine head and face.

The dreamer himself says at the end (in what I find to be a poignant and convincing fashion) that "something has healed in my life." As

I imagine this dream for myself, I find a similar sense of profound healing and change, and so *the "healing" this dream reflects and promotes is not
limited to the dreamer alone.* At very least, my own relationship to the archetypal "Snake" is healed by imagining and working on my own imagined
version of this dream for myself. There is also a direct, symbolic implication that the archetypal qualities of "snake" itself are being offered the
opportunity to try on new forms in the process.

Not only am I changed, the Snake allows himself to grow and evolve
into a symbolically more conscious and accessible form. The dream
reminds me of those stories (most particularly Hokusai's brilliant, funny
illustrations of those stories) where a wandering Buddhist monk (or in
some versions the Buddha himself) confronts and converts various traditional demons and cannibal monsters of Asian folk tradition. He preaches
the Four Noble Truths to them, and in the process turns them into good
Buddhist vegetarians, complete with straw hats and begging bowls. The
snake acquiring a taste for "oatmeal" is clearly in this same, archetypal,
"monster transforming" tradition.

The acquisition of a larger spiritual view than I could previously see
or comprehend—one that awakens the possibilty that there might be
more to life than my own fears and desires—sets the stage for the archetypal drama of Willing Sacrifice. In this dream, the dreamer manifests
such a transformtion. His dream gently opens the way for this metamorphosis by setting it all at a safe distance away in the dream, as a "story."
Like all dream stories, this one has the very real potential to heal the lis-
teners and the participants alike.

### The Universality of the Drama of Individuation,
### Both Personal and Collective

Over the years, I have done a great deal of work in foreign countries
where the majority of workshop and seminar participants spoke only languages other than English. Alas, although I speak fairly fluent "dream," I
can make myself understood verbally only in English, so I must work in
either simultaneous or sentence-by-sentence translation, back and forth,
between me and the dreamers and the various audiences of non-English
speakers.

Recently, I have been doing a great deal of work in South Korea.

Ever since 2003, I have been invited by multiple hosts to return each summer for at least a month to do projective dream work and dream work training in a number of different venues all over the country, particularly in and around the cities of Seoul and Degue.

These repeated invitations to do repeated projective dream work and dream work training in languages and cultures other than my own do not prove anything of and by themselves, and at the same time, it is clear to me that there would have been no invitations to come in the first place, let alone return on a regular basis, if the projective way of work I practice, and particularly the "if it were my dream . . ." suggestions about the collective, transpersonal, archetypal levels of meaning in the participants' dreams, had not fallen on eager and receptive ears.

If the symbolic language of dreams were not, in fact, at its deepest levels, *universal,* none of this would have happened. Dreams are so much *more* than just a symbolic reflection of the particularities of language and culture (which, of course, they also are). If this were not the case, then the insights generated by the work I do with the dreams of non-Engliah speakers from widely diverse cultures would not have touched the dreamers at all, let alone convinced them to invite me to come back and do it again multiple times.

Koreans in particular have always lived and participated in a self-conscious "culture of dreams," even before the time of their earliest recorded history. They have paid a great deal of attention to their dreams, and continue to do so in their quickly evolving contemporary society. South Korea today is also a nation and culture in the midst of immense, some might even say cataclysmic, change. The collective, social, and cultural awareness and consciousness of Koreans, of necessity, are also in a parallel state of tremendous transition, and the conscious self-awareness and worldviews of individual Koreans are also evolving quickly in an apparent struggle "to keep up" with these dizzying collective, historical, political, economic, and cultural developments. All this is, of course, regularly reflected in their dreams.

This collective reality forms the collective background for one of the most dramatic examples I have heard of a dream that simultaneously reflects the development of the personal levels of consciousness in the dreamer, and also the potential for the evolution of collective human consciousness as a whole. This dream comes from a Korean educator who attended one of my seminars in Seoul in the summer of 2008.

> In my dream, I am riding on a railway train along a winding river. We are riding through beautiful, very steep, wooded mountains, like in a classical Chinese painting.
>
> We are riding in an open train car with no roof, and nothing gets in the way of our view. The train is traveling very slowly. It seems to me that it is going at just the right speed for us to see and appreciate the beauty of the mountains and the river and the sky.
>
> There is a huge mountain right next to us, on the other side of the river, and as we slowly pass by, the mountain comes alive. It develops "arms" that reach out to embrace us, and it bends over and bows to us as we move by. For a moment, I am very shocked and amazed, and then I realize that the mountain is welcoming us, bowing to us and greeting us, and I am filled with awe and joy.
>
> I decide that I want to return to the mountain and bring six or seven of my friends with me to show them the beauty of the place. It is still midsummer when we return, riding on the same train with the open cars, only this time for some reason, huge snowflakes, as big as your fist, come drifting gently down out of the sky.
>
> The mountain comes alive again, and reaches out its "arms" and bows down to us again as we pass by. We ride the train to a village right in the middle, halfway up the mountain. We arrive and get out onto very muddy and slippery ground, where we are greeted by the village chief, a man who looks like a Native American. In the dream, I have the thought that he is a former president of Korea who was a victim of conspiracy and was impeached.
>
> The man greets us, and takes me with him across the muddy space to a garden pavilion with a traditional sloping roof and no walls. We sit together in this pavilion and talk together for a long while. In the dream, it is a wonderful conversation, and I understand everything. It's very exciting and moving, but when I wake up, I can't remember *any* of it . . . !

Once again, we can see the same archetypal pattern of the "fascinating, deep, important communication" (cf. "church service," "conversation," "revelation") that is crystal clear in the dream but defies the dreamer's ability to recall in any detail upon awakening. This is, I believe, essentially the same pattern of future developments of the dreamer's consciousness casting their individual and collective shadows before them in the dreamer's dreams before the dreamer's current state of conscious waking self-awareness has developed to the point where the "details" can be fully *remembered* and rendered into words and images in waking life.

Other elements of this dream also point quite clearly to the dream's being a reflection and a celebration of the dreamer's own evolving consciousness and to the fact that these "personal" developments also have significant echoes and implications for the corresponding developments of collective human consciousness. The "huge mountain" is, for example, a symbolic image that evokes the collective archetype of Nature herself, as well as the "mountains" of personal experience, trials, and tribulations that almost every person (particularly any person engaged in conscious individuation) collects over the course of a lifetime.

For an image of that archetypal size and collective implication to "come alive" in a dream, and "grow arms," and "bow and greet and embrace" the dreamer suggests that a great deal more than "merely personal" energies are at work and in play in this image and this dream.

When asked about the man who "greets" the dreamer and takes her to "talk" in the pavilion, she spoke about her projections on Native Americans as inheritors and carriers of a kind of "natural spirituality." This is also something of an archetypal projection in itself, filled with collective echoes, as well as personal implications for the dreamer's deep concerns about the collective/archetypal issue of the degradation of the world environment in general, and the delicate Korean ecosystem in particular, as that country plunges ahead in its postwar recovery and its rapid shift from traditional farming to industrialized agriculture and manufacturing (although these momentous developments are all still dominated and "run" by a handful of medieval clans and families).

She also said that she did not have any particular Korean ex-president in mind when she was "reminded" in the dream of the "the national leader impeached and deposed" by his political enemies. This lack of a particular historical referent for the image of the "impeached leader of the whole nation," to my mind, makes the collective, archetypal implications of this image even clearer. "The impeached ex-president who also looks like a Native American" comes to stand for the whole archetypal idea of "collective leadership with serious and profound ecological sensibilities" and how such leaders are symbolically "set up" to be vulnerable to "attack and discredit," particularly when they are associated with and advocate as-yet-not-fully-integrated collective ideals and ideas, like giving priority to the long-term health of the environment over short-term profit and personal/family gain.

The "pavilion" where the energizing but not easily remembered conversation takes place between the dreamer and the collective "leader/ teacher" is also something of an archetypal setting in itself, suggesting at yet another level that the "important but not remembered conversation" taking place there has importance beyond the personal. In Asian folk material and sacred narrative, pavilions of this sort are the immediately recognizable setting for the calm observation of nature and for crucial conversations with the teacher/guide/wise person/"guru" that are destined to change not only the course of the student's life but the course of the the the whole society as well.

I also suspect, although I do not know many details of the dreamer's life and history, that there are also experiences of being "attacked" and "impeached" in her personal and professional life that are echoed in this image as well. In my imagined version of this dream, part of the unremembered conversation in the "pavilion" is most likely focused, at one important level at least, on how emotionally hard it is to be attacked and discreditied by adversaries who do not share the same basic assumptions about what's truly important and what is simply a consequence of momentary opportunity and greed. Such are the risks that must be faced by any person willing to hazard her/his life and creative energies in acts of "Willing Sacrifice" in order to serve a higher purpose than holding on to personal safety, comfort, and status.

I do know that one of the dreamer's greatest goals and "dreams" in her life is to help found a series of "eco-villages" in Korea, where the basic organizing principles will be sustainability and long-term care for the land, as well as the needs of the people who live on and respect the land. Any enterprise of this sort is drawn to the surface of individual consciousness and galvanized into collective, organized effort by large historical and cultural forces that are beyond the personal, even though they must take personal shape in the lives and creative actions of individuals. To the extent that these visionary individuals are successful in their efforts, they change the shape of society, and collective awareness and consciousness are altered and encouraged to grow and develop further in the process.

The "snowflakes as big as your fists" and the "muddy ground" of the initial meeting both suggest that "the path," both to the personal goals and to the collective consciousness change, is not, never has been, and will not ever be easy or simple. The "fist" metaphor suggests to me that there is "anger" accumulating in "my" unconscious, as the dreamer of this dream—most likely anger born of frustration at being "conspired against" and "impeached" in waking life. At the beginning, this anger is more or less "frozen," because later, "when it melts" and begins to "flow" again, it makes everything "muddy" and "slippery." In this connection, it is also important to remember that "anger" is the emotional energy that most often drives and sustains the "Prophetic Voice." The archetypal "prophetic voice" is what any reformer and anyone who would change the way the world thinks must cultivate and embrace, despite the inevitable "willing sacrifices" that it invariably demands.

Another collective implication of this dream that I find very interesting and compelling is the twice repeated presence of the "train with the open observation car." Traditionally, journeys of this sort "to see the teacher/guru in the beautiful pavilion" are undertaken alone and on foot. The presence of the railway train "traveling at the perfect speed," together with the multiple friends whom the dreamer invites to accompany her, suggest to me that the dream itself is suggesting at an important level that the development of a new collective consciousness and awareness of the absolute importance of ecological issues need not be achieved at the cost of trashing and abandoning technological advancement.

If I had to pick a single image to stand for the whole enterprise of technology and how it has shaped and changed the world, the railway train would certainly be on my short list. In my imagined version of this dream, the "railway train" carries this kind of symbolic resonance and plays just such a gentle and benign role in delivering the pilgrims to their desination. When the "mountain comes alive" and reaches out to "embrace the dreamer" and her friends, it embraces and extends its archetypal greeting to the railway train as well. (It is a dream, after all, and if the dream had not wished to include the railway train in its "welcoming embrace," it could easily have had the train simply dissolve away and disappear before the mountain "embraced" the travelers.)

This gentle and sane affirmation of the value of technology and mechanization is certainly at odds with the angrier, Luddite factions of the world ecology movement. It points to the possibility that the transition of collective consciousness from the suicidal embrace of industrial exploitation of "natural resources" to a more conscious steward-ship of the "beautiful world where even the mountains are alive" can be accomplished without the apocalyptic destruction of technology and a return to the kinds of barbarism of isolated, competing communities that have thus far taken up so much space in the popular imagination.

The presence of the unknown but important "companions on the journey" further emphasizes the collective nature of the conciousness and wisdom that is evolving in this dream in symbolic form, as well as reflecting the reality of successful community organizing in the waking world.

If we are to make the necessary and increasingly urgent transition from modern industrial barbarism to postmodern planetary stewardship and cooperation, individuals must change their basic assumptions about the nature of civilization, the "natural world," and the place and quality of creative human enterprise. We must find ways to communicate with one another that acknowledge and accommodate our collective unconscious nature, as well as our conscious cleverness. Projective understanding of both dreams and waking life can offer specific strategies and practices that allow us to meet our deeper selves, to embrace one another, and to take greater collective, conscious responsibility for preservation and nur-turing of the ecosystem itself. In my view, this must be done with compassion. We must come to understand that all living things, even "ugly" ones that we have difficulty liking, are "entities" worthy of individual and collective respect and emotional identification.

Our individual consciousnesses are evolving as we each face greater and greater challenges in the waking world. These struggles and accomplishments of individuation can and do impact on the development of the potentials for human consciousness and community as a whole.

We are all dreamers, whether or not we pay conscious attention to these mysterious, spontaneous interior experiences. Awake and asleep, we encounter the world through the "frame" of our own unconscious selves, just beyiond the edge of our peripheral vision. If a sufficient minority of us continues to extend our understanding of the archetypal world of dreams, and to raise our awareness of the corresponding unconscious symbolism of waking life, then we will make a significant and necessary contribution to the evolution of a more creative, responsible, conscious way of being in and for the species as a whole.

To that end, this book, and all my energies, hopes, prayers, efforts, and desires are dedicated.

SUGGESTED STEPS FOR PROJECTIVE DREAM WORK IN SMALL
GROUPS (4 TO 12 PEOPLE)

1. Make sure that all group members are present. (In general, a group shouldn't have to wait more than five minutes for members who are late for the announced beginning time of the group.)

2. Once everyone is present, the group should join in a brief centering exercise (or prayer), silent or spoken, depending on the group's preference and/or the preference of the designated facilitator, if there is one.

3. When the prayer/centering exercise is complete, each group member should have the opportunity to "check in" and tell the rest of the group how he or she is feeling and what's on his or her mind and to share the brief, descriptive "headline"-style title of a dream. (Preferably, this should be the title of a dream that the dreamer is willing to work in depth with the group. This does not have be a recent dream—any dream that stays vivid in the mind of the dreamer, no matter how long ago it first occurred, is announcing its relevance to the dreamer's current life circumstances.)

4. Once every group member has "checked in" and shared a condensed dream title, the "laws of fairness" should be consulted to determine whose turn it is to share a dream and explore it in depth. Among the "laws of fairness" are: (a) Whose dream seems most emotionally pressing? (Usually, "nightmares" should take precedence over "ordinary dreams.") (b) Who worked most recently? (Except in unusual circumstances, no one should work a second time until all the people in the group have had a chance to work once). (c) The group time spent working dreams of different members should be more or less equal, etc.

5. When the group has come to consensus about whose dream(s) will be the focus of their attention, the dreamer should share the dream, telling it out loud in the present tense, no matter how long ago the dream first occurred. It is a good idea to keep all dream records in the present tense. Many groups prefer to have a written photocopy of the dream *in addition* to hearing it out loud, particularly if the dreamer has made any drawings, maps, floor plans, or other graphic representations of the dream.

6. When the dreamer has shared his or her dream and related materials, it is best to focus initially on questions of clarification— about the actual experience of the dream, about the dreamer's waking life, about the dreamer's history, etc. (Sometimes a person will be so taken with a projection that he or she will be compelled to share it right at the beginning, without prefatory questions. This is okay, but it should not become a habit.) In general, I prefer to ask questions in the "if it were my dream" form and in the present tense, in order to emphasize that questions are just as much projections as ideas about symbolism and deeper meaning are. (For example, I believe it is better to ask *"As the dreamer of this dream, how do I feel when . . . ?"* rather than *"How did you feel when . . . ?"*) Whenever a group member is tempted to ask a question the answer to which he or she thinks he or she may already know, it is a very reliable indicator that it is time to switch from questions into projective "in my imagined version of this dream . . ." suggestion and commentary. Questions are always permissible at any point in the proceedings, and the dreamer is *always* free to either ignore or respond to any and all questions and comments.

7. *"The name of the game is dreamer's choice."* This means that the dreamer is always free to ignore any questions or comments and not respond to them at all. It also means that group members are free to ask about *anything*, provided they are willing take "no" or silence as an answer. If it is appropriate, and the dreamer cares to do it, it may be valuable for everyone to hear the dream a second time.

8. The remainder of the time should be focused on the dreamer and his or her dream, offering projections about what the deeper meanings and implications of the dream may be. Remember, only the dreamer can say with any certainty what the deeper levels of meaning may be in his or her dream. The only reliable touchstone of truth is the dreamer's own aha of insight and recognition. Since we always do our own work in projected form using the gift of the dreamer's narrative, any aha that anyone has in the course of exploring someone else's dream is *true for the person having the aha,* whether it is confirmed by the original dreamer

or not. "My" aha is always about my own imagined version of the dream and is therefore true for "me," even it fails to resonate with others.

9. When everyone in the group has had an opportunity to project on the dream, and the dreamer has had an adequate opportunity to respond, *if he or she cares to*, it is time to bring the work to an arbitrary close. All endings of dream work are arbitrary; *there is no closure in working with dreams.* There is always more that could be said and brought "up" into the light of consciousness. In order to make the inevitably arbitrary ending a little less abrupt, two final questions are very useful.

10. First question, to the whole group: "Does anyone have anything to add to the work with this dream that views in from a different angle, that sees it at another level, and/or that projects another archetypal drama at work in addition to the ones we have tried to name?"

11. When group members have added their last thoughts, feelings, and intuitions about the possible multiple meanings and layers of implication in the dream(s) they have been exploring, and the dreamer has had a chance to respond to them, *the last question always goes to the dreamer* (because the dreamer always ought to "have the last word" on his or her dream work). "Is there anything else that you would like from the group regarding this dream—any place in the dream itself where you would like a little more input from the group, or anything more related to things that percolated up to the surface of awareness while we were working on unpacking the dream, and/or anything that you would like either to do or say?" (It's cumbersome, but it has a lot of territory to cover.)

12. When the dreamer has had an opportunity to ask, say, and do whatever he or she desires at the end, it is appropriate for the group to thank the dreamer for the opportunity to work and play with the dream. It is also a good idea to hold hands in a circle and close with a prayer or centering exercise, again, either spoken or silent, depending on the desires of the group and/or the facilitator, if there is one.

### SMALL DREAM GROUP PROCEDURES—SHORT FORM

1. Start on time.
2. Begin with a short prayer or centering exercise
3. Have participants "check in" with how they are feeling generally in their waking lives, and share a short, "headline"-style dream title.
4. Decide whose dream would be best to work.
5. Have the dreamer tell/read the dream, preferably in the present tense.
6. Ask questions of clarification about the dream/the dreamer's life. *The name of the game is dreamer's choice.* If it is appropriate and desired, have the dreamer reread/retell the dream.
7. Shift over to projective, "if it were my dream . . ." style commentary and suggestion. (Questions are still appropriate at any point in the process.)
8. When everyone has had a chance to project on the dream, and the dreamer has a chance to respond, *if he or she cares to*, begin to bring the work to a formal, arbitrary close by asking the two closing questions.
9. First question: "Does anyone have anything to add to this work that views the dream from a different angle or at a different level, or sees another archetypal drama at work/play in addition to the ones we have tried to name?"
10. Second question: "Does the dreamer" (who should always be offered the last word on his or her work) "have anything that he or she would like to ask the group about, and/or say to the group, or do with the group?"
11. When the last two questions have been asked and responded to, the group should hold hands in a circle and pray or center again, either silently or verbally, depending on the preferences of the members of the group and those of the group facilitator, if there is one.

*Appendix I*

# SUGGESTIONS FOR FURTHER READING & OTHER RESOURCES

*You can learn things from books.*

—RINGO STARR

(in *A Hard Day's Night*)

I f you have enjoyed this book, you might also enjoy two of my other books that are still in print at the moment: *Dream Work, Techniques for Discovering the Creative Power in Dreams*, Paulist Press, Mahwah, NJ, 1983, ISBN 0-8091-2525-0, and *The Living Labyrinth—Exploring Universal Themes in Myths, Dreams, and the Symbolism of Waking Life*, Paulist Press, Mahwah, NJ, 1998, ISBN 0-8091-3766-6. The latter book is essentially a user's guide to "archetypes in contemporary dress." Both of these books also include extensive bibliographies and recommendations for resources for continuing to explore dreams and dreaming, with an eye to discovering more of their deeper meanings and significance. Some of the suggestions for further reading in those books are now truly out of print, but all of them are worth chasing down on the Internet, in used bookstores, and through that wonderful service of civilized society, the interlibrary loan.

The following more current, in-print, and up-to-date recommendations are based primarily on my own taste and experience. When I undertook writing this book, I did send out a request to a large group of friends and colleagues to help me with an updating of "Suggestions for Further Reading," and what follows owes a great deal to their generous response. Thanks again to all of you who contributed to this effort.

## Overviews and General Surveys of Dreams, Dreaming, and Dream Work

For a general overview of the field of dream research and actual styles and strategies for practical dream work, I highly recommend *An Introduction to the Psychology of Dreaming*, by Kelly Bulkeley, Praeger Publishers, Westport, CT, 1997, ISBN 0-275-95889 (hardcover), 0-275-95890 (paperback). This book provides the clearest, most balanced, and concise overview that I am aware of of the whole field of the psychology of dreaming of any book attempting to summarize, compare, and contrast various schools of thought about dreams, dreaming, and *working with dreams*. Like almost all the books suggested and recommended here, this book also has a very broad, intelligently selective, and useful bibliography.

Another potentially useful and interesting book is *Our Dreaming Mind*, by Robert Van de Castle, Ballantine Books, New York, 1994, ISBN 0-345-39666-9. Dr. Van de Castle is one of the premier dream researchers in the world today. This is his magisterial summation work, published on the eve of his retirement from full-time academic life. It emphasizes the particular interests that fueled his groundbreaking research and addresses in particular the question of how he and his colleagues researched and documented "psi" (i.e. "psychic") aspects of dreaming.

Another magisterial overview of the field is provided in *The Discovery of the Unconscious*, by Henri F. Ellenberger, Basic Books, NY, 1958, ASIN: BDDDOLB9Z (and still in print, I believe). Although this book clearly favors a Freudian view of the unconscious and tends to belittle other major contributors (such as Carl Jung and Alfred Adler), the material it presents is quite comprehensive and valuable, particularly from a historical point of view.

A most informative and extensive collection of 150 exceptionally pithy quotes and passages from the dream interpretation literature of a wide array of world traditions, stretching from the dawn of history to the present, can be found in Leland Shields's *Dreamwork, Around the World and Across Time—An Anthology*, Blue Dolphin Publishing, Nevada City, CA, 2008, ISBN 978-1-57733-171-1. The book also includes scattered short commentaries, which attempt to set context and point to cultural

paradigms out of which the dream insights grow. The book has the ines-
timable advantage of presenting the ideas of these spokespersons in their
own words for the many and various traditions and points of view.

### Dream and Symbol Dictionaries

It is worth recalling that the oldest fragments of writing extant in the
world today are fragments of dream and symbol dictionaries. In the *Epic
of Gilgamesh*, the oldest written narrative we possess from the so-called
"dawn of civilization," the hero Gilgamesh goes to his mother and asks
her to interpret his dream. Her interpretation foreshadows and furnishes
the foundation upon which all the subsequent actions and developments
depend. An uninterrupted literary tradition of dream and symbol dictionaries exists from these earliest texts and fragments to today's ambiguous, multilingual cornucopia of dream and symbol dictionaries. It seems
to me that any literary activity with such a long and unbroken global
history deserves our serious attention (even though many of the current examples often appear trivial and counterproductively narrow and
doctrinaire).

If one keeps in mind that *only the experience of an "aha!" of insight is
to be trusted in the process of exploring dreams for more of their deeper meanings*, then even the most simplistic, cheaply printed, and *déclassé* drugstore
dream dictionary can, and often will, provide flashes of insight, recognition, and inspiration. (I believe this is due in large part to the tendency of
archetypal images to carry similar implications and associations, regardless of when, where, and in what context they appear.)

The dream and symbol dictionaries that many of my colleagues and
I have found most useful over the decades and that are still in print are as
follows:

*A Dictionary of Symbols*, by J. E. Cirlot, Dover Publications, New
York, 2002, ISBN 0486425231.

*The Penguin Dictionary of Symbols*, by Jean Chevalier, Penguin, New
York, 2003, ISBN 0140512543.

The *Encyclopedia of Archetypal Symbolism* (two volumes), published
by Shambhala, Boston & London, in cooperation with ARAS, the
Archive for Research in Archetypal Symbolism, deserves mention
here as well. Even though they are quite expensive, together they form
one of the best, and certainly the most visually beautiful, references

available today for increased understanding of the transpersonal, archetypal symbolism and dreams, myths, sacred narratives, and world culture.

Volume One, edited by Beverly Moon, published in 1991, ISBN 0-87773-479-8, touches on the whole range of archetypal symbolism with succinct clear essays and beautiful, full-page (9"x12"), full-color illustrations. Volume Two, titled *The Body*, edited by George Elder, 1996, ISBN 1-57062-096-2, follows the same elegant, readable format and focuses more directly on those archetypal symbols and images that derive directly from the universal human experience of physically embodied life. Both are wonderfully clear and well written, and filled with valuable information. (If you can't afford to own them and keep them around to refer to at your leisure, at least persuade your local library to acquire a set.)

*The Dream Book: Symbols for Self-Understanding*, by Betty Bethards, New Century Publishers, New York, 2001, ISBN 0967979013. This book has found an important place in many ongoing dream groups, assuming the role of "an honorary member." It is quite concise and regularly offers multiple paths of expanding association, leading to multiple interpretations. It also regularly mentions possible spiritual implications of the images it addresses.

Recently, I picked up another "slim volume" of dream symbolism, *The Complete Idiot's Guide—Dream Dictionary*, by Eve Adamson and Gayle Williamson, Alpha/Penguin Books (USA), new 2008 (no ISBN listed—I came across at a checkout-stand impulse item in our local supermarket). As is true of Betty Bethards's *Dream Book*, most of its suggestions spread outward in multiple directions, instead of focusing on only one possible layer of meaning. I also found all of the entries to be quite clear and succinct, and accurately reflective of many profound and reliable archetypal truths.

### On Projection

On the crucial issue of projection, some of the resources I have found useful over the years include *Projection and Re-Collection in Jungian Psychology: Reflections of the Soul*, by Marie-Louise von Franz, Open Court Publishing Company, Chicago, 1987, ISBN 0875484174.

*The Wounded Healer: Countertransference from a Jungian Perspective*, by David Sedgwick, Routledge, London, 1994, ISBN 0415106206, is also a valuable resource.

*The Mystery of Human Relationship: Alchemy and the Transformation of Self*, by Nathan Schwartz-Salant, Routledge, London, 1998, ISBN 0415153891, does a reasonable job in describing and analyzing the dynamic of unconscious projection at an interpersonal level.

*Awakening and Insight: Zen Buddhism and Psychotherapy*, by Polly Young-Eisendrath, Routledge, London, 2002, ISBN 0415217946, also addresses the question of projection quite clearly.

I would also recommend Robert A. Johnson's book on Bright Shadow projection: *Inner Gold, Understanding Psychological Projection*, koa books, Maui, HI, 2008, ISBN-978-0-97733-382-0.

### Spiritual Aspects of Dreams

Those of you who are interested in the place of dreams and dreaming in the history of the world's religions and in the spiritual aspects of dreams and dreaming in a global context cannot do better, in my opinion, than to look into Kelly Bulkeley's new book (yes, he is the same person who I said had written the best overall introduction to dreams and dream work as well) *Dreaming in the World's Religions—A Comparative History*, New York University Press, New York, 2008, ISBN 0814799574.

At the more practical level of working with the levels of dreams that address the search for reliable spiritual perspectives in the dreamer's life, you may also be interested in my own extended discussion of using dreams in spiritual guidance and counseling. These are included in *Sharing Sacred Stories: Current Approaches to Spiritual Direction*, edited by Robert Frager, Crossroads, New York, 2007, ISBN 0824524462.

*Dreams: God's Forgotten Language*, by John A. Sanford, HarperOne, San Francisco, 1989, ISBN 006067055X, is an acknowledged classic in the field, and of particular interest to Christians of all flavors. (It looks to me as though it is still in print, and even if it isn't, used copies abound.)

### Carl Jung's Contributions to Dream Work

As mentioned earlier, I have found Carl Jung's insights into dreams and dreaming generally more useful and productive than those of any other single practical dream worker or dream theorist. Princeton University Press is the official publisher of Carl Jung's works in America (thanks to a generous endowment from the Mellon family). Occasionally, it publishes collections culled from the *Collected Works* that are focused on particular areas of interest. The Princeton University Press collection entitled

*Dreams*, Princeton (NJ) University Press, 1974, ISBN 1-0691-01-792-1, contains many of the most important and significant selections of Jung's work on dreams. Another version of this same collection of edited portions of Jung's *Collected Works* addressing the deeper meanings and implications of dreams has also been reprinted under the title *Dreams*, by MJF Books, New York, 1974, ISBN 1-56731-135-0.

Of particular interest is the new book recounting Jung's work with children's dreams, *Children's Dreams—Notes from the Seminar Given in 1936–1940*, edited by Jung's grandson, Lorenz Jung, and Maria Meyer-Grass, Princeton (NJ) University Press, 2008, ISBN 978-0-691-13323-2. The appearance of a *new* book by Carl Jung, forty-seven years after his death, is an event of some significance, and thanks are due to the Philemon Foundation for providing the financing for this long-overdue publication. The book itself is full of wonderful insights about the archetypal nature of dream imagery and symbolism, not just in the dreams of children but in the dreams of adults as well.

### . . . And Speaking of Children's Dreams

Working with the dreams of children is a very important and underserved subcategory of dream work. The best book on this topic that I am aware of is *Dreamcatching: Every Parent's Guide to Exploring and Understanding Children's Dreams and Nightmares*, by Alan Siegel and Kelly Bulkeley, Three Rivers Press, New York, 1998, ISBN 0517887886.

*Windows to Our Children: A Gestalt Therapy Approach to Children and Adolescents*, by Violet Oaklander, Gestalt Journal Press, Gouldsboro, ME, 1988, ISBN 0939266067, is an acknowledged classic in the field and is worth chasing down in a used copy, if you find it out of press or out of print.

### Biographies of Jung

Jung's life and work still remain controversial, in large measure because of the blunt accusations of Nazi sympathy and anti-Semitism made against him by Sigmund Freud shortly before Freud's death (in 1939), and also because of the persistent rumors about his compulsive womanizing that still continue to circulate, almost fifty years after his death. Because of my lifelong commitment to progressive, pacific social action and cultural change, and my view of the incredibly useful insights Jung had to offer about the personal and transpersonal unconscious factors that shape our collective, historical, political, and cultural predicaments, it was very important for me to find out for myself, early in my career as a teacher, writer, community organizer, and dream worker, what basis, if any, these rumors and accusations had in historical fact. For these reasons, I have read (and continue to read) virtually all the biographical material about Jung available in English. If you, the reader, share any of these concerns, then on the basis of this lifelong study of Jung's life, as well as my appreciation of his immense contributions to the field of dream work, I would recommend the following:

(1) Jung's own "autobiography," dictated to and edited by his personal secretary, Anielia Jaffé, *Memories, Dreams, Reflections*, Pantheon Books, New York, 1973 (no ISBN listed). This is certainly the best place to start, even though it turns out that this work was significantly "cleaned up" and bowdlerized by Jung's heirs, even before his death (see Bair, below, pp. 610–617).

(2) Claire Dunne's beautifully written and illustrated biography, *Carl Jung: Wounded Healer of the Soul*, Morning Light Press, Sandpoint ID, 2000, ISBN 0-930-40750-4 (paperback), is the best short biography around. She grasps and conveys much of the depth and significance of Jung's work in an insightful and concise fashion. (If Jung's own dense and somewhat convoluted prose in *Memories, Dreams, Reflections* is a little much for you, then I would recommend starting with Dunne's short biography.)

(3) Laurens van der Post's biography *Jung and the Story of Our Time*, Pantheon, New York, 1975, ISBN 0-394-49207-2, is excellent. (This work is particularly valuable, in my view, because of van der Post's willingness to face the issue of Jung's involvement with the Nazis head-on, rather than ignore it or attempt to sweep it under the rug, as so many of his other positive biographers are too inclined to do.)

(4) To my mind, the best biography in English to date is Deirdre Bair's scholarly and evenhanded *Jung—A Biography*, Little Brown, New York, 2003, ISBN 0-316-07665-1. Weighing in at

881 pages (more than 250 of which are substantive endnotes in tiny print), her work is not something I would recommend as a starting place Once you have a general grasp of the broad outlines and mythic shape of Jung's life (if you're still interested), Bair's meticulous investigations and clear prose are most welcome and revealing Her research and scholarship are impeccable, and she answers, to my satisfaction, the two most pressing questions regarding Jung's personal life: Was he a Nazi sympathizer? (No, he was not—in fact, he was an active anti-Nazi). And was he a compulsive womanizer? (Yes, alas, he was, and Bair's research proves—again, to my satisfaction at least—that his womanizing extended far beyond his fairly well known affairs with Sabina Spielrein and Toni Wolff.)

### Two Other Favorites of Mine (& Others)

I cannot end this section on published resources without mentioning two more of my favorites that don't fit into the categories: *Dream Exploration: A New Approach*, by Robert P. Gongloff, Llewellyn Publications, Woodbury, MN 2006, ISBN 0-73870-818-6, and *Mindful Dreaming, A Practical Guide for Emotional Healing Through Transformative Mythic Journeys*, by David Gordon, New Page Books, Franklin Lakes, NJ, 2007, ISBN 1-56414-922-6. These two books are not just favorites of mine; they were also mentioned by several of my friends and colleagues who responded to my request for resources that have proved to be particularly useful and enjoyable in their dream work practices.

### Dream Network

The oldest, most reliable, and most heterodox, regularly appearing periodical focusing on dreams and dreaming aimed at the general reading public is *Dream Network—"Evolving a Dream Cherishing Culture."* Subscriptions and back issues may be obtained from the editorial office located at 1025 Kane Creek Boulevard, P.O. Box 1026, Moab, Utah 84532. The publication appears at least four times a year under the able editorship of Roberta Ossana. *Dream Network* (originally *Dream Network Journal*) predates the founding of International Association for the Study of Dreams (IASD) and regularly presents dream-inspired art and poetry, as well as a wide variety of articles, news stories, networking lists, and dream-oriented advertising.

*The International Association for the Study of Dreams (IASD)*

I am particularly pleased, as one of the original four founders of the International Association for the Study of Dreams, that IASD has sustained itself for more than twenty-five years, offering a wide range of services to its even wider range of members. IASD celebrated the twenty-fifth anniversary of its founding in 2008, and appears to be headed into the twenty-first century with growing strength and broadening vision.

IASD publishes two journals: *Dreaming*, an academic journal that has done its stalwart part in establishing "dream studies" as a legitimate field of academic interest and study, having become the journal of record for interdisciplinary studies involving dreams and dreaming in a number of other specializations as well as dream studies. IASD also publishes *Dream Times*, a more informal and broadly focused journal for its growing membership. IASD also puts on one big, international interdisciplinary conference in a different part of the world each summer, in addition to sponsoring a number of other local and regional conferences during the rest of the year.

Individual memberships are available to all, and a growing number of non-English-language and national associations for the study of dreams is springing up in other parts of the world and becoming affiliated with IASD. The URL for IASD is *asdreams.org*, where the reader will find a number of discussion threads, research projects, "cyber conferences," online classes, and answers to frequently asked questions.

*The Marin Institute for Projective Dream Work (MIPD)*

I have always maintained that to do dream work with your friends, and in relatively informal volunteer settings like summer camps and church basements, no particular training beyond grasping the "basic hints" for dream work presented in all my books, classes, seminars, and workshops is required. Many people have gone on to form their own dream groups, a number of which have lasted for decades and are still percolating along, having become "extended families" and primary support groups for their members. This is all without any more training or preparation than reading a book like this one or attending a class or workshop.

However, more and more people have come to me over the years saying that they have really gotten into their dream work and now wish to extend their dream work practice into the world, either by hanging

out a shingle as a "professional dream work practitioner" or by gain-
ing employment doing dream work in institutions like schools, churches,
hospices, prisons, executive training seminars, and healing consortia.
For that reason, in 1991, my wife, Kathryn, and I founded the Marin
Institute for Projective Dream Work and pulled together an inexpensive, seven-part curriculum to teach basic projective skills and archetypal
knowledge. For years. I have been giving certificates upon demonstration
of satisfactory acquisition and display of such skills and knowledge. The
details of this certification program are all laid out clearly on my website,
jeremytaylor.com. Over the ensuing years, many have taken advantage
of this program to get certified and have moved further into establishing
themselves as employable, professional dream workers and dream group
facilitators.

*Various Other Dream Education and Dream Work*
*Training Programs*

### John F. Kennedy University

One of the most reliable indications that the organized study and
exploration of dreams is "an idea whose time has come" is the recent
proliferation of institutes and university programs devoted to it. John F.
Kennedy University in Pleasant Hill, California, jfku.edu, was the first
accredited academic institution to offer a freestanding "Dream Studies"
program. That program is now enfolded as a "specialization" into the
"Consciousness Studies" division of JFKU.

### The Haden Institute

The second most long-lived, and currently the most successful,
program offering professional training and certification for dream workers (as well as spiritual directors) is the Haden Institute, hadeninstitute
.com, in Flat Rock, North Carolina. Founded by a retired Episcopalian
priest, the Reverend Bob Haden, the Haden Institute has been training
dream leaders and spiritual directors since 1994 for successful professional
work in the world. The Haden Institute also sponsors an annual summer
conference at the Kanuga Camp and Conference Center in Hendersonville,
North Carolina, that draws Christian dream group leaders from all over the
southern United States and, more recently, from all over the world.

Institute for Dream Studies

The Institute for Dream Studies, founded by Justina Lasley, one of the early graduates of the Haden Institute, can be found at: dreamswork. us/institutefordreamstudies.htm. It is centered in Charleston, South Carolina, and offers certification to those who wish to be employed as professional dream workers in schools, churches, hospices, churches, medical groups and prisons, among others.

Chaplaincy Institute for Interfaith and Arts Ministries (ChI)

The Chaplaincy Institute for Interfaith and Arts Ministries chaplaincyinstitute.org, founded in 1999 by the Reverend Gina Rose Halpern, offers certification both as a dream worker and as a spiritual director, as well as ordination as an interfaith minister and/or chaplain. Projective dream work and dream arts are fully integrated into all ChI's offerings, as well as forming a separate, freestanding certification program.

Miriam's Well Program in Applied Projective Dream Work

Recently, Miriam's Well, a spiritually oriented retreat and training center in Saugerties, New York, in the Hudson Valley north of New York City, miriamswell.org, established a dynamic training and certification program for "spiritual activist dream workers." The Miriam's Well program has adopted a curriculum fundamentally similar to that of MIPD (see earlier), with the addition of a "compassion practicum" component (modeled on the "compassion practicum" requirement for graduate studies at the University of Creation Spirituality, under Matthew Fox).

Wisdom University

Wisdom University, wisdomuniversity.org, under the leadership of Jim Garrison, has also recently instituted a program in "Archetypal Studies and Projective Dream Work" that offers both certification as a professional dream worker and, in collaboration with their doctor of ministry program, ordination as an interfaith minister.

Other Programs Offering Dream Studies

Many other institutions, while not offering separate programs in dreams and dream studies, are adding various dream studies classes to their other curriculum offerings. The Pacifica Graduate Institute in

Cerpenteria, California, pacifica.edu, just outside Santa Barbara, offers a program that includes training in what founding director Steve Aisenstadt calls "dream tending." This approach to embracing and appreciating dream experience is aggressively noninterpretive (à la James Hillman), and occasionally Pacifica graduates end up seeking further training and certification, while at the same time treasuring the insights and spiritually respectful attitude toward dreaming that was nurtured in their time at Pacifica.

The Depth Psychology Program at Sonoma State University in Santa Rosa, California, sonoma.edu/paychology/depth/program.html, also offers a number of courses for both groups and individuals that involve extensive dream work.

# SOME BASIC HINTS
# FOR WORKING
# WITH YOUR DREAMS BY YOURSELF

PROSPERO: *[Aside] It goes on, I see*
*As my soul prompts it—*
*Spirit, fine spirit! I'll*
*free thee within two days*
*for this!*

—WILLIAM SHAKESPEARE
(in *The Tempest*)

B y far the best way to work with your dreams is to share them and look for the aha of recognition in the comments and projections made by others, but sometimes this simply isn't possible, and you have no choice but to begin exploring the dreams on your own.

When you are working alone, you will frequently experience an initial set of ahas when you first look at the dream. These initial insights always tend to be "old," things you have already consciously thought or felt. The basic "trick" of solitary dream work is somehow to get beyond these initial ahas and find new eyes in yourself with which to view your dream. If you succeed, this approximates the genuinely new eyes that others bring to your dream. The suggestions that follow have proven useful in overcoming some of the inherent selective blindness and pre-conscious self-deception that limit those working alone.

The aha of recognition still remains the only trustworthy indication of discovering an accurate, authentic interpretation, but in working with your dreams by yourself, look for a sense of *surprise* accompanying the aha. This sense of surprise usually marks the more authentic aha, which takes you beyond what you already knew.

Here are several techniques that often produce startling insights for the dreamer working alone:

1. *Draw the dream.* As suggested in Chapter 4, even the crudest stick-figure drawings and diagrams of the dream's characters, settings, and events bring the visual system into active play. Visual associations will often unlock startling ahas that would be difficult to obtain with verbal or bodily explorations. The more energy and care you put into your creative interactions with your dreams, the more they will respond and reward you with insights and renewed vital energies. Do not let any thoughts like "Oh, I'm not an artist" have any effect on how elaborately or spontaneously you draw or paint or sculpt your dreams. As my colleague Brian Swimme is fond of saying, "Follow your allurements."

2. Separate out the emotional narrative so that it can be seen as distinct from the dream events associated with it. One way to accomplish this separation is to go back through your written narrative and underline all the emotionally descriptive words in red. Then list these words in order, in a vertical column down one side of a separate sheet of paper. Sometimes, this activity alone will reveal repeating patterns of emotional association that were not immediately apparent when the words were embedded in the dramatic narrative of the dream. If there is no immediately visible pattern, try listing free associations to the emotionally descriptive words in the spaces opposite the words. This too often reveals previously unrecognized patterns.

3. *Do Gestalt work and active imagination with characters and figures in the dream other than the original "dream ego."* One of the most effective ways of "surprising" yourself with some of the hidden levels of

feeling and meaning is to reenter the dream in waking imagination. The best way to do this is to reexperience the dream from
the point of view of some dream figure other than the "me" of the
original dream. This can be done by writing in a journal, or by
the more active method of talking out loud to yourself. One classic method from the Gestalt school is to set two chairs facing each
other and move back and forth between them as you "speak for"
different characters and objects in your dream. In this way, the
body is directly stimulated to "feel the difference" between one
embodied energy and another.

4. *Embody and act out the dream physically.* Again, this exercise is best
   undertaken with the help of others, but it can also be done alone
   with positive results. Instead of just moving from one chair to another, talking and asking questions, as in the previous exercise,
   move around and act out the events of the dream as fully and
   expressively as possible. Often new insights pop forth directly
   from the body in the midst of these dramas (as they did for Celeste
   in the dream theater work described in Chapter 7).

5. *Find the image or situation in the dream that carries the greatest energy for
   healing and increased awareness, then bring it forth into waking life in some
   concrete/expressive form.* Often, your dream will have particularly
   strong images or events that you feel call for concrete expression in
   waking life. Turn these images into works of expressive art, dances,
   songs, private rituals, and the like. It may also be a good idea to simply *play* with the more important images in the dream. For example,
   if you find yourself conversing with a wise serpent in your dream,
   you may want to drop by a local pet store and simply hold a live
   snake in your hands and feel into the dream while you're holding it.
   Such exercises in waking, "shamanic" acting out of the dream are
   sometimes called "dream tasks." My former colleague at St. George
   Homes, Strephon K. Williams, original founder of the Association for the Study of Dreams and author of *Elements of Dreamwork*,
   Element Books, 1990, is a major exponent of this technique.

6. *Make a mask of one or more of the most important characters in your
   dream and wear it while "being" that character.* Mask making is an
   ancient archetypal shamanic spiritual discipline, practiced all over
   the world, in all periods of history and prehistory. The energy of

a dream character is often clarified and focused by turning it into a mask and wearing it while acting out that energy. Try doing this in front of a mirror. Masks have an extraordinary tendency to transform your habitual sense of your limited waking self, just as they transform your appearance. You can hang the masks around on the walls of your living space and gain a greater and more immediate sense of the multiple energies and characters that inhabit your interior world.

Sometimes, if a dream character is particularly troublesome or "stuck" or enigmatic, you can make the mask, act the character, and then conclude the exercise by burning the mask. In this way, the evolution of the energies that appeared as that character in your dream will be facilitated and accelerated. This is a particularly valuable technique for helping young children cope with the energy and distress of their nightmares. It is equally effective for adults.

7. *Pray and meditate while focused on your dream.* Prayer and meditation produce states of consciousness that are more sensitive to and permeable by unconscious energies than ordinary waking awareness is. Holding the experience of a dream in mind while practicing these disciplines often leads to flashes of insight.

However, it should be noted that intensity of feeling is not the same thing as surprise. The primary problem with praying and meditating over one's dreams in solitude is that the already known feelings and emotions are often dramatically intensified. For this reason, prayer and meditation can ironically block and "blot out" any new insights as the "old" feelings bubble up with renewed intensity.

8. *Look up images in one or more "dream symbol dictionaries."* The "dream dictionary" is one of the oldest literary forms on the planet. An unbroken tradition of looking up dream images in "the sacred books" extends back to the origins of writing in ancient Egypt and Mesopotamia. "Dream books" have been around for so long because they serve a strong and real human need to find wisdom and instruction from outside authorities. Over the millennia, some authentic wisdom about the patterns of the archetypes has found its way into almost all of the dream dictionaries, no matter how silly and doctrinaire. As mentioned earlier, if you hold on to the knowledge that

only your own "tingle" or aha can be relied on to separate the wheat from the chaff, then even the most aggressively trivial and pretentious dream dictionary can occasionally provide valuable flashes of insight for the solitary dream explorer. Looking up the same image in several different symbol dictionaries often enhances the insights.

9. *Rewrite the narrative adding the phrase "part of me" to each of the images.* This simple and mechanical technique can be surprisingly powerful. It emphasizes the fact that I am everything in my dream, an awareness that is easy to misplace when working alone.

For example, I dream that:

> I run through the forest, chased by unknown pursuers. I hide from them in a hollow log and hear them as they rush past. From the sound of their passage, I cannot tell if they are even human.

I draw a blank on any part of the meaning of this dream, so I try this exercise. I rewrite the dream as follows:

> I run through the dark forest part of me, chased by unknown parts of me. I hide from the unknown parts of me in an old dead hollow-log part of me and hear the unknown parts of me rush past. I can't tell if the unknown parts of me are even human parts of me.

From this rewritten narrative, I may have surprising ahas about what the dream is trying to tell me. What do I identify as "the dark forest part of me"? What do I recognize as "an old dead hollow-log part of me"? How do I "hide" in that part of myself? And from what? What parts of myself do I imagine "may not even be human"? Instincts? Religious intuitions? Sexual desires? Anger and rage? All of these?

This exercise often leads to surprising insights that might not be reached without the seemingly mechanical exercise of rewriting the dream.

10. Finally, *incubate further dreams to clarify and amplify the dreams you are working on.* The dreams themselves remain the best and most generous source of insight and self-knowledge we have. If you are working alone, chances are you may feel frustrated from time to

time in your efforts to glean the gifts your dreams are offering. Sometimes this sense of frustration can be overcome by writing a letter to your dreams in your dream journal, asking as specifically and emotionally as you can for insight into what the dreams are trying to tell you.

In my experience, the dreams always respond to such requests, but their responses may be playful, ambiguous, and enigmatic. The responses may even deepen the mystery at the same time that the dream answers my question. Whether the dream responds clearly or mysteriously, it always invites me further into the discovery of my deepest self, and to my truest relationship with the world and to the cosmos as a whole.

# AN EXEMPLARY DREAM GROUP MEETING: DREAM WORK (MORE OR LESS) VERBATIM

HAMLET: *Do you see yonder cloud that's almost in the shape of a camel?*
POLONIUS: *By the mass, and 'tis like a camel indeed.*
HAMLET: *Methinks it is like a weasel.*
POLONIUS: *It is backed like a weasel.*
HAMLET: *Or like a whale?*
POLONIUS: *Very like a whale.*

—WILLIAM SHAKESPEARE
(in *Hamlet*)

This appendix has been assembled from notes and accounts of an actual dream group meeting in northern California in the early 1990s. It is presented here to fill out the sense of what group dream work is like in actual practice. If another meeting of the same group or a meeting of a different group had been used, the details of the meeting, the dreams shared, and the subsequent work with the dreams would all be very different. However, behind all the differences there is a deep similarity. I hope this account will give you a better sense of what the basic experiences of group dream work are like, dressed up in the particulars and peculiarities of one group of unique personalities.

The people in this group have been doing dream work together regularly for several years and have become good friends. Their current practice is to meet once every two weeks, on Sunday nights, starting around six with informal touch-in, conversation, and a shared meal, followed by more focused dreamwork after dinner. Years ago, their regular weekly meetings began later in the evening, and they did not dine together. However, beginning with occasional extended meetings at holiday times that included festive meals, they have evolved to the present less-formal pattern.

The group was composed of seven people: Rupert and Margaret, a university professor and his novelist spouse; their old college friend Larry, a videographer; Jane and Louise, both psychotherapists; Katie, an actress; and George, a performing musician and composer. Jane was the oldest member of the group at fifty, and George the youngest at thirty-three. The group included other members at different times, but these seven consistently participated for years.

Rereading and rewriting this last section for this new book has filled me with both joy and sadness, as I sit in my dormitory room at Pendle Hill, the Quaker retreat center in Pennsylvania, on the third of July 2008, having just completed facilitating another intense, weeklong dream workshop. The joy is for relationships with those boon companions and for the love and work we have shared. The sadness is for some of the ways the passing years have treated us. Katie and George are both dead (one from cancer, and the other through misadventure), and Jane and Larry have both quit smoking.

Those of us who remain are still close, and still share and work our dreams and the details of the outer and inner lives when we see one another (which is less often than before) and exchange e-mails (which is more often). The deep psychospiritual issues of our respective lives have evolved and matured, and sometimes seem to have become more profound, and occasionally even seem a little clearer and easier to deal with. The necessities of life (as well as the depredations of aging) have scattered us across the state and around the planet. Our worries that night about "war in the Middle East" have certainly been borne out, and some of our youthful enthusiasms and concerns occasionally appear to have evolved into varieties of wisdom and compassion.

I considered writing a whole new "verbatim" account of a more recent group at a more recent gathering for this book, but on balance it seems best to reproduce this little slice of our lives in our little voluntary dream community at that time, since this account still seems evocative of the essential process and of the "timelessness" that is often achieved in group dream work. This account even seems to be made a little more vivid by the ever-increasing distance from that particular evening.

On the beautiful autumn evening in question, the group as a whole is in a cheerful, upbeat mood, despite the fact that Rupert, Margaret, Jane, and Louise have all had recent bouts of illness. Margaret's illness was so severe she had to spend several days in the hospital; several other members of the group visited her there. She was released about a week before the meeting.

Touch-in over potluck dinner reveals that in addition to shared concerns about health and the possibilities of war in the Middle East, Louise is afraid that her live-in male companion of several years may leave her. Margaret and Jane are both struggling with the emotional letdown and necessary reevaluation of their lives occasioned by their respective only children "leaving the nest" to attend college. Larry is concerned about the worsening economic climate and its impact on his video business. Rupert and George both express concern that their respective creative lives are being "squeezed out" by the daily demands of earning a living. Katie is concerned about the faltering course of the rehearsals of the latest theater piece she is in, but thinks it will "pull itself together" as always.

Jane and Larry are both smokers, so after the meal they take a short walk and have a cigarette.

At about seven-thirty, the group convenes formally and holds hands in silence for about a minute before starting to share dreams.

Katie begins with a dream about hiking in the wild with friends and seeing a woman and her male companion about to commit "suttee" sitting on a funeral pyre.

Rupert follows with a dream about seeing the sun and the full moon right next to each other on the horizon and his hiding from scary marauders.

Next comes Louise, who shares a dream about a surgical operation being carried out on a woman in a cave full of cats, some of which are also being operated and experimented on in nasty ways.

George tells a dream about flying and seeing a black couple fighting and finding a "black fountain" in an isolated rural "temple."

Jane says that she hasn't been able to remember any dreams since the last meeting but tells a "fragment" that is actually quite long, involving a meeting of women and a strange furry animal with no legs and no mouth.

Margaret tells three short dreams from the past week, all of which involve descending into the earth and encountering people she knows are dead, including Lucille Ball.

Larry ends the initial dream-sharing go-round with an account of being in the desert near Kuwait in a commando raid across a "Zen stone garden" that is turned back by a tremendously powerful, unseen, but distinctly feminine force.

No one seems to be in greater need of the group's attention and support than anyone else, so, since the person who has gone the longest without working one of his dreams in depth is Rupert, he becomes the focus.

RUPERT: Okay? You want me to tell my dream again?

*(General assent)*

RUPERT: Here are the pictures I drew in my journal.

*(He passes his journal around the circle as he retells the dream so that the others can look.)*

RUPERT: A bunch of things happen that I can't remember, then my memory picks up. I am staying with rich friends at their "summer mansion." It's high up on a hill overlooking a beautiful, big ocean bay dotted with green islands. It feels like around here, with dry, bleached grasses and dark-green coast oak trees scattered around.

My hostess is a pleasant young third- or fourth-generation rich person. She shows me around the grounds. She shows me a well-worn dirt track leading to the top of the hill behind the house. I see that a lot of construction is going on up there, and I gather from her that the family, or maybe some close family friend, is building a new, modern-architecture mansion on the higher ground, and this beautiful old 1920s-style place will become a "guesthouse."

We walk along to the right for quite a ways down a shaded path to another vantage point overlooking the beautiful bay and the islands. I look back up the hill behind me and see construction here as well. I am amazed at what a *huge* house this new mansion will be.

I have a brief vision of the finished place. It takes over my mind for a moment—elegant and open and all white—like the Greek-island mansion in that weird Elizabeth Taylor film *Boom!* if you ever saw it—but my attention is suddenly drawn back to the horizon.

There I can see two huge bright lights: one appears to be the full moon, and just a few degrees to the left, the other appears to be the disk of the sun, split by the horizon, either just rising or just setting—I can't tell much. I am very disoriented.

"Look at that!" I say in astonishment.

I know in the dream that it is impossible for the sun and the full moon to appear together like this. Whenever they appear this close to one another, the moon has to be dark, or just a tiny sliver crescent. I calculate in the dream that this strange vision is appearing in the east, but since it is so bizarre, I can not tell if the sun is rising or setting. I am also surprised to see that my companion has changed from a young woman into a young man. He communicates to me telepathically that "we should go down and get a closer look."

I also find this a bizarre suggestion, since we should be able to see the horizon more clearly from a higher vantage point. My first thought is that we should climb the hill behind us and take a look from the construction site, but at the same time, I have this wordless feeling that for some unknown reason my companion is right—we should go down.

We hurry down the hill to the shore of the bay. I can see the bottom under the water covered with rounded rocks, almost like cobblestones. He and I are now in agreement—we should swim across to the first island to get a better look. Even though we are both fully dressed, we plunge into the cold, invigorating water and swim across to the island shore. Even though I know in the dream that this is an ocean bay, the water is not salty. It feels and tastes much more like the water of a northern Canadian lake.

When we get to the island, we walk around to the far side and stand on the shore to look. The sun is redder and lower, with only a small arc showing above the landmass on the far side of the bay. Clouds surround the scene but do not obscure it. It looks like the background of a Grünewald painting.

Suddenly, the shining shape of the full moon separates and divides in two. One image stays where it was, next to the sun, and the other comes hurtling across the sky toward us and over our heads at unbelievable speed.

"A flying saucer!" I say out loud with great excitement.

"Yes," my companion answers telepathically, "the last days have begun!"

In the dream I am struck by the ominousness of this message, but at the same time, I also feel strangely enthusiastic and excited. Right in the dream, I remember Jung's stuff about the "flying saucer" being a mandala of hope and divine possibility seen in the distance, and I have the thought that, once again, it looks as though Jung was right.

My friend says that we should return "to the family compound" because "the natives" may take advantage of the decay and breakdown of the old social order to pillage and "take revenge" against the rich.

We return to the channel we swam across to get to the island, only now we see that farther up to the left, the water has become so shallow that we can walk across without even getting our ankles wet. We hurry and run and splash across the water to the far side.

Then we see the first groups of lower-class looters. They are dressed like "punks," and I am struck in the dream by how their shaved heads and spiky hairdos make them look like the nasty Pawnee raiders in *Dances With Wolves*.

We hide in some large bushes until they pass, but my companion tells me telepathically that since they are so close to the house, they will undoubtedly climb the hill and raid the mansion. We have to decide what we are going to do—how we will respond. My first thought is that we should hide and try to avoid all contact with the raiders until they leave, but my friend points out that the mansion is built on a very desirable and defensible spot and that they will probably decide to take up residence and make it their hideout. No, he suggests to me firmly, we either have to gather together what we can carry and no more and leave, or we have to fight. Given how close to the house they are already, we may not even have the option of running away, since we can not abandon "the women and children" to the "Pawnees."

I have the sinking feeling that he is correct about our options, but I also have the clear thought that we don't know what "the flying saucer people" will do. I am certain they will land on the top of the hill where the site has been cleared for the construction. This thought is so energizing and exciting that I start to wake up.

As I am coming awake, I have the thought that this whole place may be called Pioneer Point.

JANE: Doesn't Jung say somewhere that dreaming the sun and the full moon together in the sky like that is a sign of psychosis?

*(Laughter)*

RUPERT: I remember that he reports one of his psychotic patients having a dream like that.

MARGARET: The thing that strikes me most about it, hearing it the second time like this, is how many opposites come together in the dream. You know, the young woman turns into a man, you have to go down instead of up to get a better view, the salt water is actually fresh.

LARRY: And the setting sun is in the east instead of the west.

RUPERT: I guess the sun is setting; I never have that clear sense in the dream, though.

LARRY: I thought you said that when you got to the other side of the island, the sun was lower in the sky—just a little bit showing over the horizon?

RUPERT: Yeah, I know, but in the dream I still can't tell if it's coming up or going down. I have the fleeting thought in the dream that it may just look lower because we've come down so far to look at it.

MARGARET: Yes, that whole business with the sun and the moon— they never come together in the sky like that, but in the dream they do. Opposites come together all over the place.

JANE: *Coincidentis oppositorum.*

GEORGE: What?

LOUISE: "Coincidence of opposites"—it's Latin. Another one of Jung's phrases.

RUPERT: Yes. He says it's a characteristic of the archetypes—they always bring together things that seem like opposites.

KATIE: And it happens in insanity and creativity both!

LARRY: Masculine/feminine, up/down, sunrise/sunset, salt/fresh . . .

there's even a suggestion of rich and poor coming together, since at the end there it looks like the poor folks marauding around are going to go up and live in the mansion.

MARGARET: Well, I have a really strong hit on it all. If it were my dream . . . What's that line the young woman who's turned into a man says there in the middle?

RUPERT: "The last days have begun."

MARGARET: Yes! "The last days have begun." And you're not upset. It's a little ominous, but you really feel excited, right?

RUPERT: Right.

MARGARET: Well, if it were my dream, it would be all about entering the second half of my life—the last half of my life. "The last days have begun," and it's a little ominous, but mostly it's really exciting.

*(General exclamations of interest and recognition)*

LARRY: It works for me!

RUPERT: Yes, strong aha!

JANE: I had another idea. In my version of the dream, there's a pun on the "1920s" building becoming a "guesthouse." If I had dreamed it, it would be about my house becoming a "guesthouse" for my daughter when she's nineteen and in her early twenties. My old house is going to become a 1920s guesthouse.

*(Laughter)*

RUPERT: Yes! That's right! And that means that, at one level, anyway, the big, modern construction on the top of the hill is the new life that Marg and I are building now that Rose [their daughter] is off at school, and only coming home . . . oh, yes, that makes even more sense about how it's a *summer* house—she'll only be coming for any length of time to the "guesthouse" in the summers.

JANE: It ties up with what Marg was saying. There's nothing like having your kid leave to make you feel as though your life is more than half over and "the last days have begun"!

*(Laughter)*

KATIE: And if it were my dream, the sun that's setting in the east and the moon that becomes the flying saucer are all about how now, in this new phase of things, the traditional masculine role of father I've been playing while Rose was at home is fading, and the new energy in my life is more feminine.

LARRY: And "setting in the east" like that might also mean that I'm not so focused on what people on the East Coast think about me and my work—maybe moving away from that whole East Coast competition and success ethic.

RUPERT: I don't know about that. Having Rose in school is making even greater financial demands on us than when she was living at home. It feels to me as though the "success" demands are even greater.

MARGARET: Well, if it were my dream, all that would have to do with the "lower-class 'Pawnee' raiders." They would be shadow figures all tied up with money, and having to earn even more money, and "revenge on the rich." Now that I'm "rich," I can't be a hippie anymore, and now I'm putting all these pressures on myself to make even more money, right at a time when what I really want to do is relax and ease off a little.

RUPERT: Well, I certainly do feel that tension in my life these days, just as I was saying at touch-in.

KATIE: And going down instead of up "to get a better view" would be a joke about inner work, if it were my dream. You know, I have to go "down" into my unconscious depths in order to really get a better look at what's happening on the new horizon of my life.

LARRY: Yeah! I might *think* that the best way to do it is to go "up" and see it all from a more "elevated" and intellectual and rational perspective—"Let's see, now that Rose is gone, what's the best way to restructure my life?" . . . but what's really required is a trip down.

RUPERT: Yes, down into the underworld—like in Marg's dreams of this week since she got home from the hospital.

MARGARET: I had a couple of those while I was still in the hospital.

RUPERT: Well, I guess I can't say that you're the only one who's suffering from the "empty nest" now that Rose has gone.

*(Laughter)*

LOUISE: Really! If it were my dream, it would be coming to let me know just how much I am feeling my daughter's departure, even though I thought that it was more "a woman's problem"! That would have to do with the sun setting and the moon splitting in two—becoming *twice* as important. These "feminine" feelings are coming up in me and changing the whole way I am in the world.

GEORGE: If these "Pawnees" really are images for the pressures to earn even more money, then they are tied up with the struggle between the masculine and the feminine in me. They're shadow figures, just the way they were in the movie. There was all that sensitive attention to the Sioux, but the Pawnee just get shown as brutal creeps.

RUPERT: I don't know. . . . There's that scene where they trap the Pawnee warrior in the stream, and he yells and does the same sort of heroic suicide ride that the Kevin Costner character did at the beginning, in front of the Confederate troops. Right then, he doesn't seem like a monster.

LOUISE: Well, if it were my dream, just what you're saying would make it even clearer that they are shadow figures. That would be part of the secret joke about these seemingly horrible marauder characters. They would be shadow figures, and for that reason alone, they would have some sort of terribly important and valuable gift to give me that I can't see in the dream because I'm so afraid of them and repulsed by them.

LARRY: Like what?

LOUISE: Well, I don't know—I'm not a man—but I imagine some sort of heroism and strength that I'm afraid to own in myself. Maybe some sort of heroic willing sacrifice that's all bound up with my masculinity and that I'm afraid to own because I don't want to be—what did you say before?—"a brutal macho creep."

GEORGE: I didn't say "macho," but it fits.

RUPERT: Yes, it does fit, for me too.

KATIE: What do you imagine is going to happen when the flying saucer people land upon the top of the hill?

RUPERT: Oh, I don't know. . . . Some sort of amazing new way of looking at everything. When you ask the question I get a flash of the punks and me and my friend, and the young woman and everybody all standing on the top of the hill watching this shining thing, and the shining people getting out of it, and realizing that we are all the seeds of some sort of totally new, advanced civilization and that we have no reason to be afraid and fight with each other. We have to work together to restore peace and harmony to the world. The flying saucer people give us this sudden bigger vision about what our lives are really all about, and we stop fighting with each other.

KATIE: Well, that sounds like a spiritual vision to me. If this were my dream, one of the things it would be saying is that this new life that I am dreaming about—the second half of my life—is going to have some spiritual developments that will change everything, especially the way I view these obstreperous "punk" parts of myself.

MARGARET: Yes! And for me, all this spiritual development comes about because I see my responsibilities to "the women and children" as being as much a part of my new life as they were in my old life. It would be about the parts of me that are deep and don't change as I grow older and mature more as well as the parts that do.

RUPERT: Yes. . . . The responsibilities of family life on the outside and the responsibility to look after the feminine and creative new growing parts on the inside—yes, there's an aha with that too.

JANE: If it were my dream, there'd be another level to it too. It would mean that whatever conscious or unconscious consideration I had given to leaving the relationship with my spouse, "now that the kids are gone," would end up affirming that I want to stay in the relationship. You know, when the last kid leaves is a classic time for long-term marriages to break up. When this companion part of me says that we can't desert the women and children and leave them to the marauders, that's a voice from way deep inside me, and the dreamer/me doesn't argue with that, or anything. I just know that that's right—we can't do that.

GEORGE: Wow, yes.

RUPERT: Well, there's a tingle with that too!

MARGARET: Well, I should hope so!

*(Laughter)*

LOUISE: What about the young woman before she turns into a man? You say she's "a third- or fourth-generation rich person"? I was really struck with that phrase both times you told the dream.

RUPERT: Yes, it's just a thing that I know about her in the dream.

LOUISE: What does it mean? How is she different because she's a third- or fourth-generation rich person?

RUPERT: That's interesting . . . how is she different? Well, for one thing, she's not at all pretentious. She's not nouveau riche—she just wears comfortable clothes and no jewelry. The main thing is that her family has been rich for generations, and they're not all dazzled by it anymore. She just knows that she has the resources to do whatever she wants, and the only real issue is "Who am I really, and what do I really want to do?" . . . Yes, that's it—it's her calmness about money—it's just not a big issue. It's just a means to an end. She can spend millions building this new house, if that's really what she decides she wants to do, but she can drive around in a reliable old car and not be alienated from people because she's rich.

LOUISE: Well, then, if this were my dream, that's sort of the overall frame of the whole dream. There's a place inside me where I feel totally secure and confident about my creative energies and my ability to do anything I want, as long as I can get clear about who I really am, and what it is I really want to do with this next phase of my life.

LARRY: And in my dream, there's also a level of it having to do with actual money. I'd see it as an assurance from my unconscious that the things I'm doing really will be well received and that I will make money on them. And I don't need to worry about how success may spoil me and turn me into a jerk. I'll still be able to drive around in an old reliable car and wear comfortable clothes. I just won't have to *worry* about where the money is coming from—for Rose's education, for the car repairs, for the house payments, or any of it.

RUPERT: I sure hope so!

*(Laughter)*

KATIE: Since the dream says that maybe it's "a friend of the family" that's building the mansion on the top of the hill, maybe it *is* about you!

*(Laughter. The laughter dies down and no one speaks.)*

RUPERT: Well, one more thing. Does anyone have any hints on this business about crossing the water to the island to get a better view? If it's just a question of going "down," I've already gone down. What's this swimming and then wading back all about?

*(Pause)*

JANE: My first thought is that it's something to with actually getting in touch with the "watery" emotions—not just "looking" with the eyes and the mind but "feeling" with the body and the emotions. Something like that. . . . The supposedly salty waters are actually fresh and you even said "invigorating"—the waters of life—it is the great ocean, but is also fresh and invigorating.

MARGARET: Yes. And in my version of the dream, there's this tension all the way through the dream between "family" and self. If it were my dream, it would be what Jane just said plus the fact that I have to get in touch with what *I* really feel and want. There would be a pun on "island"—it would be "I land." I have to go down and cross over the waters, away from the "family land" over to the "I land" before I can get a true picture of what's really going on. It's only after I do that that I can see the "flying saucer/moon" and have any idea about the larger possibilities of my new life. Then I can cross back and reaffirm my relationship to the "women and children" and think about how to deal with money-grubbing "Pawnees."

RUPERT: That's hot!

*(Laughter)*

GEORGE: Well, that really gives me an aha. And in my dream, the stones at the bottom of the channel are like "cobblestones" because this is like a sunken civilization. The "I land" is just the tip of the iceberg. There's a whole sunken city down there, like Atlantis, or Mu, and I'm going to get my creative inspirations from down there as the water recedes.

*(Rupert nods.)*

LOUISE: And all through this, every time anyone said "mansion," I kept having the thought that this mansion on the hilltop is *really* big—big enough to hold "many mansions."

RUPERT: That's right!

LOUISE: So, it keeps reinforcing for me what you said [addressing Katie] about the spiritual layers of this dream. "In my Father's house are many mansions . . ."

RUPERT: *(Laughs appreciatively)* Yes!

MARGARET: I don't know. It's probably just because I've been so sick, but you've been pretty sick too, and when you asked about the crossing over and coming back, I flashed on the "cobblestones" under the water too, but to me they suddenly became cells in my body, and especially my lungs, and when I crossed over the first time, I was still fighting off the pneumonia, and the fluid and congestion in my lungs, and when I came back, I was much healthier, and the fluids were returning to normal.

RUPERT: That's great! Thanks! This has been wonderful! Lots of ahas. Thanks!

JANE: And there's that thought while you're waking up—the whole place is named Pioneer Point. In my dream that's a pun too; I'm at a "pioneer point" in my life—a place that I haven't been beyond before.

RUPERT: Yes!

At this point the group took a brief break and moved around to use the bathroom and refill the tea and coffee cups. They resumed and did another piece of work with Louise's dream of the surgery in the cavern with the cats. The group concluded a little after ten-thirty P.M. with a quick round of brief thoughts and projections on the other dreams that they hadn't had a chance to work with in depth that evening. They agreed on the time and place of the next meeting, held hands, exchanged good-byes, and went their respective ways for another two weeks.

# INDEX

Trans- Siberian Orchestra
"Christmas Eve Sarajevo"